LIBRARY

Tel: 01244 375444   Ext: 3301

CHESTER COLLEGE

This book is to be returned on or before the
last date stamped below. Overdue charges
will be incurred by the late return of books.

WITHDRAWN

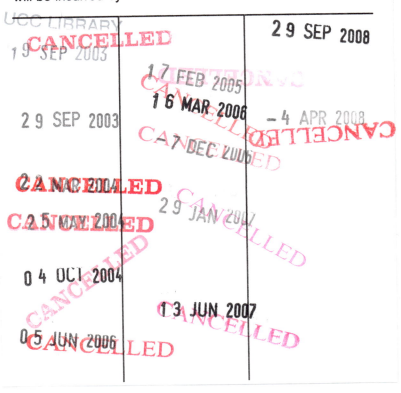

READERS IN CULTURAL CRITICISM
General Editor: *Catherine Belsey*

Posthumanism	*Neil Badmington*
Theorizing Ireland	*Claire Connolly*
Postmodern Debates	*Simon Malpas*
Reading the Past	*Tamsin Spargo*
Performance Studies	*Erin Striff*
Reading Images	*Julia Thomas*
Gender	*Anna Tripp*

Readers in Cultural Criticism
Series Standing Order
ISBN 0-333-78660-2 hardcover
ISBN 0-333-75236-8 paperback
(outside North America only)

You can receive future titles in this series as they are published by placing a standing order.
Please contact your bookseller or, in case of difficulty, write to us at the address below with your name and address, the title of the series and the ISBN quoted above.

Customer Services Department, Macmillan Distribution Ltd
Houndmills, Basingstoke, Hampshire RG21 6XS, England

Theorizing Ireland

Edited by Claire Connolly

First published 2003 by
PALGRAVE MACMILLAN
Houndmills, Basingstoke, Hampshire RG21 6XS and
175 Fifth Avenue, New York, N. Y. 10010
Companies and representatives throughout the world

PALGRAVE MACMILLAN is the global academic imprint of the
Palgrave Macmillan division of St. Martin's Press, LLC and of Palgrave
Macmillan Ltd. Macmillan® is a registered trademark in the United
States, United Kingdom and other countries. Palgrave is a registered
trademark in the European Union and other countries.

ISBN 0–333–80396–5 hardcover
ISBN 0–333–80397–3 paperback

This book is printed on paper suitable for recycling and
made from fully managed and sustained forest sources.

A catalog record for this book is available
from the British Library.

Library of Congress Cataloging-in-Publication Data

Theorizing Ireland / edited by Claire Connolly.
    p. cm.—(Readers in cultural criticism)
    Includes bibliographical references and index.
    ISBN 0–333–80396–5—ISBN 0–333–80397–3 (pbk.)
    1. Ireland—Civilization. 2. English literature—Irish authors—History and
criticism—Theory, etc. 3. Ireland—Intellectual life. 4. Ireland—In literature.
I. Connolly, Claire. II. Series.
DA925 .T45 2002
941.5—dc21

                                                              2002026761

10   9   8   7   6   5   4   3   2   1
12   11   10   09   08   07   06   05   04   03

Printed and bound in Great Britain by
Creative Print & Design (Wales), Ebbw Vale

Contents

General Editor's Preface

Culture is the element we inhabit as subjects.

Culture embraces the whole range of practices, customs and representations of a society. In their rituals, stories and images, societies identify what they perceive as good and evil, proper, sexually acceptable, racially other. Culture is the location of values, and the study of cultures shows how values vary from one society to another, or from one historical moment to the next.

But culture does not exist in the abstract. On the contrary, it is in the broadest sense of the term textual, inscribed in the paintings, operas, sculptures, furnishings, fashions, bus tickets and shopping lists which are the currency of both aesthetic and everyday exchange. Societies invest these artefacts with meanings, until in many cases the meanings are so 'obvious' that they pass for nature. Cultural criticism denaturalizes and defamiliarizes these meanings, isolating them for inspection and analysis.

The subject is what speaks, or, more precisely, what signifies, and subjects learn in culture to reproduce or to challenge the meanings and values inscribed in the signifying practices of the society that shapes them.

If culture is pervasive and constitutive for us, if it resides in the documents, objects and practices that surround us, if it circulates as the meanings and values we learn and reproduce as good citizens, how in these circumstances can we practise cultural *criticism*, where criticism implies a certain distance between the critic and the culture? The answer is that cultures are not homogeneous; they are not even necessarily coherent. There are always other perspectives, so that cultures offer alternative positions for the subjects they also recruit. Moreover, we have a degree of power over the messages we reproduce. A minor modification changes the script, and may alter the meaning; the introduction of a negative constructs a resistance.

The present moment in our own culture is one of intense debate. Sexual alignments, family values, racial politics, the implications of economic differences are all hotly contested. And positions are taken up not only in explicit discussions at political meetings, on television and in the pub. They are often reaffirmed or challenged implicitly in films and advertisements, horoscopes and lonely-hearts columns. Cultural criticism analyses all these forms in order to assess their hold on our consciousness.

There is no interpretative practice without theory, and the more sophisticated the theory, the more precise and perceptive the reading it makes possible. Cultural theory is as well defined now as it has ever been, and as strongly contested as our social values. There could not, in consequence, be a more exciting time to engage in the theory and practice of Cultural Criticism.

Catherine Belsey
Cardiff University

Acknowledgements

The idea for this project originated from my experience of teaching Cultural Criticism at Cardiff University, to students who took the double risk of signing up for modules on unfamiliar Irish material and a joint degree in a new discipline. I hope this book will find its way onto the desks of other such adventurous readers.

Margaret Bartley and Jane Moore discussed this project with me in its early stages; my thanks to each for the enthusiasm with which they responded to the idea and for the advice given. Thanks also, for conversations of all kinds, to Linda Connolly, Nicholas Daly, Colin Graham, Seán Hillen, Catherine Kirwan, Chris Morash, Shaun Richards, Ray Ryan, Anna Sandeman, David Skilton and Ailbhe Thunder. The financial support of the School of English, Communication and Philosophy (Cardiff University) is gratefully acknowledged.

Catherine Belsey showed me the way in preparing this collection. In her questions on behalf of its projected readership as well as her deep commitment to *Father Ted* I found her to be a demanding, scrupulous and inspiring editor.

I dedicate the Reader to Paul O'Donovan, to whom so much of what I have learned as theory seems to come naturally.

The editor and publishers wish to thank the following for permission to use copyright material:

Angela Bourke, for 'The Virtual Reality of Irish Fairy Legend', *Éire Ireland*, 36 (1991), 7–25, by permission of the Irish American Cultural Institute and Jonathan Williams Literary Agency on behalf of the author; Joe Cleary, for 'Misplaced Ideas? Colonialism, Location and Dislocation in Irish Studies', in *The Last Ditch: Ireland and the Postcolonial World*, ed. Clare Carroll (forthcoming) Cork University Press, by permission of the author; Patricia Coughlan, for ' "Bog Queens": The Representation of Women in the Poetry of John Montague and Seamus Heaney', in *Gender in Irish Writing*, ed. Toni O'Brien Johnson and David Cairns, Open University Press (1991), pp. 88–111, by permission of the author; Seamus Deane, for 'Heroic Styles:

the Tradition of an Idea' (1984) in *Ireland's Field Day* by Seamus Deane, Routledge (1985), pp. 45–58, by permission of Taylor & Francis Ltd; Terry Eagleton, for material from *Heathcliff and the Great Hunger: Studies in Irish Culture* by Terry Eagleton (1995), pp. 123–44, by permission of Verso; Luke Gibbons, for 'Narratives of the Nation: Fact, Fiction and Irish Cinema', in *Nationalisms: Visions and Revisions*, ed. Luke Dodd (1999), pp. 66–73, by permission of The Film Institute of Ireland; Colin Graham, for 'Subalternity and Gender: Problems of Post-Colonial Irishness', *Journal of Gender Studies*, 5 (1996), 363–73, by permission of Taylor & Francis Ltd; Siobhán Kilfeather, for 'Sex and Sensation in the Nineteenth-Century Novel', in *Gender Perspectives in Nineteenth-Century Ireland*, ed. Margaret Kelleher and James H. Murphy (1997), pp. 83–92, by permission of Irish Academic Press Ltd; Richard Kirkland, for material from *Literature and Culture in Northern Ireland Since 1965: Moments of Danger*, by Richard Kirkland, Longman (1996), pp. 19–33, by permission of Pearson Education Ltd; David Lloyd, for material from *Nationalism and Minor Literature*, by David Lloyd (1987), pp. 54–72. Copyright © 1987 The Regents of the University of California, by permission of University of California Press; Christopher Morash, for material from *Writing the Irish Famine*, by Christopher Morash, Clarendon (1995), pp. 52–66. Copyright © 1995 Christopher Morash, by permission of Oxford University Press; Shaun Richards, for 'To Bind the Northern to the Southern Stars: Field Day in Derry and Dublin', *The Irish Review*, 4 (1988), 52–8. Copyright © *The Irish Review* and the Contributors, 1988, by permission of Cork University Press on behalf of the author; Clair Wills, for material from *Improprieties: Politics and Sexuality in Northern Irish Poetry*, Clarendon (1993), pp. 13–27. Copyright © Clair Wills 1993, by permission of Oxford University Press; John Hinde, for the postcard *Thatched Cottage, Connemara, Co. Galway, Ireland*. Photo © John Hinde Ltd; Liam Blake and Real Ireland Design Limited, for the postcard *Real Ireland*. Photo reproduced by permission of Liam Blake; Seán Hillen, for the image *The Great Pyramids*. Image reproduced by permission of Seán Hillen.

Every effort has been made to trace the copyright holders but if any have been inadvertently overlooked the publishers will be pleased to make the necessary arrangement at the first opportunity.

1

Introduction: Ireland in Theory

Claire Connolly

'Imagine you are in an airplane', begins Éilís Ní Dhuibhne's novel, *The Dancers Dancing* (1999). The narrative frames an aerial vision of an undulating terrain that seems to mould itself to the observer's eye:

> The landscape spreads beneath like a chequered tablecloth thrown across a languid body. From this vantage point, no curve is apparent. It is flat earth – pan flat, plan flat, platter flat to the edges, its green and gold patches stained at intervals by lumps of mountains, brownish purple clots of varicose vein in the smooth skin of the land. Patterns of fields, rough squares and rectangles, are hatched in with grey stone. The white spots, sometimes slipping disconcertingly out of focus, are sheep.[1]

Ireland is here laid out and controlled, domesticated at the level of imagery at least: hedges and fields become the squares of a tablecloth, distance helping to discipline the view. Yet although the bird's-eye perspective afforded by the narrative serves to level the landscape ('pan flat, plan flat, platter flat'), it cannot entirely flatten out the markings suggestive of both unruly body (clots, veins) and rough map (engravings, lines hatched in). This fictional attempt to achieve perspective on the island runs the risk of the picture spilling out of its frame: what will happen as the details swim back into view?

Having transported its readers 'twenty thousand feet' above Ireland, the narrative of *The Dancers Dancing* then plunges back down into the murk of everyday life, reaching subterranean levels of obscurity. Where once focus, perspective and a sense of pattern was (just about) achieved by distance, now nothing can be seen for the sheer profusion of matter:

> What you can't see is what it is better not to see: the sap and the clay and the weeds and the mess. The chthonic puddle and muddle of brain and heart and kitchen and sewer and vein and sinew and ink and stamp and sugar and stew and cloth and stitch and swill and beer and lemonade and tea and soap

1

and nerve and memory and energy and pine and weep and laugh and sneer
and say nothing and say something and in between, in between, in between,
that is the truth and that is the story.[2]

Clarity of vision has given way to confusion, an uncertainty manifest at the
level of syntax: 'What you can't see is what it is better not to see.' The move
from elegant abstraction into the specifics of the culture is one repeated by
the essays in this collection, which attempt to make sense of Ireland and its
in-between story by a turn to theoretical arguments and idioms that lend
conceptual order to cultural chaos. Each essay also, whether wilfully or
otherwise, confronts the challenge of what cannot be seen.

The aircraft metaphor helps to highlight questions of image and perspective. What does Ireland look like? Is it Ireland itself or its image that
confronts the viewer? Where do you need to be in order to get a clear
view? And, finally, is the cost of critical comprehension a rejection of the
rich texture of the terrain, or can these layered images (land, home, mountain, veins, skin, paper) themselves enhance our interpretations?

Before moving into these difficulties, however, I wish to hold on to
(momentarily, at least) the pleasing illusion of perspective. Certain questions
now occupy the critical centre of Irish Studies. Is Ireland postcolonial? How
should the past be remembered? To whom does the term Irish apply? An
additional topic addressed in this Reader is the extent to which these queries
belong to the public, prone as they (or we) are to loose emotions and an
inattentiveness to the finer points of economic data, or to specialized commentators, who will read and digest the relevant documentation on every-
one's behalf.

Is this distinction even a viable one? A recent fashion for Irish Studies
scholars to write their autobiographies does at least have the virtue of
reminding readers that, as one historian modestly puts it, 'senses of the
past shared by the culture at large filter through to the academy'.[3] Rather
than treating popular perceptions as a hindrance, then, one of the possibilities raised by the essays gathered here is an understanding of culture that
makes space for confusion and misunderstanding as well as exactitude and
objectivity: 'the chthonic puddle and muddle of brain and heart and kitchen
and sewer and vein and sinew and ink and stamp . . .'

What is the subject matter of Irish Studies? The desire to seek out new
perspectives on Ireland too often retains – or rather is itself retained and
restricted by – a narrow understanding of the subject, the terms set by
political and economic rather than social or cultural history. For one
thing, not all of Irish culture arranges itself neatly under the heading
'Irish'. A great many things have happened and are happening on the island
that are not primarily concerned with nationality and its discontents: great
swathes of contemporary popular culture, multinational capitalism, migrants

and refugee seekers all participate in and are moved by global forces that traverse the island of Ireland, blind to the intricate complexities of its past. Nor is this simply a product of our globalized moment: the evidence of eighteenth- and nineteenth-century histories of society, of sexuality, of bodies, of emigration (many of which are only beginning to be compiled) is that the experience of those who lived on the island had both an Irish and an international dimension.

If one area of Irish criticism is forced to face up to these dilemmas more insistently than any other it is surely feminism. From the vantage point of feminism, it is possible to see how it is not only questions of national identity and definition that have motivated an Irish turn to theory. Sexual politics have played a key role in determining the shapes critical and cultural theory has taken on the island. With its own separate theoretical trajectory driven by questions at the heart of Western European culture since the Enlightenment, Irish feminism concerns itself with adjudicating between the competing demands of sexual difference and equal rights in an international idiom. No surprise, perhaps, that many of the social gains made by Irish women drew inspiration and succour from initiatives from Europe and beyond.[4]

Does Irish feminism desire to dispense with Irishness altogether? And if certain sections of it do so wish, is this even possible? Irish feminist debates have taken shape and form in the context of Ireland, and cannot be separated from its laws, history and culture. This has been most painfully experienced at the level of women's bodies, confined and regulated by the Republic's constitutional ban on abortion, for example, or accorded different status within the United Kingdom by Northern Ireland's seceding from the liberal abortion regime adopted across Britain.[5] Contemporary work by women writers, critics, painters and sculptors turns again and again to the interrelation between body and land, seeking to make sense, perhaps, of the embodied nature of citizenship and subjecthood.

Ireland has long been imagined in terms of female images: Mother Ireland, wild Irish girl, gentle colleen, old hag, wise woman. These have served to elicit both sexual and national desire, spurring Irish men on to activity on behalf of the nation. Such stereotyped images of idealized silent women and heroic active men are of course in many ways a travesty of the rich and complex roles played by women both now and in the past. They exert a powerful influence that has, at every point, come under the scrutiny and attack of the very writers and artists seemingly silenced by these dominant metaphors. When Ní Dhuibhne describes a landscape that is 'like a chequered tablecloth thrown across a languid body', it is worth considering how she manages to both evoke and evade these images.

Although feminist perspectives may not be easily accommodated within communities that imagine themselves in such terms, then, they have emerged, defiant, shaped by the cultural and political battles that surround them. Since the foundation of the Irish Free State in 1922, women writers such as Kate O'Brien, Edna O'Brien and most recently Eavan Boland have paid eloquent tribute to the emotional appeal of nationalism, while simultaneously protesting the narrow space it allots to women as subjects. In Northern Ireland, the 'troubles' have motivated women to organize to assert their own distinctive point of view, and, building on the success of the peace movement, there is a now a women's political party.

Recent developments in Irish women's history, in the social sciences and in folklore studies testify to a feminist move to (re)occupy the territory of Irishness, opposing versions of nationality that rely on femininity to form its metaphorical ground. This tension testifies to an ongoing struggle between women's material lives and cultural understandings of woman as metaphor.

In order to answer some of the questions raised about Ireland and its image, I propose a detour to a place that is part Ireland, part ancient myth and part postmodern fantasy. Seán Hillen's series of paper collages, *Irelantis*, created between 1994 and 1997, consist of bits and pieces of old photographs and postcards, cut up and reassembled so that they form arresting new images.[6] In Hillen's work the clichés of tourist propaganda (mountains, rivers, streetscapes, ancient monuments) are transformed under the gaze of contemporary concerns. They mesh with an eclectic range of current issues (religion, environmentalism, futurology, space travel) and morph into exuberant images of a place called 'Irelantis'.

Itself a place full of ruins, craters and chaos, Irelantis is painstakingly composed from the debris of contemporary Ireland. The resulting scenes represent both a compilation of second-hand images and a fresh artistic innovation. But where is Irelantis? Hillen's scalpel and glue montages take us on a tour of Ireland by way of Atlantis, the paradise island that Plato described as the most harmonious society to be found on earth, but said to have been lost to the Atlantic in an undersea earthquake. The *Irelantis* images lead viewers on an imaginative journey that takes in references to the lost island of myth, exploiting Ireland's geographical position on the western Atlantic seaboard.

Seventeenth- and eighteenth-century writers such as Francis Bacon and Delarivière Manley reimagined Atlantis in the service of the politics and scandal of their day. Hillen's Irelantis, however, may also resonate with viewers better versed in popular culture than philosophy – some readers will remember the 1970s American television series 'The Man from Atlantis', which starred Patrick Duffy (better known for his role in the 1980s drama *Dallas*) as Mark Harris. The drowned city's last survivor, Harris was a human with gills and webbed feet and hands whose job it was to save the world's oceans for one hour a week. More recently, Hollywood has relaunched Plato's underwater world in *Atlantis: The Lost Empire* (Walt Disney Productions, 2001). This infinitely flexible utopia acts as a kind of

Figure 1

shorthand for social and political fantasies driven by a frustrated desire to
shift the boundaries of what has come to seem acceptable.

Hillen's *Irelantis* provides an ideal viewpoint from which the ebb and flow
of cultural currents can be observed. Consider the opening image of the
collection, 'The Great Pyramids of Carlingford Lough' (Figure 1). Carlingford Lough straddles Counties Louth and Down, and opens into the Irish Sea.
This beauty spot marks, for a few miles, the border between the Irish
Republic and Northern Ireland as it meets the sea. The scene is overlooked
by an isolated individual, a young man in red who fills the foreground in the
manner of the great Romantic landscapes. This is no understated or subtle
grandeur, however. The depiction is hyper-realistic, the colours are lurid,
and the preferred style is clearly that of postcards rather than paintings. The
romantic claim to beauty is made and mocked simultaneously. The mockery

becomes (literally) more pointed in the shape of pyramids found on each side of the Lough. These ancient Egyptian monuments both complete and dislocate the scene, on the one hand comfortably, if somewhat bizarrely, belonging to a shared iconography of tourism, on the other serving to make the familiar Irish landscape exotic and strange.

Multiple borders are invoked in the image: the land meets the lough, which in its turn confronts the sea; the sea encounters sky and the skyline dramatically gives way to outer space. Boundaries and edges are the very stuff of Hillen's art, and here, as with all his collages, the lines and joins are obvious, jutting out for all to see. The pyramids are clearly pasted into the Irish landscape, itself overlaid into a global skyscape. If Carlingford Lough's strategic position on the Irish border is taken into account, the meanings of these boundaries become clearer: they inscribe a political border that is not physically present, the only clues to its existence being the juxtaposition of superimposed scenes.

That this technique of bricolage has broader cultural meanings is borne out by a brief examination of the genesis of the *Irelantis* images. The collages are usually composed of parts of postcards and Hillen told a journalist how the actual cards he cuts up for this purpose are recycled. They were first purchased and used by people who wrote to the national television station of the Republic of Ireland, wishing to answer a television quiz, participate in a competition or enter a game show: 'A lot of the cards I used were originally sent to RTÉ for postal competitions and sold on to dealers. So they've had a whole other life before I came to use them.'[7] *Irelantis* not only makes Ireland into a fantasy media-scape, then, but originates from the Ireland of mass broadcasting. It belongs, at least in part, to popular culture and the public that consumes such entertainment. Viewers of these images become active producers of their meaning(s), encouraged by the densely layered citational structure of the collages to unravel the references and decode the representation.

One of the factors responsible for delivering the interpretation of these images into the hands of every viewer is their reliance on a particular kind of postcard. Hillen views Ireland through the lens of what some of his critics and curators have called 'Hinde-Sight'. The postcards he characteristically uses are most evidently those sold under the name of John Hinde, the English commercial photographer who put his distinctive mark on the look of Irish postcards from the mid-1950s. His technicolour photographs of Irish scenes shot during the 1950s and 60s (showing the distinctive clothes and cars of those decades) sold well into the 1980s (see Figure 2). To understand their lasting hold on the imagination of artists and critics, it is worth considering the Ireland within which they were being circulated and sold. While the cards may be found in tourist shops to this day, in the 1960s and even 1970s they were just about the only postcard images of Ireland available for purchase.

Figure 2

From the late 1960s onwards, Ireland (both sides of the border) was dominated by a strong sense of the insufficiency of old images. In the Republic the policies of Taoiseach (Prime Minister) Seán Lemass and his economic adviser T. K. Whittaker had seen a decisive shift in the direction of economic and political modernization, away from red-haired girls collecting turf on the bogs and towards a future of prosperity, symbolized by factories and aeroplanes rather than cottages and carts. The outbreak of violence and the beginning of 'the troubles' in Northern Ireland made Hinde's Ireland seem even more radically out of date, images estranged from the country that produced them. By the 1980s the sense that the old images were inadequate was stronger still: economic recession, a fresh wave of emigration, the seeming intractability of violence in Northern Ireland, all conspired (among other things) to initiate a fresh critical investigation of Irish culture. It is at this moment that the earliest of the essays collected here was published.

Like John Ford's 1952 film *The Quiet Man*, described by one critic as 'a picture-postcard image' of Ireland,[8] Hinde's postcards not only represent an Ireland long gone – they also raise the question of whether it ever existed in the first place. Ford's fictional Ireland barely contains its staginess and theatricality within its own frame. Luke Gibbons has drawn readers' attention to this aspect of *The Quiet Man*, singling out for attention Sean Thornton's (John Wayne's) reaction on first seeing Mary Kate Danagher

(Maureen O'Hara). 'Hey, is that real? She couldn't be.'[9] Similarly, one commentator on Hinde's methods has observed the carefree manipulation of the scenes photographed:

> He and his photographers were happy to pump up the colours of a scene, plant appealing flora in shot, remove extraneous details, rope in passers-by to pose and even, on one notorious occasion, force an Aran fisherman to wear the 'appropriate' knitwear before he could have his photograph taken. One of Hinde's photographers on the Aran trip recalls that he took a photograph of a 'perfect' Aran cottage, only to discover that it had been built by Robert Flaherty for the filming of *Man of Aran*.[10]

This last anecdote perfectly captures the proto-postmodern sensibility present within Hinde's images, a further explanation, perhaps, of the enduring cultural interest in these postcards.

Robert Flaherty's *Man of Aran* (1934) was a documentary film that tried to capture the isolation and austerity of life among fishing communities on the western seaboard. Known for his *Nanook of the North*, a study of the Inuit people, the Irish-American director sought to capture the gritty realities that characterized the lives of shark fishers living on the Aran islands, off the coast of Galway. The actuality and authenticity that Flaherty worked so hard to convey make the film a landmark cultural document. Greeted with official approval, the film was premiered to an audience that included Eamon De Valera, then Taoiseach and later President of Ireland, and the politician usually credited with giving the Irish Free State its distinctly confessional and conservative slant. A cornerstone in this vision of Ireland was the idealization of the west, and it is worth remarking here on the Aran islands and their significance in Irish culture. Since the period of the literary revival at least, Ireland's west coast has been represented as the true source of national vitality, the repository of authentic language, manners and dress.[11] Such a vision was given official sanction by the establishment of residential schools (or summer camps) in *Gaeltacht* (or Irish-speaking) areas. It is in one such 'Irish college' that the central action of *The Dancers Dancing* occurs, in a village in County Donegal in the far north-west of Ireland that is, as the effusive narrative voice affirms, 'Not only west, not only beautiful, but all Irish as well – not half Irish, not a quarter Irish. All.'[12]

This is an enthusiasm for the beautiful Irish west with which readers of James Joyce's 'The Dead' (1914) will be familiar. In that story Molly Ivors disapprovingly teases the central character, Gabriel Conroy, because he writes a literary column for the *Daily Express*, a Unionist paper. Sensing his discomfort at being labelled a 'West Briton' (that is to say, leaning too far eastwards in his cultural affiliations), Miss Ivors suddenly changes tack and invites Gabriel to join a group of friends who are travelling west:

'O, Mr Conroy, will you come for an excursion to the Aran Isles this summer? We're going to stay there a whole month. It will be splendid out in the Atlantic. You ought to come.'[13]

Gabriel, however, has no wish to join his fellow educated Dubliners on their journey in search of their native culture ('if it comes to that, you know, Irish is not my language', he maintains), and explains how that summer he will, as usual, go cycling with some friends, 'to France or Belgium or perhaps Germany'.[14]

The fact that Robert Flaherty had built his perfect Aran cottage from scratch, and, if contemporary accounts are to be believed, taught the islanders how to fish for sharks (the custom had fallen out of practice some 50 years earlier) suggests another kind of value now attached to *Man of Aran*: because of the extent to which Flaherty's assiduous attempts to capture reality led him towards changing and even falsifying life on the islands, the film is now a touchstone text for those eager to interrogate the illusion of authenticity. Its vision of the west of Ireland is as much a fantasy as that created by the more openly fanciful film, *The Quiet Man*, mentioned above. This *mise-en-abyme* of representations (Hillen, Hinde, Flaherty, Ford) throws into relief the question of the real.

Yielding perhaps to the pressure of events, the Hinde-style postcard gave way in the mid-1980s to another kind of image, pioneered by the photographer Liam Blake and marketed under the name 'Real Ireland'. These images, as their name implies, promised the authenticity Hinde so spectacularly failed to deliver (Figure 3). Typically, favoured scenes were shot from unexpected angles, often in an intimate close-up that seemed to explicitly reject the panorama shots favoured in the cards sold under the John Hinde brand. 'Real Ireland' postcards might feature a bird sanctuary, or some cliffs shot in near focus. Contemporary images of elderly people were also selected, with wrinkles and worn faces photographed in loving detail. These included a memorable picture of an elderly woman with a seagull perched on her head. But the claim to reality was not founded so much on the scenes shown as in the new look these cards gave to the Irish landscape and people. The flatter, more realistic colours combined with the close camera work to create a prevailing sense of sober truth. There are vivid colours here, but it is the brilliance of a house painted pink or a barn made bright by the midday sun. The claim to reality is paramount.

While there is no simple critical equivalent to the Real Ireland postcards, it is nonetheless worth tracing here the move from one kind of image to another, each responding to the perceived falsities of the past, resulting in a kind of chain reaction against any narrow or constricting idea of authenticity. To return to *Irelantis* (standing here, somewhat precariously, for our present moment) it may help to reconsider the good humour with which it

Figure 3

invites viewers to smile at what remains of the gaudy and garish postcards
that once passed for images of Ireland. And yet, as Fintan O'Toole writes of
Irelantis, 'if that was all they did, the joke would wear rather thin'.[15] Instead
Hillen's collages reject what O'Toole calls 'easy mockery'. The refusal of
cynicism is the key here, and O'Toole's observation is echoed in many other
reactions to Hillen's work: reviews comment on how there is 'nothing snide'
in the images,[16] on their being 'not harsh' nor 'humourless'.[17] As the many
negatives suggest, Hillen's collages defy a well-entrenched expectation that
those who cast a critical eye on Irish culture are cynical and snide, or perhaps
anxious and embarrassed.

   Central to my project here is to show how theory has helped mark out a
space between scepticism and reverence. Hillen is not alone, and it is now
possible to identify a particular kind of amused scepticism, or a general
tendency to celebrate rather than mourn the decades of official misrepre-
sentation in the name of national identity. *Irelantis* does not offer a real
Ireland to replace the fake one generated by the tourist industry; rather it
inhabits the realm of the fake real, the arena of what the cultural theorist Jean
Baudrillard calls 'simulations'. According to Baudrillard, 'When the real is
no longer what it used to be ... [there] is a proliferation of myths of origin
and signs of reality; of second-hand truth, objectivity and authenticity.'[18]

He attests to the difficulty of attaining 'any last judgement to separate true from false',[19] such as might allow a distinction to be made between a map of a territory and that territory itself: the aerial perspective is unavailable.

This is only to isolate one strand from the richness of contemporary Irish culture, but it is a powerful trend that is, moreover, proceeding in synchrony with current critical questioning around authenticity and origin. Consider Martin McDonagh's plays, for example. In *The Cripple of Inismaan* (1997), the action of the play takes place during the filming of Flaherty's film *The Man of Aran*, while *A Skull in Connemara* depicts crafty Galway woman Mary Rafferty deceiving tourists into thinking John Ford's *The Quiet Man* was filmed in her village, so that she can sell fake souvenirs of an already bogus Hollywood version of Ireland: 'John Wayne photos, two pounds a pop'.[20]

The landscape of Craggy Island, the fictional setting for the British television situation comedy, *Father Ted* (Channel 4, 1995–9), similarly makes merry amidst the ruins of old representations. The remote location and rocky contours of Craggy Island suggest it belongs to the beautiful Irish west ironised by Ní Dhuibhne. *Father Ted* both makes and mocks this connection. Viewers learn early in the first series that the island's own west coast has 'drifted off'. The overall visual effect, from filmic style to television stage set, is quite deliberately archaic, lending the programme an air of age and decrepitude. The series does maintain a curious kind of innocence: none of the priests are paedophiles, the housekeeper is untouched by feminism (at least until the Sinead O'Connor style singer turns up in 'Rock a Hula Ted', Episode 7, Series 2) and the island setting radiates a remote calm. Yet this tranquillity is interrupted in every episode, breached in the opening sequence by the noisy establishing shot in which the viewer is brought into the fictional world as if arriving on the island by helicopter (hurtling towards land without any of the elegant distance afforded by Ní Dhuibhne's aeroplane); then disrupted by such formidable forces as the church authorities, visiting nuns and the island's Chinese community.

In a memorable episode, originally planned as the opening for the first series but eventually shown at its end, one of the central characters, the elderly alcoholic Father Jack (Frank Kelly), appears to have died. Sorrowfully remembering his choleric and foul-mouthed companion, Father Ted (Dermot Morgan) quotes a version of the closing lines from Joyce's 'The Dead':

> It's beginning to snow again. The flakes, silver and dark, are falling obliquely against the lamplight. It's probably snowing all over the island – on the central plain, on the treeless hills, falling softly on the graveyards, on the crosses and headstones, upon all the living ... and the dead.[21]

This episode of *Father Ted* features a situation comedy standard, here most directly borrowed from the classic British series *Fawlty Towers*, in which the characters have to spend a night with a dead body in order to satisfy the conditions of a will. Despite the prevailing slapstick, however (Father Jack comes back to life, shouting 'Will you shut the feck up!', just as Ted ends his monologue), the citation of 'The Dead' serves to create a many-layered televisual moment in which the grief of the past can find a voice.

This is reinforced visually by scenes which are strongly reminiscent of the beautiful and moving closing scene of John Huston's film version of 'The Dead' (1987): snow, Celtic crosses, a cemetery, all filmed in mournful monochrome. Both sombre and funny, this moment in *Father Ted* shares with Joyce's short story an attempt to convey a moment of change in Irish culture: the old images passing, fresh representations being put in their place. Attentive viewers of *Father Ted* will notice a framed black and white photograph of John Wayne as Sean Thornton in *The Quiet Man* occupying pride of place on the walls of the parochial house, hinting that the replacement images are not so much new as 'new-old'.

'The Dead' is a text that is itself suffused with death, longing and loss. Gabriel Conroy ponders the imminent loss of his personal past and realizes how little he knows of his wife's childhood in the west of Ireland. The story has become a central text in contemporary Irish Studies because of the way it captures a transitional moment, relevant in Joyce's own time but repeated in different modalities to this day: the living present versus the pull of the dead past, the detached sensibilities of the urban east opposed to the warm intimacy of the rural west, the everyday use of English contrasted with a memory of Irish.

These oppositions are not immemorial, however, and in the case of *Father Ted* they find expression by not only borrowing from James Joyce and *Fawlty Towers*, but also freely imitating hit US shows like *Seinfeld* and *The Simpsons*. Attentiveness to the east/west axis can blind us to the global configurations of Irish life, as well as to the north/south division that continues to shape and determine lived experience on the island. The border that is present but absent from Hillen's 'The Great Pyramids at Carlingford Lough' is also crossed in *The Dancers Dancing*: the central child characters undertake a journey from polluted Dublin to the magical west that involves crossing army checkpoints and subjecting their stuffed rabbits and cans of Coca-Cola to military inspection. The novel is set in 1972, a year after internment (or arrest on suspicion without trial) was first introduced in Northern Ireland, and the main action occurs in the summer in which 'Operation Motorman' saw the British Army dismantle barricades and reclaim the area that had become known as 'Free Derry'. In the magical west the girls from Dublin meet their more worldly Northern Irish counterparts, who carry the knowledge of violence and injustice with them in their present.

One enduring cliché of Ireland's cultural life is that the country is obsessed with its own past. In its Irish Tourist Board manifestation, this is a past that visitors weary with the modern world can visit and enjoy, returning to their own more complex and fast-paced societies refreshed and relaxed. In reaction to this tired truism, revisionist history earnestly sought to recapture the past in order to set in motion a more complex investigation of its contours. At the same moment, writers and critics solemnly rejected the legacy of figures such as W. B. Yeats and John Millington Synge, indicted for their unthinking adherence to the old and the traditional. The new critical strategies developed within Irish Studies in the period charted in this Reader can be quite simply understood as motivated by a desire to clear away this cliché, to expose the shallow amnesia of the state-sponsored modernization programme instituted in the late 1960s, and to reconnect Irish culture to the many and multifarious stories that make up its past. This is the most difficult task of all.

2

Heroic Styles: The Tradition of an Idea

Seamus Deane

It is possible to write about literature without adverting in any substantial way to history. Equally, it is possible to write history without any serious reference to literature. Yet both literature and history are discourses which are widely recognized to be closely related to one another because they are both subject to various linguistic protocols which, in gross or in subtle ways, determine the structure and meaning of what is written. We have many names for these protocols. Some are very general indeed – Romanticism, Victorianism, Modernism. Some are more specific – Idealist, Radical, Liberal, Literature can be written as History, History as Literature. It would be foolhardy to choose one among the many competing variations and say that it is *true* on some specifically historical or literary basis. Such choices are always moral and/or aesthetic. They always have an ideological implication.

Similarly, both discourses are surrounded – some would say stifled – by what is now called metacommentary. History as an activity is interrogated by the philosophy of history; literature as an activity is scrutinized by literary criticism which, at times, manages to be the philosophy of literature. In Ireland, however, the two discourses have been kept apart, even though they have, between them, created the interpretations of past and present by which we live. It is always possible to see in retrospect the features which identify writers of a particular period, no matter how disparate their interests. The link between Yeats, Spengler and Toynbee is obvious by now. They all speak the language of a particular historical 'family'. The same is true of Joyce and Lukács. What I propose in this chapter is that there have been for us two dominant ways of reading both our literature and our history. One is 'Romantic', a mode of reading which takes pleasure in the notion that Ireland is a culture enriched by the ambiguity of its relationship to an anachronistic and a modernized present. The other is a mode of reading which denies the glamour of this ambiguity and seeks to escape from it into a pluralism of the present. The authors who represent these modes most powerfully are Yeats and Joyce respectively. The problem which is rendered insoluble by them is that of the North. In a basic sense, the crisis we are passing through is stylistic. That is to say, it is a crisis of language – the ways in which we write it and the ways in which we read it.

The idea of a tradition is one with which we are familiar in Irish writing. In a culture like ours, 'tradition' is not easily taken to be an established reality. We are conscious that it is an invention, a narrative which ingeniously finds a way of connecting a selected series of historical figures or themes in such a way that the pattern or plot revealed to us becomes a conditioning factor in our reading of literary works – such as *The Tower* or *Finnegans Wake*. However, the paradox into which we are inevitably led has a disquieting effect, for then we recognize that a Yeatsian or a Joycean idea of tradition is something simultaneously established for us in their texts and as a precondition of being able to read them. A poem like 'Ancestral Houses' owes its force to the vitality with which it offers a version of Ascendancy history as true in itself. The truth of this historical reconstruction of the Ascendancy is not cancelled by our simply saying No, it was not like that. For its ultimate validity is not historical, but mythical. In this case, the mythical element is given prominence by the meditation on the fate of an originary energy when it becomes so effective that it transforms nature into civilization and is then transformed itself by civilization into decadence. This poem, then, appears to have a story to tell and, along with that, an interpretation of the story's meaning. It operates on the narrative and on the conceptual planes and at the intersection of these it emerges, for many readers, as a poem about the tragic nature of human existence itself. Yeats's life, through the mediations of history and myth, becomes an embodiment of essential existence.

The trouble with such a reading is the assumption that this or any other literary work can arrive at a moment in which it takes leave of history or myth (which are liable to idiosyncratic interpretation) and becomes meaningful only as an aspect of the 'human condition'. This is, of course, a characteristic determination of humanist readings of literature which hold to the ideological conviction that literature, in its highest forms, is non-ideological. It would be perfectly appropriate, within this particular frame, to take a poem by Pearse – say, *The Rebel* – and to read it in the light of a story – the Republican tradition from Tone, the Celtic tradition from Cuchulainn, the Christian tradition from Colmcille – and then reread the story as an expression of the moral supremacy of martyrdom over oppression. But as a poem, it would be regarded as inferior to that of Yeats. Yeats, stimulated by the moribund state of the Ascendancy tradition, resolves, on the level of literature, a crisis which, for him, cannot be resolved socially or politically. In Pearse's case, the poem is no more than an adjunct to political action. The revolutionary tradition he represents is not broken by oppression but renewed by it. His symbols survive outside the poem, in the Cuchulainn statue, in the reconstituted GPO, in the military behaviour and rhetoric of the IRA. Yeats's symbols have disappeared, the destruction of Coole Park being the most notable, although even in their disappearance one can discover reinforcement for the tragic condition embodied in the poem. The unavoidable fact about both poems is that they continue to belong to history and to myth; they are part of the symbolic procedures which characterize their culture. Yet, to the extent that we prefer one as literature to the other, we find ourselves inclined to dispossess it of history, to concede to it an autonomy which is finally defensible only on the grounds of style.

The consideration of style is a thorny problem. In Irish writing, it is particularly so. When the language is English, Irish writing is dominated by the notion of vitality restored, of the centre energized by the periphery, the urban by the rural, the cosmopolitan by the provincial, the decadent by the natural. This is one of the liberating effects of nationalism, a means of restoring dignity and power to what had been humiliated and suppressed. This is the idea which underlies all our formulations of tradition. Its development is confined to two variations. The first we may call the variation of adherence, the second of separation. In the first, the restoration of native energy to the English language is seen as a specifically Irish contribution to a shared heritage. Standard English, as a form of language or as a form of literature, is rescued from its exclusiveness by being compelled to incorporate into itself what had previously been regarded as a delinquent dialect. It is the Irish contribution, in literary terms, to the treasury of English verse and prose. Cultural nationalism is thus transformed into a species of literary unionism. Sir Samuel Ferguson is the most explicit supporter of this variation, although, from Edgeworth to Yeats, it remains a tacit assumption. The story of the spiritual heroics of a fading class – the Ascendancy – in the face of a transformed Catholic 'nation' – was rewritten in a variety of ways in literature – as the story of the pagan Fianna replaced by a pallid Christianity, of young love replaced by old age (Deirdre, Oisin), of aristocracy supplanted by mob-democracy. The fertility of these rewritings is all the more remarkable in that they were recruitments by the fading class of the myths of renovation which belonged to their opponents. Irish culture became the new property of those who were losing their grip on Irish land. The effect of these rewritings was to transfer the blame for the drastic condition of the country from the Ascendancy to the Catholic middle classes or to their English counterparts. It was in essence a strategic retreat from political to cultural supremacy. From Lecky to Yeats and forward to F. S. L. Lyons we witness the conversion of Irish history into a tragic theatre in which the great Anglo-Irish protagonists – Swift, Burke, Parnell – are destroyed in their heroic attempts to unite culture of intellect with the emotion of multitude, or, in political terms, constitutional politics with the forces of revolution. The triumph of the forces of revolution is glossed in all cases as the success of a philistine modernism over a rich and integrated

organic culture. Yeats's promiscuity in his courtship of heroic figures –
Cuchulainn, John O'Leary, Parnell, the 1916 leaders, Synge, Mussolini,
Kevin O'Higgins, General O'Duffy – is an understandable form of anxiety
in one who sought to find in a single figure the capacity to give reality to a
spiritual leadership for which (as he consistently admitted) the conditions
had already disappeared. Such figures could only operate as symbols. Their
significance lay in their disdain for the provincial, squalid aspects of a mob
culture which is the Yeatsian version of the other face of Irish nationalism. It
could provide him culturally with a language of renovation, but it provided
neither art nor civilization. That had come, politically, from the connection
between England and Ireland.

All the important Irish Protestant writers of the nineteenth century had, as
the ideological centre of their work, a commitment to a minority or subversive attitude which was much less revolutionary than it appeared to be.
Edgeworth's critique of landlordism was counterbalanced by her sponsor-
ship of utilitarianism and 'British manufacturers';[1] Maturin and Le Fanu
took the sting out of Gothicism by allying it with an ethic of aristocratic
loneliness; Shaw and Wilde denied the subversive force of their proto-
socialism by expressing it as cosmopolitan wit, the recourse of the social or
intellectual dandy who makes such a fetish of taking nothing seriously that
he ceases to be taken seriously himself. Finally, Yeats's preoccupation with
the occult, and Synge's with the lost language of Ireland are both minority
positions which have, as part of their project, the revival of worn social
forms, not their overthrow. The disaffection inherent in these positions is
typical of the Anglo-Irish criticism of the failure of English civilization in
Ireland, but it is articulated for an English audience which learned to regard
all these adversarial positions as essentially picturesque manifestations of the
Irish sensibility. In the same way, the Irish mode of English was regarded as
picturesque too and when both language and ideology are rendered harmless
by this view of them, the writer is liable to become a popular success.
Somerville and Ross showed how to take the middle-class seriousness out
of Edgeworth's world and make it endearingly quaint. But all nineteenth-
century Irish writing exploits the connection between the picturesque and the
popular. In its comic vein, it produces *The Shaughran* and *Experiences of an
Irish R.M.*; in its Gothic vein, *Melmoth the Wanderer, Uncle Silas* and
Dracula; in its mandarin vein, the plays of Wilde and the poetry of the
young Yeats. The division between that which is picturesque and that
which is useful did not pass unobserved by Yeats. He made the great
realignment of the minority stance with the pursuit of perfection in art. He
gave the picturesque something more than respectability. He gave it the
mysteriousness of the esoteric and in doing so committed Irish writing to
the idea of an art which, while belonging to 'high' culture, would not have,
on the one hand, the asphyxiating decadence of its English or French

counterparts and, on the other hand, would have within it the energies of a community which had not yet been reduced to a public. An idea of art opposed to the idea of utility, an idea of an audience opposed to the idea of popularity, an idea of the peripheral becoming the central culture – in these three ideas Yeats provided Irish writing with a programme for action. But whatever its connection with Irish nationalism, it was not, finally, a programme of separation from the English tradition. His continued adherence to it led him to define the central Irish attitude as one of self-hatred. In his extraordinary 'A General Introduction for my Work' (1937), he wrote:

> The 'Irishry' have preserved their ancient 'deposit' through wars which, during the sixteenth and seventeenth centuries, became wars of extermination; no people, Lecky said . . . have undergone greater persecution, nor did that persecution altogether cease up to our own day. No people hate as we do in whom that past is always alive . . . Then I remind myself that though mine is the first English marriage I know of in the direct line, all my family names are English, and that I owe my soul to Shakespeare, to Spenser and to Blake, perhaps to William Morris, and to the English language in which I think, speak, and write, that everything I love has come to me through English; my hatred tortures me with love, my love with hate . . . This is Irish hatred and solitude, the hatred of human life that made Swift write *Gulliver* and the epitaph upon his tomb, that can still make us wag between extremes and doubt our sanity.

The pathology of literary unionism has never been better defined.

The second variation in the development of the idea of vitality restored is embodied most perfectly in Joyce. His work is dominated by the idea of separation as a means to the revival of suppressed energies. The separation he envisages is as complete as one could wish. The English literary and political imperium, the Roman Catholic and Irish nationalist claims, the oppressions of conventional language and of conventional narrative – all of these are overthrown, but the freedom which results is haunted by his fearful obsession with treachery and betrayal. In him, as in many twentieth-century writers, the natural ground of vitality is identified as the libidinal. The sexual forms of oppression are inscribed in all his works but, with that, there is also the ambition to see the connection between sexuality and history. His work is notoriously preoccupied with paralysis, inertia, the disabling effects of society upon the individual who, like Bloom, lives within its frame, or, like Stephen, attempts to live beyond it. In *Portrait* the separation of the aesthetic ambition of Stephen from the political, the sexual and the religious zones of experience is clear. It is, of course, a separation which includes them, but as oppressed forces which were themselves once oppressive. His comment on Wilde is pertinent:

Here we touch the pulse of Wilde's art – sin. He deceived himself into believing that he was the bearer of good news of neo-paganism to an enslaved people ... But if some truth adheres ... to his restless thought ... at its very base is the truth inherent in the soul of Catholicism: that man cannot reach the divine heart except through that sense of separation and loss called sin.[2]

In Joyce himself the sin is treachery, sexual or political infidelity. The betrayed figure is the alien artist. The 'divine heart' is the maternal figure, mother, Mother Ireland, Mother Church or Mother Eve. But the betrayed are also the betrayers and the source of the treachery is in the Irish condition itself. In his Trieste lecture of 1907, 'Ireland, Island of Saints and Sages', he notes that Ireland was betrayed by her own people and by the Vatican on the crucial occasions of Henry II's invasion and the Act of Union.

From my point of view, these two facts must be thoroughly explained before the country in which they occurred has the most rudimentary right to persuade one of her sons to change his position from that of an unprejudiced observer to that of a convicted nationalist.[3]

Finally, in his account of the Maamtrasna murders of 1882 in 'Ireland at the Bar' (published in *Il Piccolo della Sera*, Trieste, 1907), Joyce, anticipating the use which he would make throughout *Finnegans Wake* of the figure of the Irish-speaking Myles Joyce, judicially murdered by the sentence of an English-speaking court, comments

The figure of this dumbfounded old man, a remnant of a civilization not ours, deaf and dumb before his judge, is a symbol of the Irish nation at the bar of public opinion.[4]

This, along with the well-known passage from *Portrait* in which Stephen feels the humiliation of being alien to the English language in the course of his conversation with the Newman-Catholic Dean of Studies, identifies Joyce's sense of separation from both Irish and English civilization. Betrayed into alienation, he turns to art to enable him to overcome the treacheries which have victimized him.

In one sense, Joyce's writing is founded on the belief in the capacity of art to restore a lost vitality. So the figures we remember are embodiments of this 'vitalism', particularly Molly Bloom and Anna Livia Plurabelle. The fact that they were women is important too, since it clearly indicates some sort of resolution, on the level of femaleness, of what had remained implacably unresolvable on the male level, whether that be of Stephen and Bloom or of Shem and Shaun. This vitalism announces itself also in the protean language of these books, in their endless transactions between history and fiction, macro-and microcosm. But along with this, there is in Joyce a recognition of a world which is 'void' (a favourite word of his), even though it is also full of correspondence, objects, people. His registration of the detail of Dublin life takes 'realism' to the point of parody, takes the sequence of items which form a plot into the series of items which form an inventory. The clean and clinical detail of *Dubliners* is akin to what he speaks of in his essay on Blake, where he describes Michelangelo's influence on the poet as evinced in

> ... the importance of the pure, clean line that evokes and creates the figure on the background of the uncreated void.[5]

His vitalism is insufficient to the task of overcoming this void. The inexhaustibility of his texts is a symptom of a social emptiness, of a world in which the subject, although one of culture's 'sons', is also 'an unprejudiced observer' whose view of any communal relationship – familial, political, religious – is darkened by the conviction that it is necessarily treacherous. The disenchantment with community in Joyce is not simply the denial by him or by a 'rational' Ulysses-like hero of myths, like nationalism or Catholicism. It is the disenchantment with privacy, especially with the heroic and privileged privacy of the individual consciousness, which is, in the end, the more disturbing discovery. The literary correlative of this is the replacement of the univocal, heroic, Yeatsian style with a polyglot mixture of styles (in *Ulysses*) and of languages (in *Finnegans Wake*). Yeats's various recuperations of 'aristocratic' and 'community' forms – though occult or occluded energies, from the 'Celtic' myths to the Japanese Noh play, from a 'national' theatre to the Blueshirt marching songs – are rebuked by Joyce's consumer-world, where the principle of connection is paratactic merely and the heroic artistic spirit is replaced by the trans-individual consciousness.

Yeats was indeed our last romantic in literature as was Pearse in politics. They were men who asserted a coincidence between the destiny of the community and their own and believed that this coincidence had an historical repercussion. This was the basis for their belief in a 'spiritual aristocracy' which worked its potent influence in a plebeian world. Their determination to restore vitality to this lost society provided their culture with a millenial conviction which has not yet died. Whatever we may think of their ideas of tradition, we still adhere to the tradition of the idea that art and revolution are definitively associated in their production of an individual style which is also the signature of the community's deepest self. The fascination with style has its roots in a tradition of opposition to official discourse, but, as we have seen, it leads to that vacillation between the extremes of picturesque caricature and tragic heroism which marks Irish literature and politics in the

period since the Union. Since Swift, no major and few minor Irish writers
have escaped this fate. Even Joyce, who repudiated the conditioning which
made it inevitable, is subject to it. There is a profoundly insulting association
in the secondary literature surrounding him that he is eccentric because of
his Irishness but serious because of his ability to separate himself from it. In
such judgements, we see the ghost of a rancid colonialism. But it is important
to recognize that this ghost haunts the works themselves. The battle between
style as the expression of communal history governed by a single imagination (as applicable to O'Connell, Parnell or De Valera as to Yeats or Synge
and Joycean stylism, in which the atomization of community is registered in
a multitude of equivalent, competing styles, in short, a battle between
Romantic and contemporary Ireland. The terms of the dispute are out-
moded but they linger on. The most obvious reason for this is the continuation of the Northern 'problem', where 'unionism' and 'nationalism' still
compete for supremacy in relation to ideas of identity racially defined as
either 'Irish' or 'British' in communities which are deformed by believing
themselves to be the historic inheritors of those identities and the traditions
presumed to go with them.

The narratives we have glanced at in the works of Joyce, Pearse and Yeats
are all based on the ideological conviction that a community exists which
must be recovered and restored. These communities – of the family in Joyce,
of the Ascendancy in Yeats, of the revolutionary brotherhood in Pearse –
underwent their restoration in literature which is self-consciously adversarial. Moreover, these narratives continue to send out their siren signals even
though the crises they were designed to describe and overcome have long
since disappeared. The signals have been at last picked up in Northern
Ireland – for so long apparently immune to them – and are now being
rebroadcast.

Both communities in the North pride themselves on being the lone and
true inheritors of their respective traditions. Their vision of themselves is
posited on this conviction of fidelity, even though this is slightly flawed by
the simultaneous recognition that the fidelity might also be a product of
isolation and provincialism. The Protestant self-image is closely bound up
with the idea of liberty and with the image of the garrison. This is well-
known, but within that there are the only slightly less well-known support
images, of the elite people (sponsored both by Protestantism and by the
exclusive Whig idea of liberty as a racial phenomenon) and of the lost tribe,
adrift in the desert of the worldly and demonic. In opposition, the Catholic
self-image is expressed in terms of the oppressed, the disowned, the aristo-
crat forced into the slum, the beseiger who attempts to break down the wall
of prejudice which calls itself liberty. The stereotypes are easily recognized
and their origins in history well-documented. Both communities cherish a
millennial faith in the triumph of their own conceptions of right. For the

Catholic, that means the disintegration of the State, for the Protestant that means its final preservation. Certain social concepts, like employment or housing, have an almost totemistic significance in the reading both communities give to the British capitalist formation in which they are both enclosed. Discrimination in these areas against Catholics is for the Protestant, a variant of the garrison or siege mentality, of keeping them out. Instead of Derry's walls, we now have the shipyards or Shorts. The beseigers live in the perpetual ghetto of the permanently ominous, yet still permanently unsuccessful, environ. Within that, no less within a ghetto, lie the beseiged.

The spectacle is obviously pathological although, for all that, no less intimate with the social and political realities of the situation. The North has all the appearances of an abnormal, aberrant society. Yet it makes plainly manifest 'normal' injustices which are taken for granted elsewhere. The religious divide is not a disguised rendering of political and social divisions. It is, at one and the same time, an expression of them and, on a more intense level, a justification for them. No one denies the existence of serious injustices in the North. But there religion is given as the reason for them. This is true and false. It is true in that religion was introduced in the plantations and afterwards as a sectarian force. Whether the bible followed the sword, or the sword the bible, is irrelevant. They came, in effect, together. The very rationalizations produced to legitimize the conquest, also help to legitimize those injustices which still derive from it as well as those which are independent of it. The communities have become stereotyped into their roles of oppressor and victim to such an extent that the notion of a Protestant or a Catholic sensibility is now assumed to be a fact of nature rather than a product of these very special and ferocious conditions.

In such a situation, nothing is more likely to perpetuate and even galvanize these stereotypes than the dream of a community's attaining, through a species of spiritual-military heroics, its longed-for destiny. Each begins to seek, in such a climate, a leadership which will definitively embody the univocal style which is the expression of its inner essence or nature. But in such a confrontation, style is no less than a declaration of war. It is the annunciation of essence in a person, in a mode of behaviour, in a set of beliefs. Paisley, for example, is the most remarkable incarnation of the communal spirit of unionism. In him, violence, a trumpery evangelicalism, anti-popery and a craven adulation of the 'British' way of life are soldered together in a populist return to the first principles of 'Ulsterness'. No other leader has the telluric power of this man. On the Catholic side, John Hume acts as the minority's agent of rational demystification and the IRA as its agency of millenial revenge. The cultural machinery of Romantic Ireland has so wholly taken over in the North that we have already seen in the last fifteen

years the following characteristic paradigms repeated: – a literary efflores-
cence, ambiguously allied to the troubles; political theologies of 'armed
struggle' and 'defence of the union'; the collapse of 'constitutionalism' in
the face of British 'betrayal'; the emergence of an ancestral myth of origin, as
in the work of Ian Adamson; hunger-strikes which achieve world prominence and give to the republican cause the rebel dignity it sought; the burning
of Big Houses, attacks on barracks, a 'decent' British Army with some
notorious berserk units – the Paras, the UDR. We have had all this before.
What makes it different now is the widespread and probably justified conviction that this rerun is the last. That lends an air of desperation and
boredom to the scene. Again, there is that recognizable vacillation between
the picturesque and the tragic, between seeing the 'Northerner' in his full and
overblown self-caricature and seeing in him the working out of a tragic
destiny. The repetition of historical and literary paradigms is not necessarily
farcical but there is an unavoidable tendency towards farce in a situation in
which an acknowledged tragic conflict is also read as an anachronistic-
aberrant-picturesque one. This reading conspires with the 'modern' interpretation of the North as a place undergoing in microcosm the international
phenomenon of the battle of extremes between the terrorist and the rule of
law, to restate the problem as a particularly unfortunate combination of
both – a 'modern' problem deriving from an 'anachronistic' base.

But this is also the standard view of modern Irish writing, and one of the
apparently inexplicable features of the Irish Revival. The appearance of
what we may call an 'advanced' or 'modernist' literature in a 'backward'
country, is not quite as freakish as it seems. Throughout the last two
hundred years there has been a widely recognized contrast between the
'modern' aspects of Irish social and political structures – the eighteenth-
century parliament, the State-sponsored schemes of the nineteenth century,
the advanced industrialism of the Belfast region – and the 'antique' aspects
of the nation. The contrast was remarkable because the State and the Nation
were so entirely at odds with one another. In Yeats's programme for unity of
culture, there is a similar blend of the modern Anglo-Irish intellectual
tradition and the old Gaelic civilization. Joyce, in his 'Ireland, Island of
Saints and Scholars', remarked that

> ... the Irish nation's insistence on developing its own culture by itself is
> not so much the demand of a young nation that wants to make good in the
> European concert as the demand of a very old nation to renew under new
> forms the glories of a past civilization.[6]

There is, therefore, nothing mysterious about the re-emergence in literature
of the contrast which was built into the colonial structure of the country. But
to desire, in the present conditions in the North, the final triumph of State

over Nation, Nation over State, modernism over backwardness, authenticity over domination, or any other comparable liquidation of the standard oppositions, is to desire the utter defeat of the other community. The acceptance of a particular style of Catholic or Protestant attitudes or behaviour, married to a dream of a final restoration of vitality to a decayed cause or community, is a contribution to the possibility of civil war. It is impossible to do without ideas of a tradition. But it is necessary to disengage from the traditions of the ideas which the literary revival and the accompanying political revolution sponsored so successfully. This is not to say that we should learn to suspect Yeats and respect Joyce. For Yeats, although he did surrender to the appeal of violence, also conceded the tragic destiny this involved. Joyce, although he attempted to free himself from set political positions, did finally create, in *Finnegans Wake*, a characteristically modern way of dealing with heterogeneous and intractable material and experience. The pluralism of his styles and languages, the absorbent nature of his controlling myths and systems, finally gives a certain harmony to varied experience. But, it could be argued, it is the harmony of indifference, one in which everything is a version of something else, where sameness rules over diversity, where contradiction is finally and disquietingly written out. In achieving this in literature, Joyce anticipated the capacity of modern society to integrate almost all antagonistic elements by transforming them into fashions, fads – styles, in short. Yet it is true that in this regard, Joyce is, if you like, our most astonishingly 'modernist' author and Yeats is his 'anachronistic' counterpart. The great twins of the Revival play out in posterity the roles assigned to them and to their readers by their inherited history. The weight of that inheritance is considerable. To carry it much further some adjustment must be made. It might be a beginning to reflect further on the tradition of the idea which these two writers embody and on the dangerous applicability it has to the situation in the North.

The danger takes a variety of forms. A literature predicated on an abstract idea of essence – Irishness or Ulsterness – will inevitably degenerate into whimsy and provincialism. Even when the literature itself avoids this limitation, the commentary on it reimposes the limitation again. Much that has been written about Joyce demonstrates this. A recent book, like Hugh Kenner's *A Colder Eye*, exploits the whimsical Irishness of the writers in a particularly inane and offensive manner. The point is not simply that the Irish are different. It is that they are absurdly different because of the disabling, if fascinating, separation between their notion of reality and that of everybody else. T. S. Eliot, in a 1919 review of Yeats, wrote:

> The difference between his world and ours is so complete as to seem almost a physiological variety, different nerves and senses. It is, therefore, allowable to imagine that the difference is not only personal but national.[7]

This sort of manoeuvre has been repeated over and over again in the commentaries on Irish writing and it reappears in commentaries on Irish politics. The Irish, in the political commentary, are seen as eluding what Eliot called a 'relation to the comprehensible'. This is propaganda disguised as mystification. The sad fact is that the Irish tend to believe it. Yet the variations of adherence (i.e. politically speaking, unionism) and of separation (politically speaking, republicanism) and all the modifications to which they are subject in Irish writing are not whimsical evasions of reality. Our reality has been and is dominated by these variations and their stylistic responses. Although the Irish political crisis is, in many respects, a monotonous one, it has always been deeply engaged in the fortunes of Irish writing at every level, from the production of work to its publication and reception. The oppressiveness of the tradition we inherit has its source in our own readiness to accept the mystique of Irishness as an inalienable feature of our writing and, indeed, of much else in our culture. That mystique is itself an alienating force. To accept it is to become involved in the spiritual heroics of a Yeats or a Pearse, to believe in the incarnation of the nation in the individual. To reject it is to make a fetish of exile, alienation and dislocation in the manner of Joyce or Beckett. Between these hot and cold rhetorics there is little room for choice. Yet the polarization they identify is an inescapable and understandable feature of the social and political realities we inhabit. They are by no means extravagant examples of Irish linguistic energy exercised in a world foreign to every onlooker. They inhabit the highly recognizable world of modern colonialism.

Even so, both Joyce and Yeats are troubled by the mystique to an extent that, in contemporary conditions, we cannot afford. The dissolution of that mystique is an urgent necessity if any lasting solution to the North is to be found. One step towards that dissolution would be the revision of our prevailing idea of what it is that constitutes the Irish reality. In literature that could take the form of a definition, in the form of a comprehensive anthology, of what writing in this country has been for the last 300–500 years and, through that, an exposure of the fact that the myth of Irishness, the notion of Irish unreality, the notions surrounding Irish eloquence, are all political themes upon which the literature has battened to an extreme degree since the nineteenth century when the idea of national character was invented. The Irish national character apologetically portrayed by the Banims, Griffin, Carleton, Mrs Hall and a host of others has been received as the verdict passed by history upon the Celtic personality. That stereotyping has caused a long colonial concussion. It is about time we put aside the idea of essence – that hungry Hegelian ghost looking for a stereotype to live in. As Irishness or as Northernness he stimulates the provincial unhappiness we create and fly from, becoming virtuoso metropolitans to the exact degree that we have created an idea of Ireland as provincialism incarnate. These are worn oppositions. They used to be the parentheses in which the Irish destiny was isolated. That is no longer the case. Everything, including our politics and our literature, has to be rewritten – i.e. re-read. That will enable new writing, new politics, unblemished by Irishness, but securely Irish.

3

The Virtual Reality of Irish Fairy Legend

Angela Bourke

Irish fairy legend[1] is a vast body of narrative which still circulates in the two languages spoken in Ireland.[2] Made up of short, vivid, easily memorable and interconnecting units, it floats like a web of story above the physical land-scape, pegged down at point after point, as incidents are recounted of a piper lured into a cave here; a young girl found wandering mute on a hillside there; a lake where a cow emerged to give miraculous quantities of milk, and disappeared again with all her progeny when ill-treated; a hill where mys-terious music could be heard after dark. Hovering in this way above the human community, the web of stories is also like a kite controlled by one or many storytellers. Under the delicate shadows it casts, places are singled out for avoidance or attention; people are identified as deviant, dangerous, afflicted, or knowledgeable.

By any standards, the fairy legends that make up this fabric constitute a marginal verbal art, subaltern discourse: the opposite of the dominant modes of speech and thought, the elaborated codes by which most privileged ideas are conveyed, especially in print. Gapped and discontinuous, lacking a tradition of exegesis, they are almost entirely confined to oral communi-cation, and almost never taken seriously. They belong in social situations whose participants hold many of their experiences and assumptions in common and where much may be left unspoken, and so share the major characteristics of restricted linguistic codes.[3]

Fairy legends are told to amuse adults and frighten children, to entertain tourists, and to mark the distance we have come from the supposed credulity of our ancestors.[4] In some cases they may be shibboleths: indicators of adherence to older, repudiated modes of thinking and living, markers of contamination.[5] Even within the groups where fairy legends are most elabor-ately told, they are rated less valuable, less important, than other kinds of narrative, notably the long, episodic hero-tales and the international folktales or *Märchen*,[6] a situation noted by the celebrated Irish-language prose writer Máirtín Ó Cadhain. As a young schoolteacher, Ó Cadhain collected and published oral legends from his neighbours in Connemara, County Galway, and remarked that 'a story-teller, whose reputation has been made on his skill in telling the old-time Fenian tales or other [M]ärchen, is, as a rule, somewhat scornful of these short trifles and must be pressed to recite them'.[7] Much that has been written about Irish storytelling echoes these pejorative terms, and while they have undoubtedly served to validate the taste and preoccupations of collectors and scholars, they also clearly reflect a vernacular aesthetic, at least among those proficient in the telling of longer tales.

Still, fairy legends are so ubiquitous and so tenacious, and ultimately so consistent, that they merit serious consideration.[8] Rich sources of inspiration for poets – from W. B. Yeats writing in English to Nuala Ní Dhomhnaill who writes in Irish – by their very obliqueness they offer a possibility of expressing things that are generally unspeakable: for Yeats, a painful tension between imagination and life,[9] for Ní Dhomhnaill, violence, sexuality and language loss.[10] But these poets make explicit what is already implicit in oral tradition. Lacking only an exegesis, fairy legend is an intricate system of expression, already highly elaborated in its own terms.

Fairy legends are simple and memorable when taken one at a time – humble in their demands on the listener – yet they connect with one another in reticulated systems that are both elegant and economical. Their terms of reference are shared, roughly the same all over Ireland, and in Scotland and Newfoundland, while related narratives are found elsewhere in the oral tradition of northern Europe, as well as further afield. Broadly, they tell of encounters between humans and other beings variously named as 'good people', 'little people', 'hill people', or simply 'fairies'. Purporting to be true, they begin in the ordinary, with human protagonists engaged in everyday tasks or journeys. They move quickly to the extraordinary, as people disappear, or appear from nowhere, or meet with extraordinarily good or bad luck. These stories generally finish back in the ordinary, while the storytellers may or may not reflect on the meaning of what has happened.

The term 'fairies', although it risks distracting the modern reader, is the one commonly used by folklore scholars and the most convenient for this discussion. The fairies of Irish oral tradition have little in common with the illustrations in children's books or with the twinkling ballerina of Disney's Fantasyland. Nor are they usually imagined as homosexual, although they are mostly male and there is some evidence of semantic overlap between the categories they represent and the slang term for a gay man.[11] Instead, fairies mirror the rural society that tells stories about them, in both its seen and unseen aspects, and while some accounts represent them as tiny, most depict them as similar in size to humans. They share space and time with the human population, but use both differently. They live under the earth, or beneath the sea, or exist invisibly in the air, while among them 'a hundred years is only like a day'.[12] With some crucial exceptions, their physical and social characteristics resemble those of humans.

The fairies keep cows and milk them, ride horses, eat, drink, fall in love, play music, dance, wear shoes and clothing, play ball and card games, fight, steal, and hold funerals for their dead. But they abhor salt, iron, and the Christian religion, and whatever runs in their veins is not blood.[13] Fairies have no hope of salvation, according to the promises of Christianity, so in the Catholic world-view of rural Ireland, they are forever outside human culture, exempt from control by its rules. But they do hope to be saved, so instead of ranging themselves in opposition to human society, fairies are always prowling on its edges, lurking above and below it, marking its boundaries, impinging on it from time to time with consequences that make the material of stories. They abduct people (mostly children and young women) and cows. They borrow milk and other goods and ask for human help in various enterprises, from delivering babies to shoeing horses and fighting battles. When displeased, fairies wreak havoc, causing illness and death, and blighting crops, but they generously reward those who treat them well. They are most often encountered in deserted or dangerous places: at the tops of cliffs, on lonely roads, by fishermen at sea.

Fairy legend narratives are offered to listeners as more or less believable, and much of the storyteller's effort is occupied in negotiating a claim on the credulity of the audience. Some are certainly told with a wink to the initiated, while many offer the listener a trade-off between hearing a good story and appearing gullible.

Mayo storyteller John Henry claimed in May 1976 that a legend about a fisherman who found cooked cabbage on his hook was 'a true story'. Happening close to his own home, the event indicated, according to Henry, that some sort of domestic life was being carried on beneath the sea. A few minutes later on the same evening he told a second legend, about a live baby hooked in similar circumstances. This time, however, he added the disclaimer: '*Ní thig liom a ráit anois ar fírinne nó bréag é*' – 'I can't say now whether it's true or false'.[14] John Henry's story of cooked cabbage is unlikely to be believed, but may be accepted without great cost to the listener. His second story, offered much more tentatively, raises the stakes considerably while borrowing credibility from the first. Storytellers interviewed in Ireland and Newfoundland have independently suggested that although hardly anybody of their own age believes stories like these, earlier generations did. Many confess that they themselves believed when they were younger. As fairy legends are often used to discipline children or to shelter them from disturbing realities, it is likely that each generation has tended to overestimate the credulity of its ancestors.[15]

Within any audience, some listeners will be more sceptical than others. The metanarratives of folklore recognize that the transaction between teller and audience depends on listeners' willingness to suspend disbelief if offered a good enough story. In the *Arabian Nights*, Scheherazade prevails upon her royal husband to spare her life by telling him stories. Elsewhere, in a tale that traces the delicate line between truth and fiction, suitors must entertain a princess with stories, but will lose their heads if she interrupts to say, 'That is a lie!' The successful suitor, of course, is the one who succeeds in telling her a story so outrageous that she is too fascinated to interrupt.

In the telling of Irish fairy legends, the payoff for a willingness to suspend disbelief is an impromptu excursion into the world of fiction, with all it has to offer. The teller of fairy legends asks to be believed – or at least for disbelief to be deferred – by using a low-key conversational tone, by speaking about a known and most probably adjacent landscape, and by including considerable circumstantial detail: names and occupations of people or descriptions of work and weather, for instance. But just as fairies are alive and yet not alive, so people can both believe in them and disbelieve. Some legends recount events that are merely odd, while others are downright preposterous, yet it is difficult to say when the boundary from reported fact to inventive fiction is crossed. It is partly in this ability to reconcile the impossible with the unexceptional that the legend-teller's skill lies.

Sean O'Sullivan's *Legends from Ireland*[16] offers an example which will illustrate this point. Told by Éamon a Búrc, of Carna, Co. Galway, one of the best storytellers known in Ireland in this century, it is just two pages long – representing only a few minutes' telling. O'Sullivan's translation of the original Irish is called 'Midnight Funeral from America'.[17] The storyteller never mentions fairies, by name or otherwise, but the whole sense of his narrative depends on their existence.[18]

SUMMARY

A man recently emigrated to America is on his way home to his lodging one night after a visit to Irish friends. He encounters a funeral, and according to rural Irish practice, turns to walk three paces along with it, whereupon he finds himself back home in Ireland, at the graveyard in Garomna, next to the house where he grew up. He goes into his old home, where the occupants are all out for the evening, and eats some potatoes from a pot being kept warm beside the fire. Then he goes back to the graveyard, attends the funeral, and afterwards finds himself back on the street in America, but not before driving his knife, on which his name is carved, into the ground beside his father's headstone. He writes to his family in Ireland, telling of his adventure. They remember missing some potatoes from the pot that night and, when they go to the graveyard, find the knife stuck in the ground as he has described it.

Garomna, where most of this story is set, and Carna, where it was told, are two remote communities on the deeply indented Connemara coast of County Galway, separated from each other by many miles of road, but only by a few miles of Galway Bay. Garomna is in fact an island, connected to the mainland by a causeway, but both it and Carna are literally and figuratively *off the beaten track*.

'There's no lie in it', Éamon a Búrc says at the beginning and end of his story. The knife left stuck in the ground, like the book left in the car by the ghostly hitchhiker in the modern urban legend,[19] is offered as fictional proof, as though it were physically present. The story is impossible to believe, yet we have been sucked in; but neither we nor the original audience have anything to gain by protesting, 'That is a lie!'

The essence of fairy-belief legend is ambivalence: a play between belief and disbelief, summed up in a well-known anecdote about an American anthropologist and an Irish informant. The Irish woman, asked whether she really believed in fairies, is said to have answered, 'I do not, Sir, but they're there!'.[20] However the precise location of 'there' is problematic, for the Irish fairies inhabit what is effectively *non-place*. People encounter them on boundaries: either in space – between townlands or on beaches between high and low tide; or in time – at dusk or at midnight; on Hallowe'en or May Eve. Other boundaries marked by fairy intervention are social: occasions of transition and ambiguity in human life, such as the few days which used to elapse in rural areas between formal betrothal and marriage, or the period between the birth and christening of a child.

In the legends told about fairies, the art of oral fiction works on the paradox of *space* versus *place* to turn 'nowhere' or *non-place* into a virtual place, in which things can happen. As geographer Yi-Fu Tuan puts it, 'what begins as undifferentiated space becomes place as we get to know it better and endow it with value'.[21] So these stories provide fictional characteristics for otherwise anomalous or unknowable places. They deepen the native's knowledge of her physical surroundings, but also thriftily use the gaps in the known environment for the elaboration of an imagined world where all those things that are in Heaven and Earth and yet not dreamt of in rational philosophy may be accommodated.

Fairies belong in no-man's land; they live in no time at all. In the story summarized above, the dark American city streets where the man walks home alone replace the scary, lonely, mistry, or boggy parts of the Irish landscape where most other tellings are set. Moving between his Irish friends' home and his own lodgings, this man's adventure happened as he passed through the *non-place* between two familiar and safe *places* in an otherwise alien environment. Significantly, the story was told, not in Boston or Brooklyn, but in rural Ireland – to an audience imagining emigration, not living it.

This ability of fairy legends to deal with so much of the betwixt-and-between – the liminal, the marginal, and the ambiguous, whether in time, in the landscape, or in social relations – makes them important cognitive tools. The very excesses which make them sometimes ridiculous to the literate mind are knots in a rope of memory, put there to save the stories from forgetfulness. Walter Ong's *Literacy and Orality* reminds us that people in oral cultures must 'think memorable thoughts'. Those images of hot potatoes missing from the pot on the hearth and the man's knife with his name on it, stuck in the ground by the gravestone, are wonderfully, tangibly, memorable.[22] Mention of the missing potatoes is a masterly touch. Connemara households cooked such vast quantities of potatoes daily, for human and animal consumption, that it is hard to imagine anyone noticing that a few were missing; the knife by the gravestone, on the other hand, is either there or not. However the heat and taste of the potatoes serve to guarantee their tenure in memory while reinforcing the 'proof' offered by the knife.

We must also reckon with the possibility that this story frames an elaborate practical joke, and that Éamon a Búrc could shrewdly calculate which members of his audience might be taken in by it. Leaving one's favourite knife stuck in a significant place is just the sort of symbolic or sentimental act people have always performed on the eve of emigration, especially in the days when emigration meant likely permanent exile. Such a knife would not easily be spotted in the long grass of a west-of-Ireland graveyard, but it would be there to be found when the emigrant wrote a letter home, as indeed the story says he did. The protagonist of this legend, recently emigrated from Connemara, could tell a story amazing enough to have his home community remember him, or his immigrant community take notice of him, while also giving voice to homesickness and nostalgia, emotions which might be unacceptable if more directly expressed.[23] Meanwhile, those people left at home could possess a piece of fiction through which to remember him as well as to contemplate, perhaps rehearse for, the experience of emigration.

Most fairy legends told in Ireland are short and easily trivialized, but in Éamon a Búrc's repertoire many of them become long, thoughtful, and graceful narratives, showing an adult intelligence skilfully negotiating a shared system of symbols and metaphors in a context of orality. This shared system is more than the oral-formulaic patterning elucidated by Milman Parry, Albert Lord, and their successors:[24] it is an intimate and detailed parallel of physical and social life, rendered in three dimensions and with full attention to bodily sensation – not so much a grammar of words and formulas, more a grammar of ideas. We may imagine it as a sort of garment: a precisely tailored artifact which will fit over human experience, as a sleeve fits an arm – and move with it. This image inevitably recalls the bristling helmets and gloves of virtual-reality technology, which translate human impulses into a domain of fiction. If virtual reality is an imaginary environment with which the user can interact realistically, then the fairy world of these Irish legends is a vernacular virtual reality.

Stories like Éamon a Búrc's 'Midnight Funeral from America' are clever games, hugely relished by their participants, but they are much more. Preoccupied with real-life boundaries and transitional states, fairy belief or half-belief also marks symbolic boundaries, which more widely facilitate the organization of knowledge and thought outside the culture of literacy.

Sixty years ago Conrad Arensberg argued that Irish fairy tradition forms 'a symbolic order overlying the values of social life'.[25] Thirty years later came Mary Douglas's influential *Purity and Danger*,[26] which focused on *boundaries* as essential to the ordering of human behaviour. More recently, and following Douglas, Robert Wuthnow has suggested that symbolic boundaries may be used to make sense of areas where problems in moral obligation may arise, and to explain the persistence of what he calls 'folk piety' in the interstices of modern society.[27]

My concern here, however, is not so much with the ordering of society or with so-called superstitious practice, as with the ordering of thought – the organization of knowledge in individual human minds and its exchange between them.

Most commentary on Irish oral tradition is influenced by colonial or postcolonial assumptions, which alike subscribe to binary oppositions between the literate English-speaking metropolis and the oral culture of rural Irish speakers. Rural culture has been so consistently presented as homogeneous and unchanging, often by conservative forces within the Irish state, that we are not accustomed to think about its verbal art in terms of the agency or oppositional interests of performers and audience.[28] The effects of such uncritical representation are far-reaching: long after it became politically incorrect to stereotype African Americans, Native Americans or other ethnic groups in even apparently benign ways, it is still acceptable on both sides of the Atlantic to characterize the Irish as stupid and pugnacious.[29] Irish-Americans appear to tolerate these demeaning stereotypes by containing them within cultural frames of the ludic – the St Patrick's Day Parade, the Notre Dame football game, the phrase, 'Irish for a day'. Within Ireland, on the other hand, stereotypes are deflected in typical postcolonial fashion onto less advantaged members of our own society: jokes told in England against the Irish are told in Ireland against Kerrymen (by people who don't know how good life can be in Kerry), while the full force of 'No Irish need apply' is visited with shameful regularity on Travellers.[30] Such unexamined thought-patterns also mean that labels applied to all the Irish by Victorian print-colonialism have been left sticking to Irish oral tradition, despite the elevation of folklore to the status of national icon under native governments.[31]

Well into this century, especially in Irish-speaking areas, rural Irish society accorded high status to its oral storytellers. More than simply an entertainer, the skilled storyteller was valued as outstandingly wise, thoughtful, and knowledgeable. The intellectual property these practitioners valued so highly, and to which they and their neighbours devoted so much time and energy, deserves careful attention; but such attention has not always been forthcoming except among folklore specialists. A major obstacle has been that the intellectual property in question consists of stories about invisible beings, without the respectability which an organized religion or tradition of exegesis might lend to such material. For hundreds of years, as rational discourses have ranged themselves in opposition to all forms of 'superstition', any suspicion of belief in fairies has been enough to label individuals and whole communities as backward, naïve and ignorant.[32]

Such wholesale dismissal of oral tradition by the culture of literacy is not conducive to serious study. However in *The Savage Mind*, Claude Lévi-Strauss noted that '[e]very civilization tends to overestimate the objective orientation of its thought';[33] and literate modern societies are no exception. It may in fact be more useful to imagine not that people in rural Ireland remember and tell fairy legends because they believe them, but that they tell them (and sometimes believe them) because they remember them. That is to say, being able to find one's way around such an intricately interconnected set of narratives as fairy legend provides may be a valuable intellectual practice in itself.

Lévi-Strauss discusses the minute taxonomies of botany and zoology found in non-literate, what he calls 'savage', cultures around the world, finding many species thus catalogued that hold no discernible usefulness, beauty, or danger for the peoples involved. He observes that 'animals and plants are not known as a result of their usefulness; they are deemed to be useful or interesting because they are first of all known'. They form, he suggests, the intellectual framework around which other knowledge can be organized in an oral culture.[34] An incident in a Navajo home in Utah, described by American folklorist Barre Toelken, illustrates how the traditional string-figures taught to every child perform the same function.

A teenage Navajo girl told three visiting folklorists, 'The Spider Woman taught us all these designs as a way of helping us think. You learn to think when you make these.'[35] Later, her father elaborated (Toelken's translation):

These are all matters we need to know. It's too easy to become sick, because there are always things happening to confuse our minds. We need to have ways of thinking, of keeping things stable, healthy, beautiful. We try for a long life, but lots of things can happen to us. So we keep our thinking in order by these figures and we keep our lives in order with the stories. We have to relate our lives to the stars and the sun, the animals, and to all of nature or else we will go crazy, or get sick.[36]

String-figures in Navajo culture, like fairy legends in Ireland, are at once games, works of art, illustrated textbooks, metaphors, and mnemonics.

'An oral culture has no texts. How does it get together organized material for recall? This is the same as asking, "What does it or can it know in an organized fashion?".'[37] Operating within the culture of literacy, we find it difficult to grasp modes of thought which do not find their analogy in the two-dimensional world of the printed page and the linear logic of the book. But in the last years of the twentieth century, as pointing and clicking on icons takes over from the linear perusal of printed texts, it may be possible to bypass the linear thinking of chirographic and typographic literacy. Instead we can look at traditional narratives as reflexes of a three-dimensional system for organizing knowledge in oral culture, simultaneously responsive to aesthetic, intellectual, and practical requirements. Irish fairy legend, especially among people who do not write, constitutes a shared intellectual resource, available for many functions from amusement to the modelling of intractable abstract problems. Meanwhile, our increasing familiarity with the way computers work offers a way of sidestepping the constraints of literate thinking to understand oral modes of thought.

A commonplace of folklore scholarship is that good storytellers possess remarkable memories. Folklorists also accept that oral cultures manage memory in ways largely inaccessible to the world of literacy.[38] And most commentators acknowledge that oral performers are artists, fully in command of their material.[39] In the last twenty years, however, as the literate world's familiarity with computers has grown, the received sense of the word *memory* has shifted, from something immaterial, even spiritual, to something finite that can be measured, filled, emptied – even added to.[40] Paradoxically, such an instrumental view of memory invites a return to understanding its workings in the terms of pre-literate culture. It becomes possible again, as it was for the rhetoricians of the Middle Ages, to think of memory as an art.[41]

The insights into oral tradition and memory-management made available by the work of Milman Parry, Albert B. Lord, and their successors depended heavily on sound-recording technology.[42] Later, Walter Ong's work on orality in the 1970s and early 1980s drew attention to the phenomenon he called 'secondary orality', fostered by the electronic media, including the telephone.[43] Secondary orality has profound implications for cultural expression by formerly colonized or potentially marginalized groups in the late twentieth century. Inexpensive cassette-tape recording has allowed migrant workers from the Philippines to stay in touch with their families back home without first negotiating the world of literacy; it permits traditional musicians in Ireland to learn songs and airs from people they may have met only briefly, or not at all. In these instances, the weary detour through the tortuous – and distorting – passages of the written or printed word has been avoided. The result is not the same as in an uninterrupted oral tradition:

people don't speak to (or listen to) a tape-machine exactly as they do to an interlocutor who is present; a song learned from a tape will be based on just one performance in identical repetitions, rather than on a series of perform-ances.[44] Nevertheless, for illiterate migrant workers and for traditional singers and musicians, as for many blind and partially sighted people all over the world, cassette tapes deliver the possibility of an autonomy undreamt of when print ruled the world.

In the last twenty years, computers have begun to offer the same kind of freedom from large centralized institutions as cassette recordings do, but on a far more complex scale. Meanwhile the cultural criticism that has developed as a discipline hand in hand with the rise of the personal computer has drawn attention to the invisible assumptions and intellectual models which underpin so much of our received knowledge. For over a century, many of the dominant ideas in metropolitan culture have been expressed in terms of linear progress and hierarchical structures. Lines could be traced to where they converged in a single point of origin, but that model is now being superseded.

A hundred years ago the train was not just an important mode of trans-port and communication; trains and railways held a central place in the popular imagination. We have only to think of model railways – of Anna Karenina and all those trains, of Sherlock Holmes and his Baedeker. Now-adays, however, a similar symbolic importance attaches to the World Wide Web. As more and more people experience it for themselves, the Web penetrates into ever more areas of everyday speech, thought, and metaphor. This substitution has far-reaching implications for the culture of literacy and for our understanding of other modes of thought.[45]

At the end of the nineteenth century, the train was a powerful symbol of progress, and the 'modern' world was mapped with the branching black lines of railways, along which progress and newspapers could be delivered from metropolitan centres to outlying areas as literacy spread among ordinary people. In America the train was an instrument of colonization, which enabled the displacement of native inhabitants and their replacement by European settlers. In Britain and Ireland, however, trains changed the lives of people who were already there, for population displacements had taken place centuries earlier. But everywhere the railway brought with it a sense of authority derived from elsewhere; of standard clocks and time-keeping, of subordination to a series of urban centres, increasing in density and import-ance as the line drew closer to the metropolis. Small towns were no longer the centres of their own hinterlands, but points on a line, polarized up and down. It is surely no coincidence that the railway map with its hierarchical structure so remarkably resembles other nineteenth-century institutions like the Darwinian model of biological descent, the *stemmae* of manuscript scholarship, the derivation of the Indo-European languages, and the family tree as reckoned through the male line – not of course a nineteenth-century invention, but much invoked then, and used as a powerful metaphor of colonization.

The effect on oral storytelling of what we may call the mental railway map was cataclysmic. Walter Benjamin's 1936 essay, 'The Storyteller: Reflections on the Works of Nikolai Leskoy', begins with the words: 'Familiar though his name may be to us, the storyteller in his living immediacy is by no means a present force. He has already become something remote from us and something that is getting even more distant.'[46] Benjamin committed suicide, believing he was about to be captured by the Nazis, in 1940. At that time, Éamon a Búrc, whose legend about the fairy funeral we considered above, was alive and well, though elderly, telling stories to appreciative and discerning audiences. Benjamin was right nevertheless: Búrc lived in a remote part of Ireland, a neutral and self-sufficient country where draconian censorship kept most European news at bay.[47] The environment which valued his stories *was* remote from the metropolitan world, and already all but forgotten by it, although this storyteller was an avid radio listener and deeply interested in world affairs.[48]

Benjamin identified two kinds of background for the storyteller: travelling and staying at home, both of which Éamon a Búrc had done by the time he began to tell stories. The Irish aphorism, *siúlach, scéalach*, gives this same idea of the traveller as one who has something to relate. We might render it as 'travellers tell'; for a traveller is an observer, whose eyes stay open in wonder, even after they should have closed in sleep, and s/he may have amazing stories to tell – *far-fetched tales*, in both senses of the word. But just as print dealt a serious blow to oral tradition and to the Irish language, to which it came late, so mass transportation almost did away with travel.

When the railways came in the nineteenth century, commuters began to replace travellers.[49] Bored repeaters of the same journey, commuters have no tales to tell. Instead they read. In Ireland and Britain from the 1840s, railway-station news-stands fostered a huge expansion in periodical publication, which led in turn to the rise of the short story (ideal for the commuter's journey) and the novel, written in weekly instalments for those same commuters.[50] In Ireland, literacy levels rose steadily after the Famine of the 1840s: the proportion of people aged over five who claimed to be able to read increased from 47 per cent in 1841 to 53 per cent in 1851, and to almost 90 per cent in 1911. Letters written and newspapers and magazines read increased as well, and the number of newspaper editors and writers quadrupled between 1861 and 1911.[51] With negligible exceptions, literacy in this period meant the ability to read English, not Irish. As in England, where the booksellers W. H. Smith made their fortune in railway-station concessions, the growing prosperity in Ireland of their counterparts, Eason and Son, was due to improvements in both literacy and transport facilities.[52]

Universal literacy was a democratic ideal at the end of the nineteenth century, a means by which all men – though not necessarily all women – would eventually share in the decision-making which affected their lives. Just as the railways carried modern men dryshod across bogs and rocks, so the printed word delivered to them certainties and regulations, the answers to all questions. In this world of advancing popular literacy, the fairy legend fitted awkwardly at best, an embarrassing relic of a discarded way of thinking.[53] A hundred years later, however, with the rise of fragmented and specialised 'Englishes' and the decline of reading, universal literacy is beginning to break apart.[54] How may we now understand the fairy legend?

This essay has offered various analogies and metaphors in an attempt to answer the above question by releasing it from the preconceptions dictated by reading and by print. Most of them, notably the central analogies of the Web and of virtual reality, offer three-dimensional imagery in place of the two dimensions of text. This contrast – between two-dimensional and three-dimensional thinking – comes better into focus if we consider the life and art of a single storyteller.

Éamon a Búrc (1866–1942) was a man of remarkable intellectual and personal resources, with none of the simple-minded credulity which popular colonialist discourse associates with the Irish teller of stories about 'the little people'. He lived alongside, but not through, the transition from orality to mass literacy in the late nineteenth and early twentieth centuries, for according to the best information available, he was unable to read.[55] Both trains and nets – webs? – played important parts in his life.

When Éamon Liam (Éamon, son of Liam) was born in April 1866, in Carna, County Galway, it was an almost monoglot Irish-speaking community, more easily reached by boat than by road or rail. His father, Liam, was a noted storyteller, but when Éamon was a child, the family emigrated from the rocky seaside landscape of Carna, with its small thatched houses and subsistence farming and fishing, to the United States, where they settled far from the ocean, in St Paul, Minnesota.

The Twin Cities of Minneapolis and St Paul were growing rapidly, just beginning to attract immigrants from Europe, and building the prosperity they still enjoy. By 1871, St Paul, on the east side of the Mississippi, was connected by railroad both to Duluth on Lake Superior and to Chicago. It was the gateway to the prairies, the last link with the East Coast. Many of the new Irish immigrants worked at building the railways, which were opening up the West during this period, and several commentators have remarked on the numbers of serious injuries they sustained. By 1883 the Great Northern Railroad linked the Twin Cities to Seattle and the West Coast; and Éamon Liam, at the age of seventeen, had lost a leg in a railroad accident.

His family brought him back to Ireland, to his home parish of Carna, where he lived for the rest of his life. He was trained as a tailor (as lame boys often were, just as blind boys were taught music), but much preferring to be outdoors, he worked most of his life as a highly skilled sailor and fisherman. He could move around freely, easily vaulting, with the help of his crutch, the stone walls that are everywhere in Connemara. Once, in his early thirties, he sailed a three-and-a-half ton traditional fishing-boat through a severe storm with only two young boys as crew. In his account of that ordeal it is hard to say which is more impressive: his seamanship or the vigorous, precise language in which he narrated his experience to Liam Mac Coisdeala in 1938.[56]

Mac Coisdeala, who became a fulltime collector with the Irish Folklore Commission in 1936, first came to the Carna area in 1928 as a twenty-one-year-old teacher interested in collecting folklore. He soon discovered Éamon Liam, who at 62 was well known among his neighbours as the most talented storyteller for miles.[57] From then until the storyteller's death in November 1942 at the age of 76, Mac Coisdeala visited the area regularly and wrote down or recorded some 200 stories from him, one of which ran to 34,000 words and took three evenings to tell.[58]

Although his fame in his own lifetime depended on his ability to tell long, formulaic, swashbuckling hero-tales and *Märchen*, Éamon Liam was also a consummate teller of fairy legends, creating enigmatic narratives that are full of striking visual detail as well as remarkable psychological and social insight. His protagonists are believable characters, the practical details of whose ordinary lives play an affecting counterpoint to the extraordinary events which befall them. One is a net-maker, so outraged by the fairies' abduction of a human child that he blocks the way in and out of their hill by constructing a web of ropes across it, in a narrative that addresses questions of love and bereavement against a background of conflicting obligations. Another is a young girl, whose alienation from her family is expressed in the language of fairy metaphor.[59] Still others are fishermen who come into contact with a world beneath the sea, behind the refraction of the water's surface that can make a straight oar appear to hinge in the middle.[60] Its fairy inhabitants are at home in that dangerous and unknowable environment in which Éamon Liam as sailor and fisherman was such a fearless expert. As storyteller, however, we can observe him contriving to preserve for future generations a wealth of technical detail and practical information, by the simple expedient of using them as scaffolding for fantasy.

If the literary short story is a form which offers us fully furnished lives, briefly glimpsed before disappearing from sight, it may be because of the effect on the middle-class imagination of those sudden views into lit railway carriages bound in other directions, where a tired mother tries to control a child, people quietly play cards, or a man appears to strangle a woman.

Generally speaking though, traditional oral storytellers are not regular commuters; nor do they live in city apartments. We do not expect them to produce stories like Alfred Hitchcock's *Rear Window* (1954). Éamon a Búrc's acquaintance with the railroad in Minnesota left him with only one leg. As a result, instead of spending his adult life in the forward progress of the American Dream, he returned to Ireland and spent the rest of his days among nets and networks, as a tailor, shopkeeper, sailor, fisherman and storyteller. The world of his fiction was not in other people's lit windows; it was in the shared tradition of what is imagined beneath the surface of the everyday.

4

'Bog Queens':
The Representation of Women in the Poetry of John Montague and Seamus Heaney

Patricia Coughlan

I

This essay investigates the construction of feminine figures, and the vocabulary of roles allotted to them, by two prominent contemporary Irish poets, John Montague and Seamus Heaney. Feminine figures and more or less abstract ideas of femininity play a major role in the work of both: how should this centrality of the feminine be interpreted? Is it, as it most usually announces itself, to be taken as a celebration? Or does it flatter to deceive, as has been remarked about Matthew Arnold's perhaps analogous celebration of the alleged Celtic virtues of passion, sensuousness, non-rational insight? I have chosen to discuss the work of male poets, believing strongly that both 'gynocritics' – the 'naming', recovery and revaluing of women's writing – and the persistent demystifying of representations of women in men's work must continue in tandem. The social and cultural construction of gender is a continuously occurring process, in which it is certainly not yet time to stop intervening. I shall argue that even able and serious contemporary work is deeply and dismayingly reliant upon old, familiar and familiarly oppressive allocations of gender positions. Our celebration of this work must therefore be inflected by this question as to its effect: can poetry's implicit claim to universality of utterance and to utopian insight be upheld in the face of a reader's awareness of its gendered and therefore (perhaps unconsciously) partial perspective?

The representation of femininity which occurs most insistently in this material takes the form of dualistically opposed aspects: beloved or spouse figures versus mother figures, which are in turn benign and fertile or awe-inspiring and terrible. Very much as in the actual social construction of femininity, the various feminine functions are sometimes made to coalesce bewilderingly, sometimes set in opposition to one another. In Heaney, for example, the nature-goddess is simultaneously spouse, death-bringer and nurturer. This invocation of a *magna mater* figure is celebrated by some readers as an empowerment of women, but it is only dubiously so if the agency described is a death-bringing one; such representations of feminine power ultimately arise from a masculine psychological difficulty in acknowledging woman's subjectivity as a force *in itself*, and not merely as a relation to man's.

[. . .]

A particular contradiction is discernible in Montague and Heaney between the project of speaking for a politically oppressed and therefore hitherto unspoken group, Northern Catholics – a project important both intrinsically and to the reception of these poets – and their failure, in general, to perceive their own reliance upon and tacit approval of the absence of women as speaking subjects and of female disempowerment. Their female figures function as crucially important forms of validation-by-opposition of the individual poet's identity, in a (sometimes almost comically blatant) neo-Oedipal struggle. In Heaney, this wresting of a speaking ego from the *magna mater* which is also the land is interestingly complicated by specifically political Irish/English stereotyping: the (necessarily, if self-expressing) male poet (phallically) digging and ploughing like his ancestors becomes the culturally female voice of the subjugated Irish, about to inundate the 'masculine' hardness of the planters' boundaries with 'feminine' vowel-floods (see 'A New Song', *Wintering Out*, 33; and 'Undine', *Door into the Dark*, 26).

Irish ideology tends to an idealization of rural life. This is often centred on female icons of ideal domesticity, especially mother-figures, who are associated with unmediated naturalness. The feminist critique of this ruralist ideology must investigate the designation of spheres and human subjects as natural or cultural and their respective valuation. It is also necessary to bear in mind the way ideology has effectively denied women the freedom to develop a fully self-conscious ego and therefore to participate in civil society by allocating them a fixed position within the domestic sphere, and by the celebration of domestic virtues as constitutive of femininity. Feminist psychoanalytic demonstrations of the construction of human subjectivity as male and Oedipal also afford a perspective on which I have drawn.[1]

In the poetry I discuss, as in the culture which produces it, women are typically associated with that which is material, and defined in opposition to mind. They are nevertheless seen as possessors of a form of knowledge hidden from the masculine speaker; but this they mutely embody and cannot themselves expound. In Montague's and Heaney's lyrics each masculine

speaker characteristically celebrates the domestic as immemorial and relishe
it as sensually and emotionally satisfying, but defines himself in the performance of his most characteristic activity, poetry, in contradistinction from it.
Woman, the primary inhabitor and constituent of the domestic realm, is
admiringly observed, centre stage but silent. She is thus constructed by a
scopic gaze, her imputed mental inaction and blankness being required to
foreground the speaker's naming and placing of her.[2] What ostensibly offers
itself as a celebration may rather be read, then, as a form of limiting
definition, in which certain traditional qualities of the feminine are required
to persist for a fit wife, mother or Muse to come into being. The constant
naming of autobiographical 'originals' for these figures effectively masks this
nearly ubiquitous blotting out of the individual qualities of *actual* women by
the dominant – and stereotyped – *ideal*.

The reader may feel a general resistance as such to the mythicizing
mentality this exemplifies: that is, to the dehistoricizing effect of discerning,
in some notional way as a truth *beneath* the actualities, an immemorial status
quo which is represented as implicitly superior to modernity; and further, to
the accompanying aestheticization by the observer of the actual deprivation,
suffering and hard work of others in the name of celebration. This objection
applies whether it is farming life, Irish political violence or gender roles
which are in question, and indeed in Montague and Heaney all three of
these are, in fact, intimately bound together. Such mythicizing moves are
discerned as false ones by Montague himself in a moment of the 'Epilogue'
of *The Rough Field* in the lines 'Only a sentimentalist would wish / To see
such degradation again . . .', and Heaney's work is perhaps more open to this
charge than Montague's own. Yet Montague falls back upon just such
sentiment later in the poem, when agricultural labour is once again interpreted as part 'of a world where action had been wrung / through painstaking years to ritual' in apparent nostalgia for the imputed absoluteness of
such humble lives. The poem's ending stresses the poet's 'failure to return'
for all his 'circling' round his rural origin (*The Rough Field*, 82–3). The point
is the necessary exclusion of the speaker *as* poet from this rural scene – even
if it had not been 'going'. The very practice of cosmopolitan literary expression marks off the poet-figure from his material throughout Montague's –
and indeed Heaney's – work, however much rural *pietas* it shows. This self-
exclusion from the whole rural world as it might be understood on its own
terms is particularly focused in the female figures this poetry constructs, who
cannot even be manipulated, as the men can, into role-models for the
apprentice to poetry-making, divided as they are by gender and its assigned
functions from the son-figures who construct them. Heaney's digging and
ploughing ancestors can be, however transiently and superficially, nomin-
ated as ur-makers, but baking, praying, home-making women – icons of
domesticity whether vibrant (mothers) or ruined (spinsters living by wells) –

are set apart from and by the poet who is concerned with conscious self-definition: an activity which must be pursued in explicit opposition to the encompassing space of a home.[3]

[...]

II

Each of the two poets inflects this conventional material with a slight difference. Let us take Montague's version first, starting with the crone-cum-chthonic mother. Hag-figures recur many times in his work, from 'The Sean Bhean Bhocht' in his first collection to 'The Music Box' in *The Dead Kingdom* (1984). The title of that first poem in which such a figure appears links it openly with popular historical representations of Ireland, by means of the 1798 ballad beginning 'Now the French are on the *say*, says the Shan Van Vocht'. In this first version, the link lies relatively inert; the description in the poem is heavily freighted with realistic detail: '... bread soaked in brown tea / And eased between shrunken gums. / Her clothes stank...' (*Poisoned Lands*, 12). But nevertheless the two essential elements of what will become a familiar conjunction are present: the distaste of the observer for what he has found physically repulsive and even terrifying, and the sense nevertheless of the old woman's access to some form of knowledge which is by definition hidden from him. In 'The Sean Bhean Bhocht', this secret knowledge is explicitly rendered as 'racial memory', curse stories and legend retellings, and in the last stanza the physical abjectness of the woman's material existence is almost cancelled by a glorious landscape vision re-situating her tales in the bright freedom of a natural setting:

> But in high summer the hills burned with corn
> I strode through golden light
> To the secret spirals of the burial stone
> The grass-choked well ran sluggish red –
> Not with blood but ferrous rust –
> But beneath the whorls of the guardian stone –
> What hidden queen lay dust.
> (Poisoned Lands, 13)

A hag or witch figure plays a role too in 'Like Dolmens Round My Childhood, The Old People', in the same collection: an Old woman living 'surrounded by animals', described as a 'well of gossip defiled' and 'Fanged chronicler...'; and once again she and the remaining 'old people' listed in the poem are mysteriously elevated to 'that dark permanence of ancient forms' by the conceit named in the title's simile. Later, in 'The Wild Dog

Rose', 'The Music Box' and 'Procession', the same lineaments recur to compose further solitary old women, though the implicit evocation of the Cathleen Ní Houlihan figure sometimes plays a more muted role (*The Rough Field*, 77; *The Dead Kingdom*, 36, 84).[4] In 'Procession', the woman is the poet's grandmother, and once again distaste ('Hawk nose, snuff stained apron') mingles equivocally with a compassionate vision of her victim status ('Still hatred and division / stain that narrow acre / from which you sprang').

Mythical appropriations play an increasingly important role in Montague's work in the mid-1970s and early 1980s. The very tentative mythicization of 'The Sean Bhean Bhocht', giving only a rather vague indication of her access to wisdom, which seems to be something not very precise to do with an earlier Ireland (spells, legends, a buried queen) becomes more insistent. In *The Dead Kingdom*, for example, with its Sheela-na-Gig prominent on an opening page, 'The Music Box' rehearses the speaker's childhood memory of an old and frightening woman who lived beside a well which she kept clear of leaves and insects and of which she is described as the guardian. The epigraph of this sequence specifically signals the use of Old Irish material:

> I cast a pebble down, to
> Set the well's walls echoing.
> As the meniscus resettles
> I see a strange face form,
> A wrinkled female face,
> Sweeney's Hag of the Mill,
> The guardian of the well,
> Source of lost knowledge.
>   (24)

This hag is from the Irish tale *Buile Suibhne*. She is a rather puzzling figure who challenges the mad Suibhne to a leaping contest, harries him, and is eventually destroyed by overleaping herself off a cliff.[5] One might suggest that this hag has a role in relation to Suibhne resembling the Sphinx's to Oedipus, with leaping in place of riddles, and the same result, the defeat of an earlier, baleful and originally divine female presence by the male hero. The oedipal parallel contributes to my general argument that an intense urge to self-definition in contradistinction to a feminine principle, cloaked as admiring celebration of women, is a main motivating force in these poets' work. In any case, the Hag of the Mill is evidently intended here to stand behind the poet's memory of old 'Mary Mulvey', thus making her a challenger to be defeated, according to the legendary allusion. When we look at the poem, we find the blend of half-guilty retrospective compassion and mild disgust familiar from the earlier hag-poems; the woman is '...cramped /

and horrible as some toothy witch. / We clattered stones on your roof . . .'
(*The Dead Kingdom*, 36). Her one 'secret', a music box with a silver dancer
swirling on top, which delighted the children, becomes her moment of
'grace', just as the dead-queen tales were that of the 'sean-bhean bhocht' in
the earlier poem: the challenge to the remembering masculine persona is to
discern that grace underlying the woman's alien terrifying presence. A further
legendary resonance in 'Mary Mulvey's' living by the well clarifies this
challenge: it may recall the Irish tales about a young man being challenged
by a crone for a kiss when he comes to draw water. This crone turns, once
her desire is granted, into a young and beautiful woman, and espouses him.
This female figure, with her two conflicting aspects of ugliness and beauty, is
a sovereignty-goddess, and in espousing her the man can become king of the
land. Her association with water links her with the idea of perpetually
renewed fertility.[6] Thus Montague's poem attempts to establish a connection
between the circumstantial detail of the actual old woman, autobiographi-
cally validated, and an immemorial legendary event, whose metaphorical
recurrence is implied by such means: the poet standing, presumably, for the
young king-figure, and the twin aspects, horror and grace, of the woman
being represented by her age and her music-box. How should we read this
palimpsest of actual and mythical?
[. . .]
     Montague constructs other female figures as guardians and sources of
wisdom also, particularly his kinswomen: his aunts, foster mother and
mother. Such figures are associated paradoxically in his work both with
death and with origins. This contradiction is not, of course, peculiar to his
work, nor indeed to Heaney's, but it is focused with peculiar and intriguing
clarity in it. Montague's collection *The Dead Kingdom*, for example, represents on the level of realistic narrative a journey to the North of Ireland for
the funeral of the poet's mother.[7] But it also rehearses a penetration of an
under- or other-world, which is simultaneously the past, Ulster; the earth,
nature; and, as we have seen, the well of knowledge. The dead mother in the
poems (who is bitterly accused on a personal level of inflicting a 'primal hurt'
in giving away her son, the future poet, to be fostered) is also death as
mother, and mother as death, part of the general *topos* in literature of the
destroying mother.[8] This is ultimately a metaphorical way of understanding
creation and destruction as unified; it is important to notice, however, that it
depends upon a projection of woman as *necessarily* contradictory.[9] In *The
Rough Field* (1972), 'The Leaping Fire' marks the death of another maternal
figure, the poet's foster mother, who like the earlier hag figures arouses
mingled distaste, fear and compassion in the poem's persona. The constellation of her features is significant. She possesses a quasi-magical skill, to do
with renewing and sustaining life, which is shown in her daily rekindling of
the fire:

'Each morning, from the corner
    of the hearth, I saw a miracle...'.
                            (19)

Her distance from sexual activity and her religious devotion are stressed and
linked with her physical grotesqueness in the speaker's mind:

    a frail body grown monstrous,
    sighing in a trance
    before the gilt crucifix.
                            (21)

And his anxious distance from such an existence is registered in his apotro-
paic assertion of his own sexual drive by masturbation ('The sap of another
generation / fingering through a broken tree'). The 'broken tree', however, is
numinous: at the end a bird-cry over Paris is read as the announcement by a
spirit voice, banshee-like, of the woman's death, arousing a momentary
reinhabiting of her thought-world by the adult, secularized, metropolitan
speaker: 'I crossed myself / from rusty habit.... / A hollow note'. In this
poem, the neo-mythicizing impulse is salutarily opposed by the accidence of
memory, so that the image of an actual woman at least impedes the totalizing projection of a notional female spirit as immemorial adversary. Though
this representation remains one from the outside, and despite the narcissism
of the masturbation scene and the allocation of rootedness and domesticity
to the female and cosmopolitan secularity to the male realm, it retains a
certain grace in the poet's acknowledgement of the mystery attending another existence, a rival autonomy.
    Such complexity deserts Montague at his more Gravesian moments,
which are frequent in the 1975 collection *A Slow Dance*. Two poems in the
title sequence of the collection (beginning: 'I: Back. Darkness, cave / drip,
earth womb...' and furnished with prehistoric monuments and early Irish
references) explicitly employ the conceit of landscape as female body. One is
the litany-like 'For The Hillmother', which invokes a benign chthonic presence as sexually welcoming and fertile:

    ...Moist fern
        Unfurl for us...
    Freshet of ease
        flow for us
    Secret waterfall
        pour for us
    Hidden cleft
        speak to us

Portal of delight
  inflame us
Hill of motherhood
  wait for us
Gate of birth
  open for us.
         (10)

The other poem is 'Message', which constructs a more unsavoury and threatening female figure ('her secret message, shaped / by a wandering wind / puts the eye / of reason out'), but nevertheless ends with a form of self-insertion into a scarcely metaphorized vaginal crevice:

ease your
hand into the
rot-smelling crotch
of a hollow
tree, and find
two pebbles of quartz
protected by
a spider's web:
her sunless breasts.
         (10)

This passage neatly manifests a disassembly and arbitrary redistribution of the female body characteristic of fetishization, of which these poems, and also Heaney's bog-goddess poems, especially *North*, are good examples. It is difficult to know how readers with a different, non-fetishized or unobjectivized understanding of women's being – female readers, and surely many male ones – should interpret these poems, whose perspective must strike them not merely as gendered, but as disturbingly close to a figurative dismemberment.[10] In the same collection, whose title sequence is said by the publisher's cover copy to 'mime a deep psychic experience of intimacy with the earth', the poem 'The Hero's Portion' grafts onto a Roman description of Celtic feasting customs a strikingly brutal passage. The hero summons a waiting woman 'to squat across his lap': his harper mauls a feminized instrument ('pulled / his long curved nails / through the golden hair / of his harp...'. The harper's song ends:

sing the sword
so fierce and tall

sing the ladies
whose bowels crave

its double edge
of birth and grave.
(*A Slow Dance*, 36, 37)

The poem lacks any indication of ironic distance from these sentiments (such as is evident in the late Yeats work which it recalls), and indeed is admiringly described by the publisher, presumably with the author's sanction, as displaying 'elemental energies'.

Not all of Montague's middle and late work is as blunt as this. A less disturbingly invaded and less limitingly gendered version of a chthonic being is later invented in 'The Well Dreams'.[11] Based on a discreet and witty personification, this poem has all the tact and inclusiveness lacking in the rather bruising writings I have been discussing. The well 'recomposes' itself after water is drawn there, supporting an 'unpredictable ballet' of water-spiders and washing a coin thrown in. A site of votive offerings, it is metonymically associated both with the saint whose cult it represents and with the 'neutral realm' of midland Ireland where it is set. The coin it renews is 'queen of the realm, made virgin again', and above all it has a self-sufficient life, expressing in 'small intensities of mirth, / the hidden laughter of earth' (*The Dead Kingdom*, 38–40).

The other main strand in Montague's work has consisted of personal love and erotic lyrics. Some of the former, particularly in the collection *The Great Cloak* (1978), have been concerned to construct a female spouse-figure who takes the form of an icon of domestic attachment, comforting and anchoring the hitherto wandering male figure. The ecstatic celebration of this figure does not, however, dispel the reader's impression of her as predominantly an aspect of the speaker's lyric autobiography and an adjunct to his self-investigation. It may be because she, somewhat like the mother-figures we have been discussing, is imaginatively constituted *in the poetry* through mythological and legendary parallels, and also because she is praised as a consumable item, like sumptuous fruit. 'A Dream Of July' merges these two procedures with particular clarity:[12]

Like a young girl
Dissatisfied with
Her mythic burden
Ceres, corn goddess . . .

. . .

Her abundant body is
Compounded of honey
& gold, the spike
Of each small nipple
A wild strawberry.
(*The Great Cloak*, 44)[13]

Beauty and seductiveness may be lavishly bestowed on this figure, but not rational distance or self-determining will; she is described as 'Fulfilled in / Spite of herself', underlining the division of labour between understanding, naming and empowerment on the part of the male, and intuition and embodiment on the part of the female. A later poem, 'The Well-Beloved', shows a conscious recognition of the process of mythologizing projection upon women which has been constitutive of so much of Montague's work, but does not forego its continuance, perpetuating the categories of that process even in the moment of recognition.

Despite the first line of the stanza, this passage leaves the reader with an unmistakable impression of the poet's belief in the objective existence of these 'disguises':

> Raised by the fury of our need,
> supplicating, lusting, grovelling
> before the tall tree of Artemis,
> the transfiguring bow of Diana,
> the rooting vulva of Circe, or
> the slim shape of a nymph,
> luring, dancing, beckoning:
> all her wild disguises!
>   (*Mount Eagle*, 46)

Montague's other autobiographical erotic poems also represent a fetishized female body. Though without pastiche mythology, they too offer a vision of woman as landscape, spatially organized: 'Snowfield' reads her as a 'white expanse' over which the male lover makes 'warm tracks' at which afterwards he 'gaze(s) happily' (*The Great Cloak*, 11).[14] In 'Don Juan's Farewell', the hero recalls multiple female partners, who are again objectivized and discounted as separate selves by their synecdochic representation as 'sweet shudder of flesh / behind shadowy blinds' and as 'warm mounds of / breathing sweetness'. They are also marked, almost in a Sadean sense, as erotic objects by 'long bars of light / across tipped breasts'. The poem emphasizes the existential isolation of the Don Juan character, who at the end tells himself that he has been 'searching through / another's pliant body' for 'something missing / in your separate self' (*The Great Cloak*, 19). Here in the erotic, as elsewhere in the domestic interior, women are the silenced attendants of a masculine quest. Such poems seem to proclaim a moment of sexual liberation, but the erotic subject-positions they represent may be seen rather to offer a mere continuance of consuming masculine passions, and quite fail to encompass a mutually liberating sexuality.

III

Turning to the representation of gender roles in Heaney's work, we find that he tends towards two opposing and possibly complementary representations of gender interaction. One constructs an unequivocally dominant masculine figure, who explores, describes, brings to pleasure and compassionates a passive feminine one. The other proposes a woman who dooms, destroys, puzzles and encompasses the man, but also assists him to his self-discovery: the mother stereotype, but merged intriguingly with the spouse. Members of the first group, representing masculine domination, are 'Undine' and 'Rite of Spring', in which the man's victory is achieved in agricultural terms; 'Punishment' and 'Bog Queens', which combine an erotic disrobing narrative (as in Renaissance and other love poetry) and a tone of compassionate tenderness, with a very equivocal result; and the political group including 'Ocean's Love to Ireland', 'Act of Union' and 'The Betrothal of Cavehill', which usually rehearse narratives of rape and sexual violation. The second group contains 'The Tollund Man', 'The Grauballe Man' and the intense and intriguing 'Kinship', which merges mother and spouse as well as active and passive and, I shall argue, functions primarily as a masculine-identity myth, despite its political ending and the political criticism it has chiefly attracted.

In Heaney's first two collections, the most prominent form of attention to gender roles is what may be termed vocational: an allocation of special domains to the masculine and feminine, of a triumphantly traditional kind. Masculine actors find the greater space: in *Death of a Naturalist*, the very first poem 'Digging' foreshadows later, explicitly sexual, bog poems, with its all too relevant succession of phallic surrogates – pen, 'snug as a gun', spade – and its sensuously rich material which waits passively to be 'dug' ('He ... buried the bright edge deep', in the 'squelch and slap / Of soggy peat' [12]). The active prowess of the speaker's male ancestors is stressed, and he is concerned to present his own displacement to intellectual performance as not interrupting his place in that succession.[15] Parallel to this insistence on inheritance, however, these early poems also rehearse the construction of an individuated masculine self: in the title poem 'Death of a Naturalist', the croaking bullfrogs – 'croaked on sods' – may be perceived as an invasion of maleness into the child's pre-pubertal feminized world, governed by 'Miss Walls' the teacher, whereas two poems later in 'An Advancement of Learning' the boy successfully faces down the slimy, 'nimbling' rat in a test of courage which confirms his own masculinity (15, 18).[16]

With increasing definiteness in the successive collections, the memory of an essentially unchanging rural world is rehearsed, with its traditional crafts and trades; and as a central part of that dispensation, male and female subject-positions are also construed as immemorially fixed. Once natural threats such as those represented by the rat, or by the eel-nits in 'Vision' (*Door into the Dark*, 45) have been overcome, the speakers of the poems identify admiringly with active natural creatures such as the bull in 'Outlaw' (16), and the trout which is rendered in strikingly phallic terms – 'Gun-barrel', 'torpedo', 'ramrodding' ('Trout', *Death of a Naturalist*, 39). The trout's ballistic activity is contrasted with the neighbouring 'Cow in Calf' (38), where bulk, slowness and recurrence of the same are stressed: 'Her cud and her milk, her heats and her calves / keeping coming and going' (38).

There are human versions of such continuities: 'The Wife's Tale' with its rare female speaker is typical in celebrating, without obvious intentional irony, the separate spheres of farm and home labour: 'I'd come and he had shown me / So I belonged no further to the work'.[17] But Heaney's imagination is already dwelling more intensely on metaphors of *nature* as feminine than on the human version. Other strongly conventionalized female figures do also appear, especially mother figures signifying domesticity, intermittently from the earliest poems. But the centre of imaginative intensity is undoubtedly his curious and compelling construct of the land-cum-spouse-cum-deathbringer, with its active and passive aspects.

The hags and goddesses, classical and Celtic, of Montague's poems are replaced in Heaney's by this figure. Its more politicized version, as it appears tentatively in *Wintering Out* and assertively in *North*, represents a merging of the north European fertility goddess, whom Heaney found described in P. V. Glob's study of Iron Age bog burials, with the rather vaguely realized notion of the land of Ireland as seeker of sacrifices, from nationalist political tradition.[18] In his bog poems Heaney sexualizes the religious conceptions of Celtic and north European prehistory.[19] Gender in Celtic and other early mythologies was a metaphysical concept, one of several dyadic means of cosmic organization (male : female lining up with black : white, left : right, north : south, and so forth); a proper service to male and female divinities of earth and air was connected with successful cultivation.[20] This is, of course, markedly different from the predominantly *sexual* interpretation of gender in our culture, which sees it as inextricably bound up with individual personal identity and affective fulfilment, an understanding deriving from Christian theology, the European tradition of courtly love, and the insights of psychoanalysis, among other sources. Heaney's archaizing projection of specifically sexual feeling on to agricultural practices ('Rite of Spring', 'Undine') (*Door into the Dark*, 25, 26) and human sacrifices to a fertility goddess (the bog poems) seems to be a bid to reach past urban and intellectual social forms and their accompanying thought-world, which are implicitly judged as wanting, to a notional state of physical naturalness and 'anonymities' whether folk or prehistoric. An obvious casualty of this attempt, were it to succeed, would be the impulse to individual self-determination and reflexivity. This is an impulse noticeably present in the self-construction of poets, but it is its assumed absence as a defining figure in the lives of Irish rural people and Iron Age Danes which seems to be being celebrated. Thus a disjunction appears between the speaking subjects of these writings and their unspoken objects. In particular the female figures in this conjured world are the epitome of a general silence, at the opposite pole from the describing, celebrating, expressing poet. Whether active or passive, these figures are spoken for, and this division is a highly problematic one.

The two successive poems, 'Rite of Spring' and 'Undine' are perhaps the first examples of an attempt to project sexual feelings into a landscape (*Door into the Dark*, 25, 26). They are therefore ancestors of the more famous bog poems, but differ from them in using the second model I have outlined at the outset, one of male activity and female passivity. They project onto a water-pump and a stream respectively the figure of a sexually willing woman, who waits to be coaxed into satisfaction by farming skill: 'It cooled, we lifted her latch, / Her entrance was wet, and she came' (25). This masculine narcissism is even more apparent in 'Undine', which ventriloquizes the water-nymph's voice:

> ... And I ran quick for him, cleaned out my rust.
> He halted, saw me finally disrobed ...
> Then he walked by me. I rippled and I churned ...
>
> He explored me so completely, each limb
> Lost its cold freedom. Human, warmed to him.
>
> (26)

It is difficult to read these pieces as other than classic fantasies of male sexual irresistibility: the moist pump-entrance, the flowing irrigation drain ('he dug a spade deep into my flank / And took me to him') seem almost like a parody of the narrative of erotic wish-fulfilment, in which the frigid female gladly warms to an expert and forceful man.[21] In one sense, the guise of a representation of rural life scarcely survives this sexual excitement, though in another it is being mobilized to legitimize the work, as eternal fact. One might read this conjunction of rural and sexual utopianism, foregrounding pleasure and promising a notional return to an earlier less repressed state; but the obliviousness of most sexual revolutionaries of the period to their own masculinist understanding of pleasure also marks Heaney's version, and hinders such an interpretation.[22] The pump and the stream are (preposterously, when one puts it like that) each imagined as 'fulfilled in spite of herself', like Montague's Ceres-figure, which is to say disempowered; hence the real resemblance to pornographic fantasy. They cannot choose but be played upon, like the

'Victorian Guitar' which like its gentlewoman owner needs to be 'fingered' into pleasure (*Door into the Dark*, 33).

There is a further recurring feature of Heaney's work which connects with this nexus of ideas. This is the conceit of language as erotically enabling, joined in the following passage from 'Bone Dreams' with the female-body-as-landscape in a political conceit. The Irish poet 'colonizes' with his charm – or force of language – the 'escarpments' of a female England. He projects himself as the phallic 'chalk giant':

> carved on her downs.
> Soon my hands, on the sunken
> fosse of her spine
> move towards the passes.
> 　　　　　(*North*, 29)

The lover-speaker 'estimate(s) for pleasure / her knuckles' paving', and begins 'to pace' her shoulder: all usual amorous activities in which, however, the explorer's, 'estimator's', evaluator's position is the man's. This is blood brother to the fetishizing erotic persona of Montague's work.[23] Other instances of the association of speech with eros and energy or force in Heaney help to elucidate the topic. In 'Midnight' the eradication of wolves in Ireland is made the sign both of the seventeenth-century conquest and of emasculation. The poem ends:

> Nothing is panting, lolling,
> Vapouring. The tongue's
> Leashed in my throat.
> 　　　　　(*Wintering Out*, 46)

making a symptomatic equation of phallus, speech, predation and national strength almost too obvious to mention. 'Come To The Bower', which echoes the title of a favourite Irish parlour patriotic song, combines the traditional topos of disrobing with the richly sensuous apprehension of the landscape which is one of Heaney's most characteristic features:

> My hands come...

> To where the dark-bowered queen,
> Whom I unpin,
> Is waiting...

This land-spouse is herself rendered as a bog body, wearing the necklet or torc which stood for the goddess:

A mark of a gorget in the flesh
Of her throat. And spring water
Starts to rise around her.
                              (*North*, 31)

The welling water indicates her fertility. The unpinning and marking encode
her female disempowerment (precisely as pornographic texts do, since social
life and the aesthetic utterances it produces form a symbolic continuum) and
thus fix her role as an erotic object. At the end of the poem, she is further
named, as wealth: 'I reach ... to the bullion / Of her Venus bone'. Here the
reality of the ritual murders Heaney found recorded in Glob is metaphorized
and explicitly eroticized, in a striking and disturbing mental transformation.

'Punishment', the poem describing Glob's 'Windeby girl' – the drowned
body of a young woman with a halter round her neck – has attracted much
commentary, chiefly about the analogy it makes with tarring and feathering
in Northern Ireland. The speaker of it does to a certain degree interrogate his
own position, discerning it as that of 'the artful voyeur', but the words' overt
application here is to his sense of his political ambiguity: he would 'connive /
in civilized outrage', but understand the 'tribal, intimate revenge' being
exacted (*North*, 38).

The publicly expressible 'civilized outrage' belongs to a language which
the persona of all these poems feels is denied him and his ethnic group; he
constructs Northern Irish Catholics as, like Celts to the ancient Romans, a
race mysterious, barbarous, inarticulate, lacking in civility.[24] But, one might
argue, the result of this expressed sense of marginalization by the speaker is
to make the girl seem doubly displaced: the *object* of equivocal compassion
by a *subject* himself forced to be covert, himself the *object* in turn of others'
dominant and therefore oppressive civility. Thus the fascinated details of the
description which composes the girl as passive and observed object have the
effect, whatever the intention, of outweighing the initial assertion of a shared
subjectivity ('I can feel the tug / of the halter at the nape / of her neck ...').
The compassion is equivocal not just because of the half-sympathy with the
punishers, but because of the speaker's excitement (can we not identify it as
specifically sexual?) at the scopic spectacle of the girl's utter disempowerment ('It blows her nipples / to amber beads ...'). Hence the usual sense of
the word 'voyeur' must suggest itself strongly.

Turning to the active feminine, Heaney's engagement with a female
destructive principle is particularly intense, as an examination of his Ire-
land-spouse poems 'The Tollund Man' (*Wintering Out*, 47) and 'Kinship'
(*North*, 40) shows.[25] In the 'Tollund Man', the sacrificed corpse is described
as 'bridegroom to the goddess', who is credited with a murky amalgam of
lethal and sexual acts:

She tightened her torc on him
And opened her fen,
Those dark juices working
Him to a saint's kept body...
                    (*Wintering Out*, 47)

This, like 'Punishment', aestheticizes the horror of a murdered corpse and presents it as a natural phenomenon ('The mild pods of his eye-lids, / His pointed skin cap'). But here it is also made an effect of erotic absorption and incorporation by a female energy conceived as both inert and devouring.[26] If one turns the motif this way round, for the moment understanding it primarily as a way of thinking about woman rather than about Irish political murder, it reveals an intense alienation from the female. Eros–Thanatos pairings generally do seem to rely on a perception of woman as channel for masculine fear and desire, and this is no exception.[27] When one readmits into one's mind the poem's parallel between Stone Age sacrifices to the fertility goddess and Irish political murders in the 1970s, one's increased awareness of the erotic-aesthetic frisson in the first section makes the analogy seem all the more shaky and difficult to assent to. Can this sexual thrill really have anything other than mischief to bring to our thought about the actual perpetration of torture and murder?[28]

'Kinship' at the dead centre of the collection *North*, also represents a centre of Heaney's project. Developing a hint at the end of the earlier 'Bogland' ('The wet centre is bottomless', *Door into the Dark*, 56) it presents Ireland's bogland as above all an encompasser – ruminant, storer, embalmer, 'insatiable bride', swallower, mideen, floe. At the end of the passage is a disrobing moment: the ground 'will strip / its dark side' as if undressing. As the poem's hero pulls out, then replaces, a turf-spade in the bog, 'the soft lips of the growth / muttered and split', leaving the spade-shaft 'wettish / as I sank it upright...' (*North*, 42). Following this moment of phallic discovery (evidently granted with some reluctance by the bog) and reinsertion, recalling Heaney's many earlier digging and ploughing passages, there is an explicit merging of birth and death – 'a bag of waters / and a melting grave' – in this personified ground, a 'centre' which, unlike Yeats's, 'holds' (*North*, 43). The poet identifies himself as having grown out of this bog 'like a weeping willow / inclined to / the appetites of gravity'. In a turn to the overtly political at the end of this poem, he addresses Tacitus, Roman describer of Celtic Europe, wryly acknowledging the practice of 'slaughter for the common good' (which presumably represents both the ritual human sacrifices described in the *Germania* and Northern Ireland's deaths):

Our mother ground
is sour with the blood

of her faithful,
...
report us fairly,
...
How the goddess swallows
our love and terror.
                    (*North*, 45)

First, taking this passage politically, one might argue that the evident irony in the expression 'slaughter for the common good' does not solve the more general problem of a projection of the mythic and ritual onto history and the resulting blockage of rational understanding and possible action. The poet compulsively predicates his claim to intuitive identification with his landscape on personifying it as feminine and equating it with death ('The goddess swallows / our love and terror'). As others have suggested, this further entangles the gloomy facts of Irish political history with the heady rhetoric of nationalist ideology instead of interrogating them.[29] My second point concerns the poem's real priorities. It privatizes and sexualizes the political. Its early sections show much greater intensity than the later (which has probably contributed unnoticed to critics' questioning of the ending): the charged personal ode to the bog as mother and partner – giver and receiver of the spade-phallus – is no more than tenuously related to the political references at the end, which risk seeming merely dutiful. I think the real focus is on the speaker's private myth of identity formation, on wresting a self from the 'feminine' unbounded indeterminacy of the bog. This poem attempts a synthesis of the stereotypes of femininity: the bog-goddess is imagined as both mother and spouse, and as destroyer and provider, but it is still persistently (and in both senses) the *ground* on which the speaker's self and his very identity is predicated. The feminine is thus once again an Other but not really envisaged as an alternative subject or self: a relation of complementarity, certainly, but not of equality, and one which enshrines difference in the oppressive sense of that word.

Following the privatized and sexualized bog-Ireland poems, there is also a series of poems in *North* which mount a specifically political gender-historical narrative of English conquest and colonization in Ireland. This series includes 'Ocean's Love to Ireland' and 'Act of Union'. Both these poems employ the conceit representing political conquest by acts of sexual possession, and 'Act of Union' makes the male/English violator its speaker; and/or: it is a love poem to a pregnant spouse. There is a crucial ambiguity about the sexual act in both poems: rape (indicated by a reference to Elizabethan massacres) or seduction by a male force whose energy is attractively irresistible? The language of 'Act of Union' strongly recalls that of the exploring lover in 'Bone Dreams':

...I caress
The heaving province where our past has grown.
I am the tall kingdom over your shoulder
That you would neither cajole nor ignore.
Conquest is a lie...

(North, 49)

Her mutuality is said by the male speaker (England) to have supplanted
violation of an unwilling woman (Ireland). How ironically is that speech to
be read? Does not the tone strongly recall the gender triumphalism of 'Rite
of Spring', which, after all, enthusiastically celebrated the farmer's sexualized thawing of the pump? The speaker in 'Act of Union' regrets the pain
of his partner's imminent childbirth ('the rending process in the colony, /
The battering ram') but also reads it as the promise of a forthcoming
Oedipal struggle: 'His parasitical and ignorant little fists already...cocked
/ At me across the water'. One can credit Heaney with a vivid rendering of
the complications, the tangled intimacy, of Anglo-Irish political relations.
But one might also feel that to rehearse the narrative of these relations in
these terms is to re-mystify rather than to attempt an understanding of the
phenomena. What is especially questionable is the apparently unconscious
equivocation in Heaney's deployment of gender. The application of force
in the agricultural handling of nature, imagined as male sexual domination, is felt as deeply right. But the occurrence of the same structure in
political relations is (presumably, in the work of a poet of Catholic
nationalist origins) to be taken as reprehensible and grievous. Further, in
the structure of *North* the death-bringing goddess's claiming helpless
victims (female force) in the bog poems is matched with the rape-narratives
in the pendent colonization series (male force). The symmetry of this
deepens the sense of inevitability generated by the whole project of the
mythicization of history. The social, economic and constitutional conditions of modern Ireland are elided in this reductive narrative which merges
the chthonic personifications of the Iron Age with a presentation of gender
roles as immemorial.

The brief lyric 'The Betrothal of Cavehill' closes the series with a quizzical
moment:

Gunfire barks its questions off Cavehill
And the profiled basalt maintains its stare
South: proud, protestant and northern, and male.
Adam untouched, before the shock of gender.

They still shoot here for luck over a bridegroom.
The morning I drove out to bed me down
Among my love's hideouts, her pods and broom,

They fired above my car the ritual gun.
                    (*North*, 51)

In the second stanza, the familiar moment when the land is taken as spouse ('...to bed me down / Among my love's hideouts, her pods and broom') allows us to identify the 'bridegroom' equivocally in three possible ways: either as an autobiographical splinter of the poet, or as an IRA man on the run and living rough in the countryside, or as the rock itself 'marrying' the prone land it surveys so dominantly. So the familiar reprise of nationalist attachment to the land as a betrothal to death is complicated by the ethnically double male presence in the poem: the 'Adam untouched' figure of Cavehill, which is made to represent the culturally masculine intransigence of northern Protestantism, disdaining converse with the land-as-Eve; and the presumably Catholic 'bridegroom', who 'beds down' in the land. Even the *culturally* feminine Catholic/nationalist figure is *biologically* male: may we read this as a discreet Utopian moment in which all (males) may merge their differences in a general bedding down in the (female) land? As to politics, this may be an improvement; but as to gender, it is the status quo as in all the other poems: politics is seen in terms of sexuality, but not the reverse. The mildly humorous characterization of the rock as phallic stops short of demythicizing Genesis, however wry it is about northern Protestant no-surrendering: the gender *there* was before gender was already male.
[...]
   So must we not conclude that the poetry of Montague and Heaney as a whole is insistently and damagingly gendered? Its masculine personae, whether in the narrative of personal identity, or that of nationality, must, it seems, possess or be possessed by a counter-force personified as feminine: an encounter of the genders as of aliens – dog eat dog, possess or be swallowed up – is forever occurring, even within and beneath politics. On this evidence, it remains very difficult for men, when they imagine self-formation as a struggle, to escape conceiving that struggle, however metaphorically or virtually, as *against* the feminine. The integral self counted as so precious to the capacity for expression of these poets is won against a necessarily subordinated ground of merely potential, never actual feminine selves. In Lacanian terms, they seem to be stuck in the self/not-self dualism of the mirror stage, failing to arrive at an acknowledgement of the existence of an autonomous subjectivity in others: a structure common to sexism and racism.[30] Just as 'every document of civilization is a document of barbarism', in Benjamin's phrase, so one is tempted to conclude that every feat of self-discovery by these masculine poets entails the defeat of a feminine ego. Or as Irigaray puts it:

the/a woman fulfills a twofold function – as the mute outside that sustains all systematicity; as a maternal and still silent ground that nourishes all foundations – ...[31]

5

To Bind the Northern to the Southern Stars: Field Day in Derry and Dublin

Shaun Richards

Derry is the unhappy home of significant events whose anniversaries have resounded bloodily across centuries of the city's history; most recently the infamous 'Bloody Sunday', but most notably, and notoriously, the annual 12 August parade of the Apprentice Boys who beat their way around the city walls to celebrate the lifting of the siege of the city in 1689 and simultaneously declare the contemporary protestant refusal to surrender. Since 1980 another date has entered the Derry calendar: the third Wednesday of September on which the Field Day Theatre Company premières its annual production prior to a tour of venues in Northern Ireland and the Republic. It is the choice of Derry's Guildhall as the location of the premières, however, which strikes the symbolic note. Not only has the seat of administrative power been entered by art, albeit temporarily, but this stark Victorian gothic edifice stands outside the city walls on the banks of the Foyle and so looks out to a wider world than that admitted by the beleaguered insularity which those walls have historically expressed. On 23 September 1987, Field Day premièred Stewart Parker's *Pentecost* prior to commencing the annual tour with a performance on 28 September during Dublin's theatre festival.

Although the outward signs of the divisive sectarianism to which Field Day is opposed were limited to fading graffiti dedicated to the UVF, and a weather-worn Sinn Féin poster of Martin McGuinness, the presence of barbed wire on the walls overlooking the Guildhall testified to the continuation of violence; the previous week a grenade had been dropped onto a police Land Rover with resultant injuries to two policemen and six civilians. The Guildhall itself was gutted by bombs in 1970 and its refurbished interior, including the stained glass windows which, ironically, were remade according to the plans made as a safety precaution against the bombing of World War II, is now protected by exterior fencing which can only be entered by means of a manned security gate. To enter the Guildhall on the night of 23 September, however, was to move from an exterior bleakness for

61

which the fitting artistic reflection was the local cinema's screening of *Lethal Weapon*, into an enclosed moment of formal celebration.

The combination of black-suited front of house staff in bow ties, stewards who were almost exclusively besuited middle-aged males, along with the presence of a four-piece 'traditional' jazz band in a bar area crowded with an audience whose dress and demeanour suggested more of a Rotarian respectability, stood in sharp contrast to the radical atmosphere which might be expected for the première production of a company with the stated intention of subjecting the political crisis in the North and its reverberation in the Republic to a necessary and urgent reappraisal. The main hall, which was entered directly from the makeshift bar area, was also suitably dressed for the occasion, with the steeply banked rows of temporary red-plastic seats and black-plastic sheets on the interior windows emphasizing, rather than detracting from, the mellow wood and rich red curtains. Within that ornate space, however, albeit almost dwarfed by its height, stood a set whose dominant shade of faded browns, along with gas lamp fittings, prints and samplers, cast the mind out into those mean streets in which could be found the psychological equivalent of this stage world in which time had stood still. The entry of non-sectarian time into this frozen moment is the dramatic and thematic focus of Parker's play.

While all the action occurs within the one set – the parlour of a terrace house in protestant Belfast – the setting of the action in the period of the Ulster Workers' Council strike in 1974 sets up a series of resonances between the onstage drama of the interwoven lives of the five characters and the off-stage events which penetrate the drama, to the point that the play's conclusion sees the ecstatic fusing of on- and off-stage issues in a declaration of faith in the personal politics of what can best be described as charismatic humanism. Using the clichéd but frequently moving metaphor of childlessness, Parker merges the private plight of the characters with that public sterility which, as he effectively articulates through the character of the ghost of Lily Matthews (Barbara Adair), has disfigured Belfast for at least three generations. The entry of that public world into the domestic space of the set provides the play's basic structuring principle as well as its dramatic focus.

The first of the five scenes sees modernity enter in the form of Lenny Harrigan (Stephen Rea) who has inherited the house of the now dead Lily Matthews from a doting aunt. At the end of the first scene and the declaration 'I'll take it!' by Harrigan's estranged wife Marian (Eileen Pollock) the plot essentials are established. Harrigan is an up-dated Jimmy Porter who has abandoned responsibility in favour of a bohemian existence as a jazz trombonist. His wife, disillusioned both with her husband and what has been a successful career as an antiques dealer, is looking for an escape from the outer world which she thinks she has found in the house whose every feature denies modernity and suggests a time before the present 'Troubles'; a term which, Parker implies, is as applicable to the shattered relationships of the characters as it is to the broken community from which the house offers a frequent retreat. As the play progresses through Scenes 2 and 3 to the interval, three additional characters enter; their lives adding repetition and hence resonance to the relationship of the Harrigans which had foundered on the death of the child Christopher in August 1969. This was a 'vintage month' as the character Peter (Jonathan Kent) comments, marking as it did the outbreak of the modern 'Troubles'; and Parker adds to this the emotional sterility of Peter, 'dicking his way around the Birmingham discos' and attempting to erase his Belfast accent; the miscarriages and brutal marriage of Ruth (Paula Hamilton), estranged wife of an RUC man who, we later learn, has broken under the strain of the job and smashed his own hands to a pulp; and the character of Lily Matthews whose life and home lie at the emotional and dramatic heart of the play.

The Matthews house, brilliantly created in the set by Bunny Christie, is in a condemned terrace on the 'firing line' between the sectarian factions of the city whose feuds and divisions are replayed between the catholic Marian and the protestant Lily. As the second scene opens Marian talks to Lily's ghost, an emanation produced by her weeks of absorption in the house which, museum-like, contains all the minutiae of Lily's life, and her intention becomes to preserve the house as a perfect example of Belfast's modern history by handing it over to the National Trust. The concept of the frozen moment, however, is that to which Parker is most clearly opposed, consolidating things as they were and refusing to engage with things as they are and as they should be. As the scenes progress, the characters, most particularly Lenny, Marian, and Lily, exteriorize the deeply traumatizing experiences of child-loss which unites past and present, catholic and protestant, middle-class and proletariat, in a shared and numbing sense of grief. As Rea movingly expresses his vanished experience of love with the words 'He was my son. She was my wife', the past tense location of the familial nouns underscores that which the play addresses most movingly: lives lived in an isolation produced by an anguish which they can barely articulate.

It is anguish and anger, in fact, which informs the first three scenes, reaching a climax in the frenzied beating of the Lambeg drums which ends the first half of the play and drowns the lament of Marian for the dead child who 'was our future' in the cacophony of a historically prescribed sectarianism. To cross the sectarian divide through a process of emphatic awareness of the equally desolate experience of 'them' has been steadily foregrounded as an alternative to division throughout Scene 3 as Marian declares her need of the embittered protestant Lily and announces her intention of providing a life for her memory, as well as for herself and the equally childless Ruth. The 'barren' house now takes on the symbolic weight of the sterile politics of the province, a point underscored by Ruth's Scene 4 references to the house being in danger as she dismisses Peter's arrogant detachment in mocking rejection of his 'A plague on both your houses' stance. It is at this point that the interpretative difficulties arise; at least in so far as Parker is providing the audience with both a dramatic experience of the characters' situation and a thesis as to the means by which the 'Troubles' can be resolved.

Verbal and aural references to violence run throughout the first three scenes, ranging from Lily's memories of being burned out by a catholic mob in 1921 and the observation that the contemporary bombers take their timing devices from the street lights, to the sound of off-stage explosions. The thundering drums which end both Scenes 3 and 4, however, signal a greater proximity between on- and off-stage action as the crisis initiated by the Ulster Workers' council strike impinges directly on the characters' lives and makes political violence the matter of on-stage conversations. The speech of the then British Prime Minister Harold Wilson to which Ruth and Peter listen at the opening of Scene 4, as the blinding light and noise of an army helicopter which opens Scene 5, give precision and impact to the nature of the historical moment in which the characters are set, and leads to a conclusion which is both that of the characters and, it is inferred, one which could well be taken as a model by divided communities as much as by divided individuals. At the end of Scene 4 Marian clasps Lily's hand and asks for her forgiveness; an emotional bond being established across time as much as across the two communities. It is then for Scene 5 to establish this meaningful moment within the on-stage lives of the present day characters.

As Fintan O'Toole commented in his review in *The Sunday Tribune* on the weekend following the première:

> Having convinced us of the reality of these people and of the time and place in which they live, Parker has then to try to leap beyond realism into some kind of metaphor of transcendence. That leap has to be credible on the level of the real political world which he has delineated so sharply. And it isn't.
>
> We have been led to expect some kind of apocalyptic deliverance at the end of the play. What we get is an evangelical sermon on the 'Christ is ourselves' as the source of change. The problem is that this pentecostal image works only on the level of words. Change is evoked verbally, it doesn't *happen* on stage. What we end up with is the notion that if we were all nicer people the troubles would go away. Nothing in the play gives us much reason to believe that.

As O'Toole sharply observes, the final scene founders on the playwright's inability to find a metaphoric equivalent for the love in the future of a parallel power to the childlessness by which he has evoked the sterility of the present. The on-stage characters are finally bonded together in a complex family unit – something which Peter notes ironically – and respond to the traumatic events of the Belfast streets with individual stories of revelation. O'Toole has noted the difficulty of accepting the 'evangelical' conclusion as satisfactory, but the issue is more problematic, and even less convincing, than his review suggests.

Scene 5 is set on Sunday 2 June, the day of Pentecost, so stimulating the protestant Ruth, prompted by Peter, into quoting the story of Pentecost from *Acts*, Chapter 2. The story of unifying revelation in which national and linguistic divisions are transcended through the intervention of the Holy Ghost stimulates Marian into an ecstatic demand for a Christianity beyond the church and an end to the committing of sin. The play closes as Lenny starts to play the trombone in the yard which can be seen through the parlour window, a rendition of 'Just a Closer Walk with Thee' in which he is slowly and hesitantly joined by Peter's banjo. As Ruth opens the window to admit the music into the 'barren' house the lights dim and the spiritual swells in triumphant intensity. The play ends on a note of affirmation and unification with the earlier touching of Lenny's hand by Marian suggesting a solidarity of purpose in the present as her earlier clasping of the hand of Lily suggested a commitment to the memory of the past. Moreover, the love-making of Peter and Ruth on the front room sofa replays that of Lily and the British RAF man Alan Ferris, with the hope that this time love will not be abandoned in the face of prejudice. The issue of personal relationships is then dramatically paramount, but at no point does Parker convincingly translate the microcosmic level of the domestic onto the violent plane of the political.

What was lacking in *Pentecost* was promised in the intended companion piece in a projected double bill which would have paired Parker's domestic drama with Frank McGuinness's *Carthaginians*. Field Day had already rejected McGuinness's earlier *Observe the Sons of Ulster Marching Towards the Somme* which, as directed by *Pentecost*'s Patrick Mason, achieved an exploration of the psyche of the Ulster protestants which was as moving on the personal level as it was penetrating on the political. McGuinness's withdrawal of *Carthaginians* following that of director Sarah Pia Anderson resulted in the blunting of the self-professed analytical intentions of Field Day; intentions which, as in the vetoing of David Rudkin's engagement with the protestant predicament in the commissioned *The Saxon Shore*, have frequently lacked the support of rigorous practice. *Carthaginians* is set in a Derry graveyard where a group of social and emotional derelicts perform a play-within-a-play from a script provided by Dido, the 'queen' of Derry. The time of the play is sixteen years after Bloody Sunday, giving it a contemporaneity which, along with its setting in Derry's *demi-monde* and a juxtaposition of tragedy and farce, led Paul Allen to suggest to McGuinness, during the course of a BBC Radio 4 *Kaleidoscope* interview in April 1987, that some people would be outraged by the production. McGuinness's comment as to the underlying theme of his play supports a reading of the work as highly provocative in that it is informed by the declaration of Aeneas' Dido that 'Carthage has not been destroyed' and neither, by implication, has the all-Ireland aspirations which a contemporary rival to Rome has attempted to destroy. Parker's *Pentecost*, although purporting to engage with a moment of Ulster history and, through its characters, prescribe a solution to that province's violence, is best judged in the terms utilized by Philomena Muinzer in her critique of Graham Reid's *Ties of Blood* in *New Theatre Quarterly*: 'It appealed for humane relations between the two communities without examining the complexities which prevent them, and in this was typical of the Ulster genre, The Answer Without a Question.'

Acceptable answers are more palatable and, superficially at least, suggest a greater harmony than do awkward questions, and while the setting of Dublin's John Player Theatre, in the factory area of the cigarette manufacturer among the guest houses and corner shops of the city's South Circular Road, lacked the symbolic resonance of Derry's Guildhall, the audiences on the opening nights in both cities were distinguished more by uniformity of appearance and response than by any deep ideological divide which had to be overcome. These Field Day audiences were not being forced to confront their own political and sectarian differences, rather they were united by dimensions of class and culture in the context of which the play was ultimately providing a 'liberal' message to which no-one could object as nothing was being fundamentally questioned. That the play was well received by both its Derry and Dublin audiences is unsurprising in terms of its essentially nostalgic 1960s message, founded in the 'revelation' of Lenny in Scene 5 of the spirituality of the naked jazz singer in the sand dunes and the sexuality of the nuns in the nearby surf; an image of beatific human wholeness which has the same anti-intellectual bias as the LSD escapade through which, as Peter recounts, he and Lenny once aimed to turn Belfast on to its shared humanity by a mass spiking of the city's water supply. This essentially 'mellow' message was obscured by the christian terminology of Marian's final speech, powerfully rendered by Eileen Pollock, and the use of the Pentecostal imagery. That the humanity of the 'self' has to be realized before the individual can respond to the humanity of others is the fundamental message; one which is both inadequate as a response to a complex, but clearly materially and historically founded situation, and one, moreover, which comes dangerously close to advocating that to which the play is thematically opposed through its use of a Biblical passage central to fundamentalist protestantism.

The production is both powerfully realized and movingly performed, the domestic anguish of the piece coming over particularly strongly on the smaller proscenium stage on the John Player Theatre than in the towering space of the Guildhall. To the point that the play is given two deeply felt performances by Stephen Rea and Eileen Pollock it realizes the claim which Parker made in an *In Dublin* interview with Jonathan Philbin Bowman that he is 'very nakedly, and straightfowardly – presenting fairly powerful emotional relationships'. Doubts are raised, however, as to the play's ability to realize his *Sunday Tribune* statement that he has '[tried] to explore some kind of vision of the future'. More specifically, these doubts apply to the intellectual rigour of the analysis on which the vision is founded; doubts which are only exacerbated when considering the play as the annual Field Day production.

In the Preface to the collection of their first six pamphlets published as *Ireland's Field Day* the Company declared their objective as being '[to] contribute to the solution of the recent crisis by producing analyses of the established opinions, myths and stereotypes which [have] become both a symptom and a cause of the current situation'. Parker's play works powerfully as an expression of personal anguish, and indeed he stated to Bowman that 'it's not political, the top line of the play is not political at all'. As suggested above, however, the play is explicit as to a faith in an inspired humanist harmony ending discord on both the personal and political planes. What does not occur is analysis of either myths or stereotypes, nor is there a more informed engagement with the social, political, and economic discontents which, laid down across centuries, fuel the present crisis and frustrate the personal desire for peace. That *Pentecost* is a frequently moving and often witty dramatization of personal relations makes the play one of some distinction. When it is considered as a response to a political situation, however, its last twenty minutes lack credibility on any level other than that of the performers' ability to invest the lines with passionate conviction. That this succeeded in the John Player Theatre, but failed in Derry's Guildhall, was due entirely to the fact that the smaller area allowed a focus on the intensity of experience within the domestic, while the space of the Guildhall provided a political dimension into which the play could only aspire to enter.

The warm applause at the end of the performances in both Derry and Dublin attested to the quality of a company which has survived in a climate which is both financially and politically fraught with difficulties. That no-one appeared to be anything other than happy with an evening well spent is a compliment to the company but, given its own stated ambitions towards analysis, the audiences applauding laudable sentiments expressed on-stage need more than emotion if they are to support sentiment with informed action. As Brecht observed in *The Messingkauf Dialogues*, the issue is not simply to reproduce real-life incidents but 'to underline their causality'. It is here that *Pentecost* and Field Day are at their weakest. As Seamus Deane, one of the company's directors, stated in his Field Day pamphlet *Heroic Styles: the tradition of an idea*: 'Everything, including our politics and our literature, has to be rewritten – i.e. re-read.' What *Pentecost* presents, however, is a moving modernization of the plea of O'Casey's Juno to 'Take away our murdherin' hate, an' give us Thine own eternal love'. Not so much a re-reading as a reprise.

6

Narratives of the Nation: Fact, Fiction and Irish Cinema

Luke Gibbons

'Hey, is that real...?'
(John Wayne, in *The Quiet Man*, 1952)

One of the recurrent narrative devices in Irish cinema, from the earliest silent films to the present, has been the insertion of actuality or documentary material into improvised storylines, thereby indicating that the boundary between truth and imagination may be more indefinite and permeable than clear-cut distinctions between fact and fiction would suggest. This technique has taken many forms, from brief inserts for comic or topical purposes to a more sustained, critical use of the archive to explore the limits of both the imaginary and the real. In *Rooney* (1958), the actor John Gregson togged out with one of the teams taking part in the All-Ireland Final between Kilkenny and Waterford in 1957 to display his character's prowess at hurling, a matchless performance which gave much amusement to the assembled masses gathered to witness this founding ritual of the nation. A ceremonial ritual with somewhat more gravitas was incorporated to lethal effect in *Hennessy* (1975), one of the earliest films about the Northern conflict. In a climactic scene which led to the virtual banning of the film, Rod Steiger rubbed shoulders with Edward Heath and other dignitaries in cleverly edited footage of the state opening of parliament in London as his character attempts to assassinate the Queen. In Tom Collins's recent *Bogwoman* (1997), covering the period which led to the breakout of the Northern conflict, colour home movie footage of Derry is used to give a poignant evocation of community life before the Troubles. At a different level, grainy inserts of newsreel from the Eucharistic Congress in Dublin in 1932 throw into stark relief the contrast between the intimidating show of strength by the Catholic church in the early years of the state, and its decline in city suburbs now. Actuality footage from the War of Independence is incorporated into the action of *Irish Destiny* (1926), scenes depicting the burning of Cork City and of the Customs House being juxtaposed against dramatic uses of actual locations such as the GPO and the Curragh camp. Silent film of the

69

War of Independence, in this case a Black and Tan raid on Enniskerry, also features in Neil Jordan's *Michael Collins* (1996), but is integrated into the storyline by having people watch it at a cinema. This device recurs in a contemporary mode through the relaying of television news reportage of Northern Ireland or other recognizable material in the background of several scenes in films such as *Maeve* (1981), *After '68* (1993), *Hush-a-Bye-Baby* (1989) and *Some Mother's Son* (1995).

SIMULATING THE REAL

The recourse to the real in fictional settings is not, of course, unique to Irish cinema, and has lent itself, indeed, to a new genre of 'docudrama', exemplified by the controversies surrounding films such as Oliver Stone's *JFK*. However, as a contrast with Stone's film suggests, the use of this device may take a distinctive form in Irish cinema, calling into question many of the assumptions which underlie its deployment in mainstream docudrama. 'I am troubled', wrote one critic of *JFK*, 'by Stone's mix'n'match of recreated scenes and archival footage' because 'young viewers to whom [Stone] dedicates the film could take his far reaching conjectures as literal truth'.[1] The implication here is that archival footage is being used to confer authenticity on the director's wild speculations, to add credibility to what many historians regarded as the excesses of a paranoid imagination. 'Most moviegoers', observes historian Eric Foner of Stone's film, 'don't go to a film thinking how [it achieves its effects] – They think *JFK* is true . . . [Stone] created new footage that looked exactly like the original documentary footage, and you couldn't really figure out where the "real" documentary footage left off and the "new" documentary footage began.'[2]

The prototype for this kind of 'faction' or 'infotainment' goes back, perhaps, to the beginnings of silent cinema, and particularly to George Melies's studio recreation of news events, such as the coronation of King Edward in 1901, which couldn't be captured on camera due to the poor lighting conditions in Westminster cathedral. It is difficult not to suspect that, given the paucity of early newsreels, and hence the capacity of audiences to contrast the real and the fake, the studio recreations themselves, with their attention to detail and verisimilitude, may have carried more conviction than the use of actuality footage. (Even the King himself asked to see the record of his own coronation!) In this respect, it is striking that it was the problems presented by Irish subject-matter which first brought the question of authenticity itself to the forefront of fictional, as against documentary, story-lines. In 1910, the Kalem Company, under the direction of Sidney Ollcott and Gene Gauntier, travelled to Ireland to pioneer the use of 'real' locations, or actual places, as settings for dramatic action. As a review of their first film, *The Lad from Old Ireland* (1910) declared: 'The picture is genuine Irish and needs no labelling to prove it. It carries its authenticity on its face.'[3]

It remains to be seen, however, what exactly is rendered authentic in this situation. The narrative technique of framing fictional action against what purported to be authentic topographical or ethnographic settings derives from the emergence of the 'regional novel' in early romanticism, a genre ushered in once more by a work set in an Irish location, Maria Edgeworth's *Castle Rackrent* (1800). At the hands of its most successful exponent, Sir Walter Scott, this took the form of punctuating romantic plots with extensive descriptions of scenery and national character, duly annotated by learned footnotes citing authoritative sources for the various scenes depicted, or turns in the plot.[4] Such was Scott's success at integrating dramatic action with local colour that his novels were generally taken as faithful pictures of manners and character, as accurate historical accounts of bygone eras. As one reviewer put it in relation to *Ivanhoe*, the historical novelist 'aims to produce the conviction in his readers...that the events recorded not merely took place, but took place under such and such minutely defined peculiarities of scene and circumstance'.[5]

QUESTIONING THE REAL

However – and this is where a distinctive Irish turn is given to the quest for realism – it may turn out that instead of adding to the authenticity of a work, such historical asides or anecdotal detail can topple the whole edifice of realism so carefully contrived by the fictional narrator. The very need to provide scholarly scaffolding to support the fictional superstructure indicates that its foundations may not be secure, and in fact, may have the effect of undermining entirely the authority of the fictional narrator. This can be seen, for example, in the almost Mylesian array of personal asides, scholarly footnotes and indeed, footnotes within footnotes, with which Lady Morgan peppered the text of her sensational novel, *The Wild Irish Girl* (1806). At one point a footnote intrudes on the action to remind us: 'I have seen such scenes as the above, the dramatic effect of which exceeds all description' – which hardly reinforces our confidence in the descriptive powers of the hapless fictional narrator.[6] At another exchange between the two main characters, a long antiquarian and etymological digression throws the discussion off course, glossing the origin of the harp, and citing various scholarly sources in support of its position. But in case even this display of erudition is not sufficient, another line of defence is introduced by a cryptic personal footnote *within* this footnote: 'A few months ago the Author having played the Spanish guitar in the hearing of some Connacht peasants, they called it a

clarseach beg, or little harp' (62). At this point it is impossible to determine
who is telling the story, or what we are to believe. Instead of authenticating
the fictional narrative, the vertiginous annotations and layers of realistic
detail only serve to derail it, breaking up the seamless continuity required to
maintain the spell of fictional illusion.

This radical divergence between story and setting, narrative and history, is
seen to telling effect in one of the earliest Kalem films, *The Colleen Bawn*,
based on Boucicault's enormously successful Victorian melodrama, and shot
in Killarney in 1911. The opening titles assure us that 'Every scene, including
interiors, in this Irish production was made in Ireland, and in the exact
location described in the original play'. As the story progresses – or digresses
– the intertitles continually introduce non-sequiturs where the story is concerned such as 'The inn shown is over 100 years old', before assuring us that
we are looking at 'a real bog near Killarney's lake', and the 'exact reproduc-
tion of the original Danny Mann's cottage', not to mention in the climactic
scene depicting the attempted murder of the eponymous Colleen Bawn, 'the
exact location including the real Colleen Bawn rock and cave'. (That there
were no originals for Danny Mann's cottage or the rock and cave, as both
characters and incidents were fictitious, only adds to the ontological confusion.[7]) The *reductio ad absurdum* of this approach is demonstrated by the
complete narrative redundancy of one intertitle, accompanying the depiction
of Danny Mann's remorse after his attempted drowning of the Colleen
Bawn: 'The bed used in this scene belonged to Daniel O'Connell and was
occupied by him.' The topographical and historical asides here cut across the
ostensible story, skewing its narrative coherence by introducing what were,
in effect, other disparate narratives bound up with the landscape and history
of Kerry.

The contrast with the intercutting of fact and fiction in contemporary
films such as *JFK* is instructive here, for despite Oliver Stone's avowed
intention to deploy a *Rashamon* type structure, with competing, multiple
points of view, the film subordinates all its rapid editing and montage
techniques to an emphatic 'one-sided perspective'[8] – as befits the paranoid
style and conspiracy theories which inform its controlling vision. This is the
kind of narrative structure, with its drive towards coherence, certainty and
moral clarity, which underlies recent criticisms of attempts to impose a
similar order on the obdurate course of Irish history. According to Roy
Foster, for example, nationalist versions of the Irish past, at least in the main
nation-building phase, were characterized by 'the idea that Irish history is a
story, and the implications that this carries about a beginning, a middle and
a sense of an ending'. For this reason, Irish historians intent on demyth-
ologizing the past 'have tried to break up the seamless construction of
narrative incident which was presented as the story of Ireland, and to
analyse the moment simply rather than follow the flow'.[9] The suggestion

here seems to be that the effect of introducing narrative into history is to construe the past as a unified organic whole, the story of a mythic, enduring nation. Accordingly, the task of historians is to set the record straight, to remove the malaise of myth – what F. S. L. Lyons referred to as 'Literary Parnellism' – from the prosaic 'facts' of Irish history.

It would seem, however, that what is needed here is not less but more attention to literature and film, for writers and film-makers in Ireland have already taken it upon themselves to question the kind of omniscient or overarching narratives which Foster singles out for criticism. Some of the most distinctive – and, it could be argued, influential – strands in Irish fiction have sought to pre-empt the very possibility of narrative coherence by introducing into fiction precisely the contingency of history – the chance event, the accidental detail, the unexpected encounter, the irrelevant aside. In Irish culture, the difficulty has been not simply to elicit order from history, but even from fiction itself, at least as it evolved through the powerful counter-currents of romantic, gothic and modernist fiction. One of the consequences of this, as Foster points out, is that narratives are not only disjointed in structure – the 'deliberate gap in the narrative and [the] significant elision' become the hallmark of the Irish national tale (40) – but are also unable to achieve closure or a sense of an ending, let alone a happy ending. 'It will be a bitter day for this town if the world comes to an end', one of the shopping women remarks to Francie Brady in *The Butcher Boy*, with true apocalyptic forebodings. The actuality footage of the Cuban Crisis which dominates television screens throughout the story, and the magical realist explosion which detonates the landscape in Francie's demented imagination, also relays this rueful message.

WORLD WITHOUT END?

Within narratives of the nation in Irish popular history, this lack of closure took the form of an endless – or tragic – deferral of an ending, as in Robert Emmet's famous last words – 'Not yet! Not yet!' – and his wish to postpone the writing of his epitaph, to remain as 'the unnameable', until Ireland achieved its freedom. These sentiments form part of a historical tableau – recreated in George Melies fashion – in Walter MacNamara's rambling epic, *Ireland a Nation*, which ran, in tandem with the course of history itself, from 1916 to 1921. It is in this film that we see the full narrative implications of introducing actuality footage into fictional formats. Insofar as it attends to the past, and to imaginative recreation, the film has a clearly defined structure in the manner outlined by Foster, the heroic struggle of a nation against adversity charting the events of 1798, Emmet's rebellion, O'Connell's campaign for Catholic Emancipation and Repeal, and so on. But half way through, contemporary events catch up with the story, and the rest of the film is an ill-sorted assemblage of scenes from the War of Independence caught by the camera, ranging from de Valera's homecoming, British army raids, to extensive footage of the funeral of Terence McSwiney. This constitutes more a kind of public 'stream of consciousness' of the nation than a well-formed narrative, and because it continually opens itself up to the exigencies of events, there is no guarantee of an ending. Such closure as the film possesses, then, can only be achieved by stepping out of the action to the act of narration itself – as in the last shot which reveals that the story has been told by a grandfather to a child on his knee.

The effect of this act of closure is to draw attention to the fact that we are receiving a story, filtered through a point of view, as against the form of omniscient narration which purports to record the objective unfolding of a sequence of events. That this extension of oral culture into cinema is overtly or covertly at work in some of the most important Irish films is clear from the multi-layering of films such as *The Quiet Man* (1952) and *The Butcher Boy*, where it becomes exceedingly difficult to determine who is telling the story, or from what position it originates. The cadences of the voice assume a different form in the ballad structure of *Michael Collins*, a tale told to the camera with the narrative repetitions and refrains of ballads such as 'Old Skibbereen' and 'She Moves Through the Fair' which, indeed, frame and punctuate the action. The intrusion of history itself into the narrative – in the form of the brute reality of Collins's assassination – was sufficient to rule out the feel-good ending which would have greatly enhanced its box-office appeal in the United States, but interestingly, this ending was itself interpreted as an act of closure by some Irish commentators. For Fintan O'Toole, the film signalled the end of an era of nationalism, and the aspiration for a United Ireland, through its rehabilitation of the historical compromise of a (permanently) divided Ireland effected by the Free State. But is the ending so clear-cut as to warrant that conclusion? The fact that the hero of the film, the charismatic figure of Collins, does not come through the ordeal throws a question mark over the successful completion of his political project in narrative terms, a lack of resolution signalled throughout the film by its cyclical, repetitious structure. This raises the possibility that the cycle of violence does not terminate with the ending of the film, a prefiguring of the future alluded to by the systematic – and highly controversial – allegorical resonances with the contemporary conflict in Northern Ireland. Not least of the ironies of the concerted effort to extricate fact from fiction, and to relieve Irish history of the burden of narrative, is that the desire for simplified story lines, with clearly identified heroes and villains, linear progression and the wish for a happy ending, is now the prerogative of those who wish to draw a line over the past, and to leave history itself behind. The surge of narrative in its determination to surmount all obstacles in its path can be seen in the optimism, amounting almost to euphoria, which attended the signing of the Belfast agreement. Here at last was one narrative that was not going to founder on the irruptions of history, despite Drumcree, the murder of the Quinn children in Ballymoney, and the carnage of the Omagh bombing. If there is any lesson to be learned from the past, however, it is that narratives in Irish culture offer no insulation from history, and are only as resilient as their capacity to articulate the voices of those who have not been heard, rejecting the habits of authority which have enabled some to continually shout down others. Only then will history move beyond a story, as Paul Durcan has expressed it, 'with a middle only'.

7

Changing the Question

Terry Eagleton

> The British can never solve the Irish question because the Irish keep changing the question.
>
> (*Traditional aphorism*)

The status of Ireland in Wilde's day was oxymoronic. The country was a metropolitan colony, at once part of the imperial nation and peripheral to it. As with many a marital union, a formal parity concealed the real subordination of one of the partners. Before the Union, Ireland could regard itself as an independent nation because its allegiance lay not to the parliament at Westminster but to the Irish crown, which could be seen as distinct from the British crown even though it happened to rest upon the same royal head. But since the crown is merely metonymic of British power as a whole, this neo-scholastic manoeuvre proved peculiarly hollow. Ireland was an independent kingdom, so the theory ran, because it had its own monarch, who happened also to be monarch of Great Britain. In fact, Ireland shared a sovereign with Britain because it belonged to it; but the fetish of the crown allowed these power relations to be suppressed when it proved convenient, and necessity to be transformed into contingency.

The bond between the two nations was thus a kind of fiction. 'In this United Kingdom of Great Britain and Ireland,' writes Sir Samuel Ferguson, 'each part is governed by the whole, and neither by the other' – so that no 'free-born Irishman' could acknowledge allegiance to a *British* sovereignty.[1] The British do not govern Ireland, despite every empirical appearance to the contrary, since Ireland submits only to a sovereignty which includes itself. The Irish after the Union swear fealty not to Great Britain, but to a Platonic totality created out of their unequal incorporation into it. In this way, the conditions of their subservience become the conditions of their freedom. An appropriate analogy here might be the work of art for classical aesthetics, all of whose elements are equal and autonomous, recognizing no dominion but the law of the artefact as a whole.[2] But this 'law of the whole' is really just a mystifying name for the interrelations of the elements as such, just as the crown is no more than a signifier for actual political relations.

By a curious inversion, then, reality – the actual state of Anglo-Irish relations – has become fiction, and a palpable fiction is promoted as reality. But the fiction is doubled: for since the Revolution of 1688, the British crown had itself become progressively subordinated to parliament, making the myth of Irish autonomy harder to sustain. Since the notional independence of Ireland had been based in part on the fetish of royal authority, the exposure of one form of chimerical independence threatened to unmask another. It was partly because this changed relation between crown and parliament was nowhere formalized that the fiction could still be sustained – which is to say that the appearance of Irish independence depended in part on the absence of writing. But the asymmetry of the post-Union situation was enough to betray its fictive status. If the sovereign power of the United Kingdom contained, so to speak, an Irish admixture, then the free-born British fell as much under a certain element of Irish dominion as vice versa. It is hard to believe that many nineteenth-century Britons held that the supremacy to which they paid homage owed anything to the prognathous creatures they chuckled over in the *Punch* cartoons.

Paradox, metonymy, oxymoron: it is in terms of such tropes that the relationship between imperial Britain and colonial Ireland has to be read. What precisely is the grammar of Anglo-Irish relations? For two characters in John Banim's novel *The Anglo-Irish of the Nineteenth Century*, this is a slippery linguistic matter:

'After more than seven hundred years of identity with this country –'
'Not identity, Grady; that almost makes you speak a paradox', said the Secretary.
'Connexion, Sir?'
'No.'
'Then, Sir, conjunction?'
'Not even that, unless you mean our grammatical anomaly, a disjunctive conjunction . . .'

Which is to say that the text of the relationship is indecipherable – that there is a fundamental opacity or equivocation built into it, a subtle mismatching of perceptions by which it refuses to add up to some luminously intelligible whole. As with the modernist work of art, there is a sense of it never quite achieving the wholeness for which it strives, of some slippage of the sign or skewing of narratives which threatens to undo any totalizing logic. And this failure of assured translation between the two nations is nowhere more vividly exemplified than in the present-day Irish constitution, an Irish-language text which assumes that in the event of an interpretative conflict between its meaning in Irish and in English, the Irish version will be deemed to take precedence over the English. But the Irish text is widely suspected to be itself a translation from the English; so that, by some Derridean logic of supplementarity, the derivative takes precedence here over the original. If a discrepancy arose from the Irish document having mistranslated the English, then a mistranslation would hold sway over the translated text.[3] Flann O'Brien himself could hardly have pulled off a more improbable scenario.

Fredric Jameson has argued that the modernist sense that meaning is no longer immanent in daily experience but always elsewhere, ceaselessly displaceable to some mysteriously absent cause, can be related to the conditions of colonialism, in which 'a significant structural segment of the economic system as a whole is now located elsewhere, beyond the metropolis, outside of the daily life and existential experience of the home country, in colonies over the water whose own life experience and life world – very different from that of the imperial power – remain unknown and unimaginable for the subjects of the imperial power . . . '[4] This is one way in which the narrative of colonialism becomes strangely scrambled, as the classical coherence of metropolitan life is undermined by its absent colonial cause; and Jameson goes on to suggest that what would be needed to model this elusive totality is a kind of half-way house, an exceptional national set-up which reproduces the appearance of 'first world' social reality but whose underlying structure is in fact much closer to that of the 'third world'. The name of this laboratory experiment in modernist literature is *Ulysses*. But the problem with Ireland is that the water to which Jameson alludes is so very narrow – narrow enough to trouble the distinction between 'inside' and 'outside', and so to defeat totality in this way too.

Ireland was indeed in one sense unimaginably remote to some of its proprietors: if a few intrepid British souls set foot there for the odd vacation it was because, so Sir Jonah Barrington considered, the place was as exotically alien to them as Kamchatka.[5] Affairs in Ireland, concluded an exasperated Lord Liverpool in 1816, were 'not influenced by the same feelings as appear to affect mankind in other countries'.[6] But the island was also unsettlingly close to hand. It is not, with Ireland, simply a question of some inscrutable Other, as an increasingly stereotyped discourse of stereotyping would have it; it is rather a matter of some unthinkable conundrum of difference and identity, in which the British can never decide whether the Irish are their antithesis or mirror image, partner or parasite, abortive offspring or sympathetic sibling. A colony is not just 'other' to its metropolis but its highly *particular* other – not simply different but, as it were, antithetical. It is a point well captured in Samuel Beckett's reply to the French interviewer who gullibly enquired whether he was English: '*Au contraire*'. If Britain is the source of authority, then it is the parent and Ireland the child; but if both bow to the jurisdiction of the crown, then the two nations instantly become siblings, recomposing their relationship in the light of this fetishized Law. It is a puzzle of which we have a microcosm in *Ulysses*:

are Stephen and Bloom brothers or father and son, and if father and son then which is which?

The Anglo-Irish sometimes spoke of Britain as the mother country and Ireland as the sister nation, and sometimes of a brotherly affection between the two kingdoms.[7] Thomas Bartlett points out that whereas in the pre-Union period the Irish liked to think of their relationship to Britain as one of sisters, the British themselves thought of it in terms of mother and child – with the ominous implication that a child can always grow and demand independence.[8] The logic of the situation is incestuously garbled: your brother is really your father, and you are both sister and daughter. Indeed one might claim that incest is as fearful as it is precisely because it writes large an intolerable riddle at the root of all identity. Since all identity depends upon difference, I can only be truly myself by uniting with the other; but to achieve such union completely would be to abolish the difference between us, and along with it all possibility of identity. Difference is both the ground and obstacle of relationship: if the other ceases to be other to me, then in that very act I become alien to myself. Banim is right to see identity as paradoxical; but the logic of incest drives this paradox to an insupportable extreme, as what should be other (the parent) becomes intimate (the lover). A curious inversion is at work here, evident enough in Sophocles' Oedipus, whereby an excessive intimacy with what should be off-bounds alienates you from yourself, and so makes you a stranger to what is nearest to hand.

It is not hard to see the bearing of this paradox on Anglo-Irish relations, from either end of the power structure. At once too near and too far, akin and estranged, both inside and outside each other's cognitive range, Britain and Ireland at least shared in common the crisis of identity which each partner catalysed in the other; whereas if the Irish had been black, unintelligible and ensconced in another hemisphere, savages of the desert rather than the doorstep, their presence might have proved rather less unnerving. It was, of course, thanks to British colonialism that they were as culturally close as they were, so that when the British felt themselves confronted by backyard barbarians they were merely reaping the harvest of their own overfamiliarizing of them. The Act of Union between Great Britain and Ireland has commonly been figured as a sexual coupling; but it is a peculiarly incestuous form of congress, in which the border between difference and identity, alienness and intimacy, is constantly transgressed, and subject-positions (strangers, siblings, parents, spouses, partners) become dizzyingly interchangeable. (As far as spouses go, Oliver MacDonagh compares the influence of the Irish MPs at Westminster to that of 'Victorian women over husbands or fathers – not indeed in terms of affection and compassion, but in terms of domestic miseries that might ensue were they wholly thwarted, maltreated, or abandoned'.[9]) If your partner turns out to be a

parent in thin disguise, then it is understandable that the incest taboo will
spur you to revolt against this consanguinity, in that act of Oedipal aggres-
sion which is one feature of nationalism. Stephen Dedalus feels betrayed by
his real father and so must either, like Jesus, become his own progenitor, or
find a new parent in Leopold Bloom. Ireland, too, must throw off its false
parent, Britain, and fashion its own forebear by reinventing its ancient past –
in which case it becomes, in a familiar Oedipal fantasy, self-begotten. Yet
such disavowals of dependency must be directed *at* the parent, and so remain
a kind of negative bond or dialogue of antagonists. To disown another is at
least to credit him with the capacity to recognize your refusal, and so to align
him with oneself.

It is in this sense that separatism remains, in Lacanian parlance, a 'discourse of the Other', and not only in the more obvious sense that the very
means of Irish nationalism, from literacy and communications to education
and political organization, were largely British-made materials. Nationalism
is an affirmation of difference or autonomy; but like the Oedipal revolt it
makes sense only within the context of parental authority, and so is always
at some level a performative contradiction, qualifying its declaration of
freedom by the very situation in which it is forced to utter it. There is no
genuine independence which is forced to assert itself. And since perceiving
you as different was in one sense what the metropolitan nation did all along,
nationalism represents a discourse of the Other in more ways than one. What
you say in such circumstances is not at all to the colonialist's taste, and
exactly what he wanted to hear.

There can be no union without distinct identity, otherwise what exactly is
being unified? Identity is at once the precondition of unity, and its potential
disruption; without a degree of identity there is nothing to amalgamate, and
with too much identity no possibility of accord. It is hard to locate the
delicate point of equipoise between the two – the point where you are at once
enough something to become something else, and yet not so grossly self-
identical as to resist all reciprocity. To unite with another implies a persistence as well as a transformation of your previous identity, since it is *you* who
have united; whereas a mere act of assimilation, as of the Irish parliament to
the British in 1801, is in one sense no unity at all, since one of the terms in
question has simply been abolished.[10] From this viewpoint, the Act of Union
delivered the worst of all possible worlds. For what was at stake was not the
coupling of two securely established identities, but the consummation of a
long history in which the senior partner had so grievously undermined the
identity of the junior that, like some lunatic driven to distraction and
threatening both murder and self-destruction, the latter had to be taken
into custody both for his own protection and for the safety of those around
him. What was in one sense an act of voluntary merging was in effect one of

annexation and appropriation; indeed it is interesting here to glance back to the language of the Declaratory Act of 1720, which speaks of Ireland as being 'inseparably United and Annexed' to Great Britain. There is an ambiguity in the word 'unite', which can mean a free mutuality, or – as with 'annexed' – the mere superadding of one thing to another. 'The United States' signals more than geographical contiguity. What happened in 1801, in certain respects at least, was a union rather in the sense that a burglar can be said to unite himself with one's domestic goods, or in which a mugging can be viewed as an equitable exchange between one's wallet and a blow on the skull. Ireland and Britain were united in the sense that the latter confiscated the former's parliament, and so rather as a fish can be said to be amalgamated with a diner through the act of eating. In the words of a seventeenth-century Munster planter, the British were to 'incorporate [the Irish] into ourselves, and so by a oneness take away the foundation of difference and fear altogether'.[11]

In one sense, Ireland, rather like a minor in law, had too little identity to enter into a marriage, and would not have needed to do so if it had not; in another sense it had all too strong a notion of itself, which was another reason why it required some marital curbing. If it was to be yoked into stifling intimacy with Britain, this was precisely because it was perceived as dangerously other. At one level, the two nations were to enter into symbiotic union precisely so that one of them could be the more effectively treated as a special case. What linked them was the difference; what grappled them together, as with some tormented Lawrentian couple, was their mutual antagonism. In a case of what Theodor Adorno sees as the secret gesture of all ideology, identity was to be foisted upon non-identity; but that non-identity was itself, among other things, the product of a too-strong imperial selfhood. Britain and Ireland were now to pursue an equal, identical project of treating the latter unequally and non-identically; as with all the most effective forms of dominion, the freedom of the underlings lay in taking an active hand in their own subordination. The very difference of Ireland had created the need for a shared identity; but for those who objected to that arrangement, the difference would be merely exacerbated by it. It is in this sense that R. F. Foster can speak of the Union as preparing the way for its own dissolution.[12]

But if the Union delivered the worst of all worlds, it was because, failing to find the balance point between identity and non-identity, it treated Ireland at once differently and not differently enough. Indeed it was a familiar complaint of nineteenth-century nationalism that Britain did one or the other according to its own advantage. The Irish were different enough to require a special civil service and apparatus of repression, to be asked to foot the bill for the Famine, and to enjoy a peculiar franchise qualification. But they were alike enough to have MPs at Westminster in the first place, a privilege enjoyed by no other British colony, to contribute to the national debt, and to share with the imperial nation an exchequer, armed forces, postal services and a free-trade area. As far as economic life went, Ireland's integration with Britain had meant, over the years, gearing its production more and more to the British market – a symbiosis which then served to reinforce its industrial backwardness, and so ironically to foster its difference. On the other hand, there were several respects in which the colony was like its imperial masters, only more so. Precisely because of its difference, it could serve as a sphere for social experiments which would hardly have been readily countenanced at home, and so gained a national education system before Britain itself, one of the most advanced public-health establishments in Europe, public works and a streamlined paramilitary police force. This precociousness, needless to say, was not unconnected with the need to police and pacify a disaffected people; but some of these developments were significant advances in Irish civiliza- tion, testimony to the more positive, progressive face of the Union. From this viewpoint, Ireland differed from Britain by prolepsis, anticipating its own future evolution, and so could be seen as fundamentally identical, a mere fold in time in which the colonizing nation could view its own imminent destiny. From another viewpoint, Ireland was different from Britain because it was caught up in some archaic temporality, and had simply to enter upon the triumphal time-stream of European Enlightenment – its people happily Protestantized, its agriculture fully modernized, its barbarous customs dis- creetly erased – for its underlying identity with Britain to emerge. Each nation could thus glimpse something of its own future in the glass of the other; and the fact that the two time-streams were somewhat out of syn- chrony – that Ireland at once lagged behind the metropolitan nation and was in some ways out in front of it – was not of course accidental, since it was precisely its backward, recalcitrant nature which called for an unusual degree of state intervention. In the meantime, Britain treated Ireland differ- ently when it suited it, leaving its half-rotten boroughs untouched by the 1832 Reform Bill and its local government firmly in the hands of the landowners, and identically when that suited it too, in the imposition, for example, of a poor law grotesquely ill-suited to native conditions.

In some cunning twist of Hegelian logic, then, the union of Britain and Ireland did and did not take place. What happened was that a metropolitan narrative was overlaid on a colonial one, to produce a radically undecidable text. As far as difference and identity go, it was hard to say whether the Union had changed everything or nothing whatsoever, as with some ontological shift so profound that almost nothing of it can be detected on the surface. Though the infantile sexual imagination may fantasize that the bride, on the morning after the wedding night, will rise mysteriously trans- formed, the reality proves somewhat more prosaic. Ireland had undergone the drama of a 'legislative union', which is to say that one legislature had been abolished rather than two harmoniously coupled. At this level, the union was so deep-seated, so profoundly accomplished, that one party entirely swallowed up the other. Unity implies an exchange of identities; but in this case the exchange seemed largely one-way. It is hard to see that Britain was being hibernicized in the sense that Ireland was being anglicized, whatever the English cult of the Celt which followed in the Union's wake. As in chemical catalysis, one of the elements of the synthesis appeared mysteriously unaltered. But this was hardly the whole story. The supplement, so Jacques Derrida has argued, is no mere addition to an already complete phenomenon, but alters its nature, reveals what was lacking to it all along.[13] Politically speaking, this was certainly true of the Union: dogged by the dull insistence of the 'Irish question', the course of life at Westminster could never be the same again.[14] But Walter Benjamin's sagacious dictum that 'the fact that "everything just goes on" *is* the crisis' also had its force. Ireland was now part of a United Kingdom; but it seemed something of an afterthought, which did little to modify the already assured identity of its masters. It had been a kingdom of the crown before the Union, and was part of a kingdom still. Its colonial apparatus remained firmly in place, indeed would be reinforced; and though a Dublin without the social retinue of its parliament was a rather less glamorous place, there was a sense in which Ireland under the Union was the status quo ante only more so.

[...]

The British government further sapped Anglo-Irish authority with its informal promise of Catholic emancipation, soon to be broken; but one of its aspirations, ironically enough, was to grant an increasingly paranoid Protestantism a deeper sense of security, and so breed in it a greater tolerance for its Catholic compatriots. If this hope proved too wan, then direct rule of Ireland from Westminster might at least give Britain a more active hand in protecting the Catholics from the more arrogant excesses of their superiors. If the Anglo-Irish would not cajole the Catholics, thus leaving them dangerously open to an alliance with revolutionary France, then the British would step in and do it on their behalf, thereby robbing the Ascendancy of their political initiative in the hope of securing for them a more stable future. Two birds might thus be improbably killed with the same stone, as the ruling minority was propped up and the disgruntled majority simultaneously placated. Irish Catholics were to be emancipated within a novel political framework (the United Kingdom) within which they formed a minority, and so were to be privileged and sidelined at a stroke. In this respect, the Union was a deliberately self-defeating phenomenon; in other ways it proved more unwittingly so, nurturing unintended results and reversals it was powerless to control. If many Catholics had initially supported the Union, they were later to identify it as a major barrier to their freedom, so that what was invented as a solution to political ills became, in an inversion of homeopathy, a problem and political target all in itself. On the other hand, some of the Protestants who had opposed the Union were soon its most ardent apologists, so that religious and political divisions were disastrously deepened by the move. Many Orangemen had fiercely resisted the Union precisely because they foresaw the odious corollary of Catholic Emancipation, and thus feared that a move intended to support the Protestant nation would end up by subverting it. As the cause of national independence passed by an ironic twist from Protestant to Catholic people, the Union, far from winning the allegiance of the Catholic masses, became the focus of a militant nationalism. In this sense, an original separatism – the United Irish movement – had led to fusion, and that in turn to a fresh drive for national autonomy. In drawing Ireland closer to itself, Britain had in one sense merely underlined the contrast between this formal partnership and the inequities of colonial power, thus stoking nationalist rancour in a notably self-thwarting move. In a further irony, the newly centralized power of the United Kingdom, in extending 'modernity' to Ireland in the form of new structures of civil society, provided the nationalists both with fresh grievances and with the means of articulating them. English-bred literacy, education, communications, political forms, were all in this way to prove conveniently double-edged weapons. What had started life as a remarkably ad hoc, cobbled-together affair – the Union itself – had rapidly escalated into a fresh set of permanent political antagonisms.

[...]

It is possible, then, to see the various contradictions of the Union as symptomatic of Anglo-Irish relations as a whole, in which difference and identity are continually transformed into each another. Karl Marx understood well enough how an abstract equality could both foster and conceal injustice, crushing specific needs beneath a spurious equivalence; and this is obvious enough in colonial Ireland, where a formal principle of parity required that the country was subjected to, say, a type of British poor law or *laissez faire* economics, thus creating non-parity in the shape of a greater wretchedness. To treat others equally is not to treat them as mirror images of oneself, but to extend to them one's own freedom to become what one desires. Difference and equality are not simple opposites: the more Ireland crept closer to an equality with Britain, the more firmly it needed to be held in place. 'The more wealthy Ireland became', comments Edmund Curtis, 'and the more equality with Great Britain she attained, the more necessary it seemed to Great Britain to "manage" her.'[15] The contrast between equality and inequality is also one between intention and effect: in different social conditions, the same even-handed measures will breed divergent consequences, and so cease to be identical. Britain would legislate for itself, only to find that it had, so to speak, inadvertently legislated for Ireland too. To extend to the colony its own democratic reforms was to bring it more securely within its civilized orbit; but it was also to risk undermining the undemocratic power of the Ascendancy, and so to risk creating more instability for itself. A similar play of difference and identity can be seen in nationalism, which shifts between a demand for equality and an assertion of difference, between constitutional text and separatist subtext. And there are those who would claim that, just as colonialism is potentially self-undoing, unavoidably handing its subjects the weapons by which they might bring it low, so nationalism can advance only by adopting the methods of its oppressors, thus baffling its own demands.

The ratio of difference and equality, so Christopher Clapham argues, varies from one type of colonialism to another. French colonialism, Clapham claims, is typically centralizing and assimilationist: it regards native cultures as largely worthless, but offers its peoples the chance to integrate with an enlightened metropolis by becoming French citizens themselves. British colonialism is rather more particularist: since the natives cannot really aspire to become English, they must be ruled, in part at least, through their own cultural forms and political institutions. Imperial government, rather than seeking to raise the benightedly particular to the universal, descends to the particular and implants itself within it. The colonies have their own distinctive destinies and rhythms of development, which must become the very medium of colonial power.[16] One might see this as a distinction between the political and the cultural. For the French, the ideal goal is political citizenship, which an Algerian or Vietnamese may in principle attain; for the British, identity is essentially a cultural affair, so that the thought of a British Asian or African is merely absurd. Edmund Burke is one of the most eloquent exponents of this British particularism; but how is this concern with cultural difference to be squared with the integrationist policy of the Act of Union, a policy of which he himself was sceptical and which he did not live to see? Ireland would seem in this way too something of an anomalous case, caught on the hop between difference and identity, culture and politics, particular and universal. The Union is an uneasy compromise between French and British strategies, seeking to impose identity on what the British, in another quarter of their mind, recognize as two distinct, organically evolving cultures. There is something incongruous about the Hibernian apes of the *Punch* cartoons, creatures of a different planet and time-scale entirely, enjoying political representation in the British parliament; but this bizarre commingling of cultural orders, in which a society in the wings of history also came to hold centre stage, was forced on the British government in the heat of revolutionary crisis, and had then to be lived with as best it could.

Sylvester Douglas, former Chief Secretary of Ireland, writes in the year of the Act of Union that relations between Britain and her colony are 'in constant danger of misapprehension and dispute, and subject to the inconveniences which inevitably arise from circuity of communication, and the impediments and embarrassing modifications to which jealousy or ignorance on the one side or the other will so often give occasion'.[17] Douglas's comment is hardly a masterpiece of lucidity itself; but it pinpoints well enough the sense of some constant scrambling of communication between the two nations. [...] The history of Anglo-Irish relations is among other things the story of a ceaselessly garbled conversation, of partners speaking resolutely past each other, of obtuse or well-intentioned misapprehensions.[18] How could it be otherwise, when the two parties shared a common history, but shared it precisely from conflicting positions, and so with colliding versions of the centuries-old transactions which had passed between them? John Stuart Mill believed that Britain, of all 'civilized' nations, was the least well-placed to understand the Irish – partly because no other nation was so 'conceited of its institutions', partly because no other was so remote from Ireland in its social and economic history.[19]

Taken overall, the British response to Ireland was quite astonishingly ignorant, bigoted and thickheaded, lurching from transparently false optimism to a desperate faith that if the country were ignored for long enough it might just sidle away. As humble yet crucial a word as 'farm' could breed different meanings on each side of the water, as the British thought of well-cultivated estates and the Irish of a few acres of stony soil. That England had lost its own peasantry, indeed looked askance on the whole notion of a peasantry as anti-modern, did not help in this respect. If the British thought in terms of contract and utility, there was at work in popular Irish attitudes a doctrine of moral economy, which could generate systematic misunderstanding with their masters.[20] The triumph of the landlord was the triumph of writing: Deasy's Act of 1860 based the relationship between landlord and tenant 'on the express or implied contract of the parties and not upon tenure or service'. Gladstone's egregiously ineffective Land Act of 1870 was inspired in part by the assumption that the grievances of Irish farmers might be met by the granting of longer leases. He did not grasp that the tenant considered himself to have a natural right to his land as long as he paid his rent, and that any sort of fixed lease would limit this prerogative. In seeking contractual security for the tenant, Gladstone succeeded in dispelling a salutary vagueness in the existing arrangements which could work in the tenant's favour.

The Act was founded on a whole series of misreadings: of the causes and frequency of eviction, of the supposed superiority of Ulster agriculture and the presumed role in this of the so-called Ulster custom, of the part played by security of tenure in agricultural productivity.[21] Some of these misperceptions were particularly ironic, since Gladstone himself was well aware of the role of custom and moral obligation in the Irish countryside. It was he, not some morbidly nostalgic Fenian, who remarked that the 'old Irish ideas were never supplanted except by the rude hand of violence – by laws written on the State Book, but never entering into the heart of the Irish people'.[22] Two texts, the one written and contractual, the other tacit and traditional, were thus at loggerheads,[23] and – most unusually in the course of modern agrarian capitalism – it was the latter which was to triumph, as tenant rights became enshrined in the various Land Acts of the *fin de siècle*. It was the finale of a long-running conflict between English and Irish ways of seeing. Sir Marmaduke Travers, the returned English absentee landlord of Charles Lever's novel *The O'Donoghue*, has benevolent intentions towards his tenants but cannot understand the character of the people. Ignorant of their manners and mores, he fails to grasp that they define the 'same' material matters differently from himself; and this is a common enough motif in Anglo-Irish writing, from Maria Edgeworth's *The Absentee* onwards. It is no accident that John Stuart Mill, enlightened apologist for Ireland, should also have proposed a new science of Ethnology, which would take as its subject-matter the distinctive culture and psychology of a people.[24]

It may be that there is a deeper, more structural dimension to this dialogue of the deaf – or at least that a psychoanalytic analogy may help, if not to account for it, then at least to illuminate it. For Jacques Lacan, the demand for full recognition by the other is tragically unrealizable for at least two reasons. For one thing, the other must interpret one's demand for what it is; but one can never be entirely sure that this has happened, given that the demand itself, in order to attain expression, must pass through the defiles of the duplicitous signifier. The meaning of speech depends upon the response of its addressee; but since this response, too, must pass through the ambiguous medium of signification, we can never be entirely sure that our demand has been acceded to. For another thing, the other will receive one's demand only from within the distorting perspective of his or her own desire, which will then render it doubly opaque. It is for this reason that Lacan writes the 'other' with a capital O, to signify that structural non-reciprocity or miscommunication which we call the unconscious.[25] In seeking the recognition of the Other, I am led by this very desire to misrecognize it, grasping it in the imaginary mode. There is an Irish demand; but the British can never be sure that they have interpreted it correctly, since its form of articulation seems constantly to change. 'The Pope one day and potatoes the next', as Disraeli wearily put it. At one moment the call is for land reform or an independent parliament; then it takes the form of a struggle against tithes or godless universities, a plea for electoral reform or the repeal of the Union; next it shifts back to the land question, but adds an appeal for Home Rule or a threat of republican separatism. The British, when seized by a fit of receptiveness, attend to the demand and seek, for the most part belatedly, inadequately and under dire threat of coercion, to accommodate it; but they may find themselves here in the situation of the Lacanian adult vis-à-vis the infant, who in catering to the child's immediate needs fails to decipher the absolute demand for recognition obscurely encoded within them, and so unwittingly crushes that demand in the very act of relieving the infant's want. Since the infant can only express this impossibly general demand for recognition in narrowly specific terms, in gestures which at once reveal and conceal it, this misapprehension is built into its transactions with the parent. The infant may then, so to speak, shift ground and try again; but the same structural misprision is bound to occur; and in the rift between need and demand will germinate desire, that objectless, insatiable hankering which is born of the despair of one's demand ever being fulfilled.

A Lacanian Irish rebel song makes the point precisely:

> When we were savage, fierce and wild
> She came like a mother to her child
> And gently raised us from the slime
> And kept our hands from hellish crime
> And she sent us to heaven in her own good time.
>
> Now Irishmen forget the past
> And think of a day that is coming fast
> When we shall all be civilised
> Neat and clean and well advised
> Oh won't mother England be surprised?

It is not hard to read the sardonic humour of this as displaced rage. Ironically complying with the mother's wishes is a way of not complying with them at all – of fulfilling them only to draw her attention to the gap between her desires and expectations, and so turning the insult back on herself. The elaborate obedience with which you meet her wishes is simply a way of signalling their worthlessness. It is not that the mother has failed to attend to the child's needs; it is just that she has blandly misconceived them. And this brings us to the second Lacanian cause of the garbled discourse: the fact that the other will receive one's demand only through the distorting prism of his own desire, which is to say, in the case of Britain, of its own political interests. It is in this sense, as Lacan insists, that one always receives back one's demand from the Other, from that place where it has been refracted through a language which always precedes you. Dispiritingly enough, you will emerge into existence as an 'autonomous' subject only on the basis of that alienated image of your demand which the response of the Other returns to you. If the Irish appeal seems mystifyingly to alter from one moment to another, or at least from decade to decade, it is for good political reasons; but it is also as though it is striving to outflank this dire condition to which all human dialogue is apparently doomed, shuttling from political to cultural to economic registers in the hope of discovering the transcendental signifier which will say it all. But if the demand is finally for a recognition of your autonomy, then it cannot properly be uttered, since it will need to pass through the discourse of the Other and so will be assimilated to the very conversation from which you hope to extricate yourself. As long as the demand for independence must be addressed elsewhere, and there is no demand which is not, it is bound to constitute a scrambled message. The Irish could never be sure that they were receiving back a response to their appeal because the British had usually misunderstood the question, passing it through the defiles of their own signifiers; but this misreading is then fed back into the demand itself, which begins to revise itself in the light of its own alienated image.

We are always at some level told how and what we may ask for, and the Irish were no exception. What they wanted depended to some degree on what they thought they might get; O'Connell declared himself interested in nothing but an independent legislature, adding with swift illogicality that were someone to offer him a subordinate parliament instead he would not refuse. The discourse of the colonial is always rhetoric which overhears itself in the ears of the other, shaping itself accordingly; and as long as one's demand is in this sense dialogical, it can never remain self-identical. So it was that the Irish came to direct their own speech and actions at the British (mis)understanding of them, in ways that then introduced division and ambiguity into their own language. 'The relation between the two races', writes Elizabeth Bowen in *The House in Paris*, 'remains a mixture of showing off and suspicion, nearly as bad as sex. Where would the Irish be without someone to be Irish at?' The Irish are no doubt no more remarkable for showing off than any other people; but there was certainly a sense in which they knew themselves to be permanently on stage. And it is suitably symbolic that two of their greatest champions, Daniel O'Connell and Charles Stewart Parnell, displayed in their discourse a mastery of equivocation and ambiguity which would have been the envy of a Mallarmé. As that oxymoronic animal, a radical landlord, Parnell could offer himself as a conveniently indeterminate space in which different forces – Fenianism, constitutionalism, agrarian agitation – might temporarily congregate. He was not the only Irish leader to live his existence as a kind of symbol, converting his Anglo-Irish aloofness into a blankness in which others could find themselves conveniently reflected.

The fact that a radical demand must be expressed in the language of the present, and so in terms of what it opposes, has sometimes been used to convict it of bad faith. Irish nationalism castigated British culture, but where would it have been without it? The very processes which brought it to birth – education, the press, modern political structures – emerged, ironically

enough, from the dissolution of the traditional culture from which nationalism drew its inspiration. It was, so the argument runs, a product of the very
British modernity it so fervently denounced, and so was locked in hopeless
self-contradiction. A similar charge can be levelled at Marxism, with its
'capitalist' obsession with the economic, or at the kind of feminism which
complains of the lack of female chief constables. There is certainly a fair
amount in nationalism which mimics the power it opposes; but the criticism,
as it stands, is altogether too facile. There is no contradiction in the fact
that radical movements are products of the system they seek to contest; if
they were not, but moved instead in some metaphysically distinct space, they
would be incapable of challenging it. One can only logically speak of conflict
if two power systems share a world in common. Those who regard nationalism as the mere inversion of imperialism, or feminism as patriarchally
obsessed with sexual power, would no doubt be the first to denounce these
beliefs as idle utopianism should they seek to invent a language of their own
from scratch.

Quite who is in bad faith here, then, is a matter for debate. Such political
movements are forms of immanent critique, which find themselves installed
within the logic of what they oppose, and for just that reason are able to
press that logic through to an outside or beyond which is political emancipation. A truly radical demand is by definition one which deconstructs the
'inside/outside' opposition.[26] If the fact that it shares in what it rejects opens
a perpetual possibility of bad faith, it is also an opportunity for pressing
beyond it. In Irish nationalism, the tension implicit in the phrase 'immanent
critique' could be damagingly relaxed on either side: into a mere shadowing
of the regime it confronted, or into an ultra-leftist purism which refused all
truck with it. But that a demand for radical change must work with the
contaminated materials of the present is no objection to it, and no assurance
of its futility. It is simply a reminder that all political demands are impure;
but that, after all, is one of the first lessons of materialism, and one with
which the liberal can heartily agree.

8

Misplaced Ideas? Colonialism, Location and Dislocation in Irish Studies

Joe Cleary

The emergence of colonial and postcolonial studies within the Irish academy as a distinct mode of critical analysis can probably be dated to roughly the start of the 1980s. The social climate in Ireland at that time was one conditioned by a major exodus of the country's young population in search of work in Britain and the United States, by the social toll of constantly rising unemployment and by political deadlock and military conflict in the North. The dominant intellectual responses to these crises developed by the Irish academic and political establishments were essentially shaped by variants of modernization theory and revisionist historiography. Most modernization theories rest on a crude dichotomy between 'traditional' and 'modern' societies, and are designed to conceptualize the process whereby 'traditional' societies can acquire the attributes of 'modernity'.[1] From this perspective, the problems besetting Irish society since independence – whether political violence or sectarianism in the North or conservative Catholic nationalism or economic inefficiency in the South – are interpreted as evidence that the island still has to make the necessary transition from a 'traditional' to a properly 'modern' social order.

The popularity of modernization discourse is explained no doubt by its suppleness – a product of its tendency to detach questions of social agency from considerations of structure – and by its consequent capacity to lend itself to a wide range of political positions and agendas.[2] 'Modernity as such,' as Francis Mulhern comments, 'has no necessary social content: it is a form of "temporalization", an invariant production of present, past and future that "valorizes the new" and, by that very act, "produces the old", along with the characteristic modes of its embrace, the distinctively modern phenomena of traditionalism and reaction.'[3] The dichotomy between 'tradition' and 'modernity' that subtends modernization discourse has been used effectively by Irish liberals genuinely concerned to secularize the oppressively Catholic state culture established in the Irish Republic after independence. The same sclerotic dichotomy can also be used, however, to advance the rather different interests of neo-conservatives less concerned with social emancipation than with the emancipation of domestic and international capital from all sorts of 'traditional' constraints such as state control or trade union regulation. Modernization discourse has also exercised considerable attraction for some sections of the Irish left on both sides of the border. In a country where the electoral record of socialist and labour parties is poor by Western European standards, the explanations for Irish 'backwardness' offered in modernization discourse have seemed quite compelling to many on the left. Only when modernization through Europeanization has enabled the country to overcome 'the idiocy of rural life' in the South and the 'atavism' of sectarianism in the North so that it can become like the rest of Western Europe, some liberals and leftists seem to assume, will Irish social democracy be able to make its belated rendezvous with history.[4]

One of the attractions of postcolonial studies in Ireland as it has emerged since the 1980s has been its attempt to destabilize the cultural dominant represented by modernization discourse. Like modernization theory, postcolonial studies is concerned to articulate the systemic connections between the various crises that affect Irish society, North and South, but it does so in a manner that controverts crucial tenets of the reigning conceptual orthodoxy. From the perspective of postcolonial studies, modernization discourse is simply another variant on the nineteenth-century bourgeois ideology of evolutionary progress, the occluded side of which has always been European imperialism and the colonial subordination of the greater part of the world to metropolitan domination. By focusing overwhelmingly upon variables relating to indigenous aspects of social structure and culture, modernization theories generally have displayed indifference to the entire issue of economic and political imperialism and have usually ignored or underplayed many important external forces or constraints upon change within given societies. Even in those cases where they accord significance to external forces, modernization theorists tend to look at this 'impact' in terms of the diffusion of ideas, values and expectations as a consequence of interaction between societies, but they rarely attend to the structural mechanisms that condition such interactions. Where modernization discourses, therefore, consistently locate modern Ireland within an apparently self-contained Western European context and within a foreshortened time-span in which the past is consistently coded as calcified 'tradition' that simply acts as a barrier to progress, postcolonial discourse insists on the need to understand Irish historical development in terms both of the *longue durée* and the wider geographical span of Western colonial capitalism. Where both modernization discourse and Irish revisionist historiography stress the reactionary nature of Irish nationalism, postcolonial discourse has suggested that

Irish nationalism can only be understood contextually, as the complex outcome of local interactions with an aggressively expanding imperialist 'world' economy. Where revisionist historiography and modernization studies have both been obsessed with the 'high' history of nation and state formation, with the narrative of the political élites that shaped Irish political institutions and state apparatuses, postcolonial discourse has sought to develop a more critical understanding of the various forms of subaltern social struggles that have largely been written out of the dominant debates in Irish history, whether in their bourgeois nationalist or revisionist versions.[5]

That said, Irish modernization discourse, revisionist historiography or postcolonial studies ought not be credited with more internal coherence than they deserve. All have been coloured to some extent at least by the extended conjuncture of economic crisis in the South and military stalemate in the North. How these intellectual formations will adapt to the altered conditions of the new century which commences with the South enjoying a dramatic economic boom and with the tentative establishment of a new political dispensation in the North still remains to be tested. The intersecting social and intellectual forces that have shaped the emergence of postcolonial studies in Ireland are heterogeneous. The various intellectual currents – new transnational models of historical research such as the 'Atlantic' and 'New British' histories; Marxist dependency and world systems theories; the wider international development of postcolonial cultural analysis inspired by the work of Edward Said and others; and the study of colonial social history from 'below' associated with the Indian Subaltern Studies project – that inform the scholarship conducted under this rubric are diverse in origin and valence. Given the complex concatenation of social and intellectual forces involved, the tendency by its critics to represent Irish postcolonial studies simply as a stalking horse for 'traditional' Irish nationalism or as a renovated version of 'Celtic whinge' or simply as the latest exotic intellectual import must be dismissed as reductive.[6]

For now at least, postcolonial studies in Ireland represents less an authoritative corpus of work than the name of a still quite novel research agenda. What distinguishes the formation is that it is by far the most outward looking of the modes of socio-cultural analysis currently shaping Irish Studies. Based on the premise that it is the wider historical and geographical span of modern colonial capitalism that constitutes the proper contextual frame for the study of modern Irish society, the work conducted in the field implicitly sets down a challenge to the narrowly insular Anglo-Irish framework that has conventionally shaped Irish Studies. Given the extent to which this area studies framework has been naturalized as the constitutive disciplinary horizon for the critical analysis of Irish society, postcolonial studies by its very nature has served to dis-locate Irish Studies in ways that many find counterintuitive and disconcerting. It is this issue of location and dis-location that I want to investigate in this essay.

Since its inception, Irish postcolonial studies has been continually confronted by its opponents with a series of sceptical questions: Can Ireland legitimately be considered a colony like Britain's other overseas possessions? Did colonialism play a significant or only a minor role in Irish historical development? If Irish historical experience is to be considered a colonial one, then when did it begin and when cease to be so? Does the situation in Northern Ireland represent a continued colonial dimension in Irish politics? Such questions continually boomerang Irish postcolonial studies back to what we might call questions of beginnings, intention and method.

In a classic essay, 'Misplaced Ideas', the Brazilian cultural critic Roberto Schwarz discusses what he describes as the besetting 'experience of incongruity' that continually obsesses commentators on Brazilian society.[7] Schwartz's attempt to account for this 'experience of incongruity' centres on a contrast between the ideological function of liberal ideas in Europe (their location of origin) and Brazil (one of their places of adoption). In Europe, he suggests, liberal ideology was the expression of a triumphant bourgeoisie in its successful struggle against the *ancien régime*. In Brazil, where the fundamental productive relationship in the nineteenth century continued, however, to be based on slavery, an ideology that proclaimed the autonomy of the individual, the equality of all men, the universality of the law and the disinterest of culture was patently out of place. For Schwarz, an ideology is 'in place' when it constitutes an abstraction of the social processes to which it refers. While in Europe, therefore, liberal ideology constituted an abstraction of industrial capitalism, the import of liberal ideas to Brazil created a situation where these ideas were put to work in a social order of a very different kind. The contrast between, on the one hand, the realities of the slave trade, economic dependency, and a political system based on clientalism and favour and, on the other, a liberal discourse which proclaimed universal equality before the law and the virtues of the impersonal state created an effect of ill-assortedness, dissonance and distortion. This distortion, Schwarz contends, led simultaneously to the debasement of Brazilian intellectual life and to an almost reflex scepticism where matters of ideology were concerned since the disjunction between ideology and material reality was so vast. For Schwarz, then, the 'experience of incongruity' that obsesses commentators on Brazil ought not to be construed in terms of a clash between European 'modernity' and Brazilian 'backwardness' nor explained away by a poststructuralist relativism which assumes that the real problem has to do with the inadequacies of the European sciences and methodologies and not with Brazilian reality itself. Instead, that experience must ultimately be attributed to the constitutive paradox of Brazilian social order: a local slave-owning latifundist economy structurally integrated on a dependent basis into the 'liberal' capitalist world economy.

From the theoretical perspective that shapes Irish postcolonial studies, Irish history discloses a constitutive paradox of a rather similar kind. The suggestion is not, patently, that nineteenth-century Ireland was like nineteenth-century Brazil. What is suggested, rather, is that although Ireland belonged to the same geo-cultural locale, the same orbit of capital, as the major European imperial powers, it was integrated into that orbit of capital in a very different way to its main European neighbours. Those who contend that Western Europe represents the appropriate comparative framework for the evaluation of Irish society assume an essentially homologous relationship between the country's spatial location, its socio-economic composition and its culture. Conceived in this way, differences between Ireland and Europe are invariably structured by the conceptual couplet of 'backwardness' and 'advance'. The postcolonialist perspective, in contrast, suspends the notion of homologies, and attempts to investigate the *discrepant* ways in which Irish political and cultural life, which were obviously shaped and textured by European developments, were at the same time over-determined by the country's dependent socio-economic composition. Contrary to what its critics would claim, then, postcolonial studies is not a misplaced or out-of-place idea in Irish circumstances. On the contrary, it might be argued, following Schwarz, that an obsessive 'experience of incongruity' – occasioned by the fact that dependent cultures are always interpreting their own realities with intellectual methodologies created somewhere else and whose basis lies in other social processes – is indeed a typical characteristic of postcolonial societies.[8]

If matters are to be advanced beyond the current controversies about whether or not Ireland can legitimately be considered a colony it is imperative, I think, to understand that this issue can be posed on two *analytically* discrete levels that require different methods of investigation: one that has to do essentially with matters of consciousness, systems of representation and discursive regimes; the other with 'objective' structural and socio-cultural correspondences – though ultimately the relationship between these two 'levels' also needs to be theorized of course. I want to deal briefly here with both levels individually, setting aside for the present the more complex question of their mediation.

On the first level, the question that is essentially being posed is: to what extent did those charged with British government in Ireland as well as Irish nationalists and Irish unionists consciously consider the Irish situation a colonial one? Since British rule in Ireland extended over several centuries, during which the British Empire changed dramatically in economic character and geographical composition, and since conceptions of Empire also changed from one epoch to another, what is called for here is a very challenging kind of intellectual history: one capable of tracing the shifting ways in which the various British governing classes, Irish political élites and insurgent social movements conceived of the Irish situation over an extended period of time. While the value of a history of *mentalités* and systems of representation of this sort can hardly be questioned, some caveats need to be entered. Some scholars argue that Ireland cannot be considered a colony at some or other stage because Irish nationalists did not deploy the language of colonialism and that opposition to British domination was coded instead in the language of tyranny and denied citizenship or argued on the constitutional grounds that the country was a separate kingdom.[9] The difficulty with this line of argument, as David Lloyd has rightly pointed out, is that it assumes already the historical development of a concept whose full range of meanings emerged only gradually through the nineteenth and into the twentieth century.[10] The fact that peasants in late medieval England, Spain or Russia did not consciously think of themselves as oppressed by a feudal social system does nothing to diminish the theoretical value of the term 'feudalism'.

The argument that eighteenth- and early nineteenth-century Irish nationalists looked mostly to the white settler colonies to highlight their own grievances, and less so to the indigenous native peoples of America or Africa or wherever, also needs to be weighed in this context. The fact is that in the period between the eighteenth and the late nineteenth century (perhaps later) the most difficult struggles of the European imperialist metropoles were not for the most part with the native peoples in their colonies but with their own white settlers.[11] The major changes brought about in the whole structure of the contemporary capitalist world system as a consequence of Britain's disputes with her restive white settlers in North America and Spain's with her creole populations in South America in the late eighteenth century testify to the significance of such conflicts. In other words, the earliest and most successful anti-colonial nationalisms were those of the white settlers and creole populations in the Americas and given the international significance of such movements it is not particularly surprising that their influence was most acutely registered in Ireland at the time. The fact that many prominent Irish nationalists – John Mitchel and Arthur Griffith are exemplary cases – considered it outrageous that Ireland should be treated as a colony because to do so was to put an ancient and civilized European people on the same level as non-white colonial subjects in Africa or Asia is well established. But the fact that some Irish nationalists or some versions of Irish nationalism were capable of only a very limited and conservative critique of British imperialism is not in itself an argument that Ireland was not a colony. Were the class-consciousness and solidarity of the oppressed not something that has continuously to be struggled for, rather than something that automatically attends the subaltern condition, then oppression would not be the problem it is in the first instance.

If the concept of colonialism has a theoretical value that cannot be reduced to the subjective consciousness of the colonizer or the colonized, then why does it matter one way or the other whether either the Irish or the British conceived of Ireland in colonial terms? Even if British administrators or some Irish nationalists discerned parallels between the Irish situation and that in various British colonies this obviously does not establish that the actual conditions were indeed commensurable. Nevertheless, as Luke Gibbons has argued, it is also the case that '[u]nderstanding a community or a culture does not consist solely in establishing "neutral" facts and "objective" details: it means taking seriously *their* ways of structuring experience, their popular narratives, the distinctive manner in which they frame the social and political realities which affect their lives.'[12] Once we allow that culture is the sphere through which conflicts are experienced and evaluated then it is clear that the attempt to trace the shifting ways in which Ireland was conceived in relation to other parts of the colonial world does have its own intrinsic value and interest.

While I have stressed the importance of discourses that construe Ireland in colonial terms because they help us to understand how political agents and communities structured their own experience, no historical materialist could be content to pose the question 'was Ireland a colony?' simply at the level of systems of representation. But this reservation immediately leads to the further question: with which colonies and with what kinds of colonial processes elsewhere might the Irish situation productively be compared? Naïve objections to the proposal that the Irish historical experience can be considered a colonial one seem often to assume that there is such a thing as a typical colony and a standard or one-size-fits-all colonial experience against which Ireland's claims might be weighed and measured. The real difficulty, on the contrary, is that colonial practices, structures and conditions around the globe have been of the most varied and heterogeneous kind. The sheer diversity of lands that comprised the British Empire alone has caused scholars to question whether any substantive similarities between colonial polities can be deduced, and some have even queried whether the term 'colonialism' itself has any analytical value.[13] To avoid surrender to such positivism, which reduces everything to an eclectic catalogue of isolated singularities, Irish Studies might do well to devote more attention to the task of generating a serviceable historicized typology of colonies.

The conservative historian of empire, D. K. Fieldhouse, and, building on his work, George Fredrickson, an American comparative sociologist of race relations, have divided overseas colonies into four categories: administrative, plantation, mixed settlement and pure settlement.[14] Though often the most prized imperial possessions, *administrative colonies* aimed at military, economic and administrative control of a politically strategic region and were never settled by Europeans on a mass scale. What usually destined a particular region to be an administrative colony rather than one of the settler types, Fredrickson suggests, was the presence of a dense, settled, agricultural population with a complex social and economic system, considerable military capacity, and relative immunity to the diseases of European origin of the kind that wreaked demographic havoc on the native peoples of the New World. Where these factors obtained, European conquest would normally be difficult and costly and little land was readily available for white settlement. Hence, once they had attained dominance in the region, the European powers could economically benefit most by extracting economic surplus or valuable mineral resources from these lands without systematically destroying their traditional societies. Colonial control in such instances could best be exercised by means of indirect rule exercised by co-opting indigenous élites or by newly constructed colonial bureaucracies staffed by European administrators and civil servants or by way of some combination of the two. This category includes the colonies of South Asia as well as most of Africa and the Middle East.

In contrast to the administration colonies, where power was exercised through a relatively small, sojourning group of primarily male European administrators, settlement colonies were characterized by a much larger settler European population of both sexes whose intentions were for permanent settlement. These fall into three general types. *Plantation colonies* usually attracted relatively small numbers of white settlers, but these acquired large tracts of land, found that the indigenous population did not meet their labour needs, and imported a slave or indentured and usually non-European labour force to work the monocultural plantations. In the plantation colonies, the mode of economic production rested essentially on the forced labour of imported workers to produce specialized staples for the world market. The exemplary instances in this case are the monocultural plantations in the West Indies and in the southern region of the United States.[15]

In the *mixed settlement colonies*, of which the clearest examples are the highland societies of Latin America, the indigenous peoples were not annihilated, but the Iberian settler culture and social structures nonetheless became the dominant ones. When Europeans first intruded, these regions already had large populations and complex sedentary societies. But the drastic losses suffered by the native population as a result of epidemics, warfare and brutal exploitation allowed the European settlers, Fredrickson suggests, to monopolize control of the land and to replace native political and cultural institutions with their own. Though the racial and class strata that emerged in such situations were typically very complex, miscegenation normally occurred and gave rise to racially mixed groups that served as buffers between those of settler and indigenous descent. Labour was exploited in such situations usually by way of coercive landlord–peasant relationships – with the indigenous peasantry left in place but required to pay tribute to European landlords or political authorities in the form of labour or commodities.[16]

In the *pure settlement colonies*, of which the United States, Canada and Australia are the exemplary instances, the native peoples were either exterminated altogether or their remnants pushed onto reservations in remote or unproductive regions. European exploitation in these regions did not take the form of the coercion of native labour. Instead, an expanding settler frontier was constantly pushed back as the indigenous peoples were displaced to make way for new waves of settlers. The North American and Australian colonial economies of this kind depended in their initial phases on indentured or bonded labour and even at later stages cheap coolie labour from Asia especially continued to play a major role in their development. But because land in such instances was usually relatively cheap by contemporary European standards, and labour consequently comparatively expensive, the pure settlement economies were not structured in terms of the 'feudal' tenurial systems that characterized mixed settlement and plantation colonies where a small landed oligarchy dominated peasant masses. Instead, farmer-settlement and free white labour became the social dominant. Because of the rigid social separation between settler and displaced native and comparatively low levels of miscegenation, these societies usually became homogeneously European in cultural character. Nevertheless, since land was cheap and white labour expensive, and because there were fewer inherited institutional restraints than in Europe, these societies were also often less rigidly socially differentiated and considerably more egalitarian – at least for white settlers – than their European counterparts.[17]

Used crudely, typologies such as these can obviously freeze into Weberian ideal types. But they can also be used productively to highlight dominant settlement patterns, economic systems and state structures that emerged in particular colonial situations, and they can be adapted to account for historical transformations within a given colonial situation in response to the larger global mutations of the world capitalist system. Moreover, it is also clear that many colonial situations must be construed as composites or hybrids of the basic types rather than simply as varieties of them. The case of the United States, which can be described as a composite of a pure settlement colony in the North and a plantation type in the South, is a case in point – though several other major examples such as South Africa or Palestine might also be mentioned.[18] The chief value of such typologies, I would suggest, is that they can help to distinguish the new and varied compositions of land, labour, capital (and the attendant class, racial and cultural relations) that typically emerged and predominated in different colonial situations.

Viewed in this frame, some elements essential to any evaluation of Ireland in comparative colonial context become evident. First, Ireland was systematically colonized on a modern proto-capitalist basis in the early modern period, roughly contemporaneous with the establishment of the Spanish and Portuguese colonies in South America and the English ones in North America. None of the expanding European colonial powers in that period were strangers to conquest and colonization when they reached the New World. Portugal had already occupied the islands of the Azores and Madeira, and was establishing trading colonies on the coast of West Africa, while Castile had taken the Moorish kingdom of Granada and was completing its conquest of the Canary archipelago. Both Iberian kingdoms had also been engaged for centuries in the struggle to expel the Moors from the Iberian Peninsula. Many of the techniques developed to settle and defend great tracts of underpopulated territory, as well as the spirit of religious crusade that inspired this Reconquest, were to be carried over in due course to the New World.[19] Similarly, England had been engaged for centuries in various attempts to subjugate Ireland when it established its first colonies in North America.

The dominant economic system that shaped the early modern colonial system was state-regulated merchant capitalism (or mercantilism). Like the West Indies and the American colonies, Ireland in this period underwent an exceptionally violent and accelerated process of colonial modernization in which every aspect of the indigenous society was almost wholly transformed in a very short period. All of these colonial sites were commercially orientated towards the emerging Atlantic economy, but imperial mercantilist policy was designed to prevent the colonies from developing independent trading links with each other. Instead, trade had to be channelled through the British and Spanish imperial centres, inhibiting independent economic development and diversification within the colonies over the longer term and thereby establishing the structures that would condition future economic dependence.[20] One of the distinguishing characteristics of the colonial outposts of this emergent Atlantic economy is the velocity of their transition from various forms of pre-capitalist society to mercantile capitalist modernity, without experiencing what Kevin Whelan has called the long conditioning of other medieval European societies.[21] Thus at the beginning of the seventeenth century, as Whelan remarks, Ireland was a very lightly settled, overwhelmingly pastoral, heavily wooded country, with a poorly integrated, quasi-autarchic and technologically backward economy. By the end of the century, however, all that had changed. As it was commercially reoriented to service the expanding English mercantilist state and concurrently integrated into the world of North Atlantic trade, Ireland, Whelan argues, underwent 'the most rapid transformation in any European seventeenth-century economy, society and culture'.[22]

In all the colonial sites that constituted this new Atlantic world this precociously accelerated modernization process was accompanied by what would ultimately appear from the perspective of a more fully developed industrial capitalism, with its 'liberal' emphasis on free labour and free trade, to be apparent economic and legal-juridical 'archaisms'. These include the slave plantations in the West Indies, the southern United States and Brazil; the *encomienda* and hacienda system in South America; and the oligarchic landed estates system in Ireland – by the nineteenth century the latter would be regarded by political economists of all shades as the single greatest impediment to 'proper' capitalist development in the country. In nearly all these situations, moreover, the native populations were subjected for extended periods to legal and political constraints – though these varied in kind enormously – designed to exclude them from civil and political society and to secure the privileges of the immigrant settler communities.

The discrepancy between the precocious modernity of these colonial societies and the extent of their integration into the emergent capitalist world system, on the one hand, and some of their more 'archaic' *ancien régime* characteristics has generated considerable theoretical controversy among Marxists. One position, associated with the work of Paul Baran, André Gunder Frank and Immanuel Wallerstein, holds that capitalism as a mode of production can be equated with the penetration of capitalist market relations. From this perspective, as capitalism comes into contact with other modes of production through trade, all economic activity is increasingly subordinated to the profit-maximizing imperatives of the market. Hence all essential distinction between the capitalist mode and modes initially outside the capitalist sphere is rapidly eroded and the problem that then poses itself is that of analysing the relationships of unequal exchange that subsequently emerge between capitalist core and periphery. An alternative position, associated with Ernesto Laclau and Robert Brenner, holds that while capitalist expansion is often accompanied by the extension of capitalist class relations it may also result in the combination of capitalist and non-capitalist modes of production in ways that contribute to underdevelopment. Brenner, for example, contends that capitalist expansion may result in 'merely the interconnection of capitalist with pre-capitalist class forms, and indeed the strengthening of the latter'. Alternatively, it may also lead to 'the transformation of pre-capitalist class relations, but without their substitution by fully capitalist social-productive relations of free wage labour, in which labour power is a commodity'. For Brenner, accounts such as Wallerstein's that equate capitalism with the extension of the capitalist market will 'fail to take into account either the way in which class structures, once established, will in fact determine the course of economic development or

underdevelopment over an entire epoch, or the way in which these class
structures themselves emerge: as the outcome of class struggles whose out-
comes are incomprehensible in terms merely of market forces.'[23]

These different theoretical methodologies point to strikingly different
conceptualizations of Irish history. From the first perspective, which is
closest to that shared by most Irish economic historians, a hallmark of the
Irish economy as it developed in the seventeenth century is the accelerated
velocity of its enforced capitalist modernization through conquest and colonization and the extent to which the country is incorporated as a producer
of agricultural exports into an emergent Atlantic economy. The sweeping
aside of existing feudal custom and moral economy during the successive
conquests that displaced the old Gaelic systems is viewed in this context as
leading to an unfettered capitalist exploitation of peasant labour in Ireland.
Unrestrained by the hereditary rights and moral economy that conditioned
landlord–tenant relationships in Britain, the Irish situation in this view
constitutes not a more retarded but rather a less regulated form of capitalism
that lacked the customary checks and balances that made its British counterpart more politically stable. Ireland's specialized and dependent economy
oriented towards international export, moreover, made it more vulnerable to
the cyclical vagaries of international markets and this in turn aggravated the
political volatility of a region already fissured by colonially structured ethno-
religious cleavages.

From the alternative minority perspective, which has been argued by
Eamonn Slater and Terrence McDonough, the British conquest of Ireland
allowed for the creation of a landlord class that controlled the Irish legal and
political system to a degree unparalleled in England. In this account, conquest led to the emergence of a kind of bastardized feudalism that allowed
the landlords to extract rental payments from tenants by means of extra-
economic coercion. Notwithstanding the fact that after the Union in 1800
Ireland was constitutionally integrated into the most advanced industrial
capitalist economy of the time, Irish society remained in this view essentially
feudal or quasi-feudal in character until the very end of the nineteenth
century. It was not primarily the dynamics of the capitalist market, but the
development of class struggle within what remained an essentially feudal
mode of production, it is argued, that eventually led to the demise of this
system. After the late nineteenth-century collapse of landlordism, peasant
proprietorship replaced it with a small-farmer regime, and only then was the
stage set, and even then only unevenly, for actual capitalist production in
agriculture.[24]

Depending on the theoretical model applied, it is argued then that Ireland
either underwent an extremely rapid enforced transition to a form of
dependent capitalism constrained within a colonial relationship mediated
through London or, alternatively, that it evolved by way of a bastardized

variety of colonial feudalism that allowed only for a very late development of capitalism by Western European standards. The differences here do not simply reduce to matters of different chronologies of capitalist development; different conceptions of the character and function of the Irish state are also at issue. Despite such divergence, both models suggest that Irish historical and economic development poses theoretical questions for Marxism that cannot be grasped within the feudalism-absolutism-capitalism sequence usually applied to the core centres of Western European imperialism. Both theoretical models further suggest, therefore, that the assumption that Western Europe constitutes the natural frame of comparative analysis within which Ireland should be located is open to question. The importance of Europe as the source of many of the economic, political, cultural and intellectual stimuli that shaped Irish society is not in doubt here – though these stimuli were also felt, to varying degrees, in all the major colonies of European settlement in the Atlantic world. What a postcolonialist methodology would suggest, however, is that it is the disjunctive way in which these metropolitan influences are articulated in a socio-economic context different to those in which they originally emerged that constitutes the real interest of the Irish situation.

The development of postcolonial studies in Ireland potentially represents a considerable challenge to Irish Studies as currently constituted. Too often reduced on all sides to a drama between nationalism and its critics, its real novelty, I have tried to suggest, may well lie elsewhere. To determine how Irish social and cultural development was mediated by colonial capitalism is the goal of postcolonial studies. From its inception, the colonial process was never simply a matter of the subjugation of this or that territory. It was, rather, an *international* process through which different parts of the globe were differentially integrated into an emergent world capitalist system. Once this premise is accepted, then it follows that the determination of a specific national configuration must be conceived as a product of the global: to borrow Neil Larsen's phrase, the *part* must be thought through the *whole* and not vice versa.[25] In contrast to a nationalist conception of Irish Studies, obsessed with the discovery of chimerical 'national' identities, and a liberal area studies alternative, that hesitates to look beyond the horizon of the British Isles or Western European state formation, postcolonial critique impels Irish Studies in the direction of conjunctural global analysis. From such perspective, the national arena still remains a crucial site for social struggle, but a true understanding of those struggles can only be grasped contextually within a wider global frame.

For the most part, debates about whether Ireland was or was not a colony have rarely got beyond questions of geo-cultural location and constitutional statute. These are important, but not the decisive issues. If colonialism is conceived as a historical process in which societies of various kinds and locations are differentially integrated into a world capitalist system, then it is on the basis of the comparative and conjunctural analysis of such processes that the debate must ultimately be developed. Cultural analysis has an important role here since this is the decisive area where social conflicts are experienced and evaluated, but it is ultimately the contradictions of the wider capitalist system that shape those conflicts, whether cultural, political or economic. While I have suggested that typologies of colonialism can serve as a useful heuristic device for the analysis of colonial situations, any taxonomy that loses sight of the fact that colonialism is a historically changing process will also be reductive. As Francis Mulhern has remarked, Ireland's colonial history, by virtue of its sheer duration, can read like a history of colonialism itself.[26] In the late medieval period the country was, like Scotland and Wales, one of the ragged frontiers of English state expansion and contraction; in the early modern period, a commercial settlement plantation was developed in the same westward thrust as European expansion into the New World. At the moment of the southern state's independence it was constitutionally configured as a white 'dominion' like Canada, South Africa or New Zealand. But this status was conferred against the backdrop of a triangulated military conflict between nationalist, unionist and metropolitan British forces – in some ways redolent of the situation involving a similar tangle of forces that later emerged in Algeria – that split the island into two states. The situation in contemporary Northern Ireland is sometimes compared to that of the Basque region in Spain or to ethnic conflicts in Central Europe. But Northern republicans have also construed and evaluated their situation in terms of African-American civil rights campaigns and late anti-colonial struggles in South Africa and Palestine.[27] Similarly, the recent 'peace process' is repeatedly compared to roughly concurrent processes in the Middle East and South Africa. Even the term 'the Celtic Tiger' adopted to describe the current economic boom in the Irish Republic implicitly associates that phenomenon with the small handful of East Asian 'tiger' economies that have emerged from a colonial history to attain levels of economic development comparable to those in 'the West'. While the term infers, on the one hand, that Ireland has now attained levels of economic development comparable to those in the rest of Western Europe, it also infers, on the other, that the trajectory of that development finds its closest parallels with other non-European histories. The point, finally, is not to adduce whether Ireland is or is not really 'just like' any of these situations since no two colonial sites are ever completely identical. It is, rather, to think the ways in which specific national configurations are always the product of dislocating intersections between local and global processes that are not simply random but part of the internally contradictory structure of the modern capitalist world system.

9
Sex and Sensation in the Nineteenth-Century Novel

Siobhán Kilfeather

To dream of a hearse with white plumes is a wedding; but to dream of a wedding is grief, and death will follow.
To dream of a woman kissing you is deceit; but of a man, friendship; and to dream of a horse is exceedingly lucky.[1]

The fact is, though it is difficult for an outsider to believe it, that the whole subject of love, of passion of any kind, especially from a girl and with regard to her own marriage, is such an utterly unheard-of one amongst Grania's class that the mere fact of giving utterance to a complaint on the subject gave her a sense not merely of having committed a hideous breach of common decency, but of having actually crossed the line that separates sanity from madness.[2]

Emily Lawless, in *Grania* (1892), tackles a problem that haunts much nineteenth-century Irish fiction: how to represent the (presumably) inarticulate masses, without merely re-presenting stereotypes associated with stage-Irishry and the brogue. Lawless gestures towards a recognition of this problem in her dedication: 'the possibility of an Irish story without any Irish brogue in it – that brogue which is a tiresome necessity always'. In her heroine, Grania O'Malley, named for an almost mythical figure from Irish history, Lawless creates a subjectivity whose complexities are indicated by sense, feeling and intuition rather than articulation, a woman isolated from her community by a superior sensibility which she has no words to explain, even to herself. The grandeur of Grania's nature is mapped directly onto the bleak grandeur of the landscape – the novel's subtitle is 'the story of an island', and the frontispiece is a map of the Aran Islands. None of Lawless's characters is liberated – except in death – from the confines of what the novelist presents as a narrow and rigid world-view. Grania never succeeds in articulating her discontents to her lover or to herself. The drama of their conflict requires a richness of language in the interplay between free indirect discourse and omniscient narrative to

105

suggest to the reader the meaning of Grania's social, sexual and spiritual frustrations.

Terry Eagleton writes that in nineteenth-century Ireland 'the sexual culture of the nation belonged to a complex economy of land and inheritance, property and procreation. As far as sexuality goes, we are speaking less of the erotic or psychological than of dowries and matchmakers.'[3] At one level, Lawless's novel would seem to concur with the view that Irish sexuality is so materially located as to exclude expressions of desire and sensuality, to make such expressions seem absurd or insane. At another level, the very posing of the problem of how to articulate desire within the novel suggests that the sociological or anthropological model for recording Irish sexualities is inadequate to the lived experience of those sexualities. Eagleton argues that it is with the modernism of Moore, Wilde and Joyce that 'sexuality becomes a metaphor for political revolt'. Eagleton's description of the sociological model is true to one dominant discursive mode of constructing Irish sexualities, the sketches of Irish life that run through those texts of political economy, travel writing, fiction, memoirs, journalism and apologies that seem to look to a British as well as Irish audience. Many of these incorporate an homage to the possibility of self-representation of the masses, in so far as they include documentation such as interviews or testimonies presented in court, to journalists, or to officials such as census takers or Poor Law Commissioners. In general these texts offer a contrast between the obfuscation of Irish speech – its deviousness, its foreignness, its intrinsic absurdities – and the apparent transparency of hunger and poverty as written on the body of the peasant. I began this essay with a quotation from Jane Wilde to indicate that there was some recognition in nineteenth-century literature that popular superstitions, folklore and ballads might be some of the languages in which ordinary people articulated the complexities of desire, and that the inverted logic of dreams has a pronounced role in such articulations. I want to argue that the novel is a significant source of information about sexuality because of its special ability to incorporate conflicting discourses, without necessarily reconciling them, and that in nineteenth-century Irish fiction there are recurring dramatizations of a great silence around sex.

Terry Eagleton, *à propos* his argument that the major nineteenth-century Irish novelists are 'engaged in a kind of performative contradiction', producing texts 'colonial in their very letter', cites William Carleton as an example:

> [T]he speech of Carleton's characters can also veer from one linguistic form to the other within one sentence...Young Dalton, one of the labouring poor of *The Black Prophet* (1847), manages to produce this earthy, monosyllabic praise of the woman he loves: 'Upon my honour, Donnel, that girl surpasses anything I have seen yet. Why, she's perfection – her figure is – is – I havn't [*sic*] words for it – and her face – good

heavens! what brilliancy and animation!' Young Dalton's problem is that he has all too many words for it . . . [4]

Eagleton makes this point in a context where he argues that what the Irish *novelists* have no words for is a history so 'crisis-racked, excessive, hyperbolic, unlikely', where 'life itself is sometimes a great deal more improbable than the most sensationalist of tales'. I make no apology for returning to the question of realism in the nineteenth-century novel, since criticism has so readily agreed that this is *the* issue.[5] Although the narrative of nineteenth-century fiction is often traced from Edgeworth to Somerville and Ross, I would argue that in this debate there is an exclusion of a certain kind of women's writing and a demotion of the melodramatic and sensationalist aspects of nineteenth-century fiction that in Britain were associated with an appeal to women readers.[6] It is when he tries to describe the body of Sally M'Gowan that words fail young Dick. Nineteenth-century Irish novels have as much trouble representing bodies and sexuality as in representing famine, dispossession and emigration. This is not because sex is simply an unspeakable subject in nineteenth-century Ireland, but because Irish writers reject the domestication of sexuality in ways that disrupt and depose the conventions of realist fiction.

The use of the word 'sensation' to describe excited or violent feelings dates from the late eighteenth century and by the beginning of the nineteenth century 'sensational', like the recently coined term 'melodramatic', was being associated strongly both with popular theatre and with newspaper reporting of crime. In literary criticism 'sensation fiction' is a term very specifically applied to a group of novels published in England in the 1860s, many published by Bentley and by Maxwell, some serialized in periodicals edited by women: the best-known of the sensation novelists are Wilkie Collins, Mary E. Braddon, Mrs Henry Wood, Sheridan Le Fanu, Charlotte Riddell and Rhoda Broughton. Jenny Bourne Taylor suggests that Wilkie Collins transposes 'the disruptive and disturbing elements of Gothic fiction into the homely setting of the family and the everyday, recognizable world, thus generating suspense and exploiting undercurrents of anxiety that lie behind the doors of the solid, recognizable, middle-class home.'[7] While many critics have followed W. J. McCormack's analysis of Le Fanu into recognition of the symbolic and allegorical valences of the so-called Protestant Gothic, with its narratives of aristocratic decay, there has been a concomitant denigration of, or apology for, 'Catholic' bourgeois fiction (McCormack is an exception).[8] Eagleton, for example, recognizes Protestant Gothic as 'the political unconscious of Irish society';[9] but in discussing *The Black Prophet* he identifies a striking 'hiatus' between 'story and society': 'Carleton can find no way of anchoring his narrative in the social conditions he depicts; instead the latter threaten at times to become a mere context for the former, which irrelevantly revolves on a twenty-year-old murder.'[10] Other critics have depicted the Irish novel as undermined by these dislocations. According to Thomas Flanagan:

> The history of the Irish novel is one of continuous attempts to represent the Irish experience within conventions that were not congenial to it … The best of them, which seek to move beyond these forms, make their strongest points and exist most vividly through indirection, symbol, allusion, and subtle shifts of points of view.[11]

John Cronin precedes Terry Eagleton in finding the plot of *The Black Prophet* inadequate to its anthropological and political concerns:

> Ideally the terrible realities of the truths in his novel cried out for a study plot-structure to match them and symbols grand enough to do justice to his fearsome theme. Sadly, what he offers instead is an unconvincing story of rural murder and mystery which is intended to generate, in relation to the contemporary events of the novel, an atmosphere of tension and horror.[12]

It might be profitable to move from the presumption that these are failed realist texts to think of their sensational and melodramatic elements as the vehicles for certain kinds of critique. It is not simply that Irish life had its sensational and melodramatic aspects, for which novelists such as Carleton strove to achieve what Margaret Oliphant ascribed to the sensation novelists – 'a kindred depth of effect and shock of incident'.[13] *The Black Prophet* is, of course, exemplary of a narrative and imaginative problem foregrounded in the debate between Edmund Burke and Thomas Paine on the French Revolution, the problem of representing the suffering of the masses as dramatically or affectively as the story of an individual, particularly of a literate, self-reflective individual. Sensational fiction offered writers the opportunity to interrogate the mechanisms by which grand historical narratives invade and evacuate individual subjectivities in what are conventionally presented as the private spaces of home, family and sexuality.

I am aware of the dangers of adapting the very specific use of 'sensation fiction' to include a much larger group of generically mixed texts over a much longer period in Ireland. I have argued elsewhere that there existed amongst eighteenth-century Irish and Scottish writers a sufficient alienation from English literature to foster the development of gothic fiction as a critique of 'progress' from the margins.[14] I want to argue here that in the nineteenth century Irish writers responded to the demands of new discursive formations about Irish reality, and to the tensions of negotiating between the slightly different demands made upon them, by a variety of

British readerships and Irish readerships, to discover the uses of sensational-ism. As a specifically literary, historical argument I would identify Gerald Griffin's *The Collegians* (1829) as the foundational fictional text in this transformation. It would be mistaken, on several counts, to insist too schematically either on a rigid distinction between English and Irish novel-ists – after all, Charlotte Riddell and Sheridan Le Fanu can be incorporated into the narrative of English sensation fiction – or between sensational and realist texts. One might question the usefulness of categorizing *Clarissa* or *Emma* as realist novels, in so far as such categorization necessarily belies interesting elements of those texts. More importantly, perhaps, Jenny Bourne Taylor warns of the dangers of privileging sensational novels as the site of madness and 'otherness', 'making them the bearers of a more authentic truth'.[15] It is possible to look at the sensational aspects of writers such as Griffin, Carleton, Le Fanu, Frances Browne, Sarah Grand and George Moore without denying that they have other striking generic affili-ations, not all of which are necessarily best read in an Irish context.

Jenny Bourne Taylor describes the middle-class English home of sensation fiction as a 'secret theatre', operating behind closed doors. Irish novels place much more emphasis on open doors, from cabin to big house, but the house open to hospitality and community is also open to surveillance. In the most famous depiction of the middle-class home in nineteenth-century fiction – breakfast at the Dalys' in *The Collegians* – the room is an over-determined text, the apparently transparent domesticity riven with incongruity and contradiction. One of the novel's motifs, in fact, is spatial contrast. In terms of landscape this involves a reiterated mystique of the west, where landscapes are more dramatic and life lived at a greater pitch of intensity.[16] The nobility of Myles and the unruliness of Poll both have their true homes in the west, and it is appropriate that at the novel's conclusion Hardress is seeking his death on a westward voyage, just as Mihil is being carried to a grave in the west.

The allegorization of space is just as striking in the representation of interiors, particularly in the repeated use of adjacent rooms to house irre-concilable narratives. The chasm between the classes is represented, for example, when Hardress cripples Danny Mann by pushing him downstairs; while Hardress's muted alienation from his own class is most strikingly presented when he stands at the deathbed of Dalton, the huntsman, who is being teased by drunken revellers in the adjoining room. The organization of domestic space is also a mode for conveying several undercurrents of passion that cannot erupt into social space. In the chapters at the Dairy Cottage, for example, while Kyrle is advocating the necessity of certain social hypocrisies, he is opening his heart to Hardress, while Hardress, the advocate of frank-ness, refuses to acknowledge the anguish of Eily, pacing the floors of another room. At Poll Naughten's cottage, Eily is repeatedly represented as moving in and out of her own room, and this movement provides Danny Mann's testimony with one opportunity for evasion:

> Questioned, If he were not present in said Naughten's house, when said Eily (deceased) said Looby being then in Naughten's kitchen, did give a letter to Poll Naughten, sister to prisoner, addressed to Dunant O'Leary, hair-cutter, Garryowen, and containing matter in the handwriting of said Eily; answereth, How should he (prisoner) see through stone walls.[17]

The anti-naturalistic presentation of space also opens up possibilities for representations of the fantastic. At her first appearance Anne Chute is passing around a drawing of Castle Chute, the house in which the party is gathered, and yet Hyland Creagh does not recognize the scene. Castle Chute is the place of two 'supernatural' visions; Dan Dawley's comic encounter with the Chute family ghosts at the start of the novel is echoed by a moment towards the end when Danny Mann's guards mistake Hardress for a ghost.

Luke Gibbons, in an essay on Killarney and the politics of the sublime, argues that the recurrence of supernatural motifs in eighteenth-century Irish literature provides one of the few means by which the legitimacy of the colonial settlement can be contested, and quotes Tzvetan Todorov: 'The function of the supernatural is to exempt the text from the action of the law, and thereby to transgress that law.'[18]

Griffin presents the Irish peasantry as a people 'at war with the laws by which they are governed ... There is scarcely a cottage in the south of Ireland, where the very circumstance of legal denunciation would not afford, even to a murderer, a certain passport to concealment and protection.'[19] There is a more textually interesting association with the law in Griffin. What chiefly justifies describing *The Collegians* as sensational is the novel's relationship to crime reporting. Showalter and Taylor point out that sensation fiction in England is concurrent with a huge public interest in murder trials, particularly trials of young women such as Madeleine Smith and Constance Kent. Jonah Barrington's recollections are one testimony to Irish public interest in crime. It has been observed that Griffin's historical setting for *The Collegians* is complicated by public memory of the much more recent murder of Ellen Hanlon. Later editions of the novel reiterate that memory by printing Curran's narrative of the murder from the *New Monthly Magazine* as an appendix. The juxtaposition of novel and narrative has the effect of demonstrating how inadequate explanation and motivation are to the crime. The discrepancies within and between the two texts draw attention to the ways in which various discourses – law, reportage, imaginative fiction – stand in for and gesture towards sexual passion and domestic violence but can never sufficiently account for that excess. The seduction of Eily, as much as her murder, happens off-stage.

It has been persuasively argued that newspaper reporting of sex crimes tends to produce conservative and normative versions of appropriate female behaviour, blaming the victim.[20] It is tempting but unproductive to suggest that what has been silenced in *The Collegians* is Eily's voice. Eily's voice is, in fact, foregrounded in a bizarre call to realism within the text, namely the dream of Hardress Cregan, where he introduces Eily to his rich and fashionable acquaintances, and is shamed by 'the bashfulness, the awkwardness, and the homeliness of speech and accent, with which the ropemaker's daughter received their compliments' and at the sight of her peeling a potato with her fingers. 'He dreamed, moreover, that when he reasoned with her on this subject, she answered him with a degree of pert vulgarity and impatience which was in "discordant harmony" with her shyness before strangers.'[21] The dream, like the scene at the Dairy Cottage, suggests that Hardress is not at all free from social concerns, as he pretends, but it is tonally a very different kind of revelation from that found in dreams in other novels, where the dreamer is overwhelmed by memory or unacknowledged, even unfocused, desires. In *The Black Prophet*, Donnel Dhu dreams that Condy Dalton is hammering a nail into his coffin. Sarah Grand's *The Heavenly Twins* and George Moore's *Evelyn Innes* are just two examples of novels featuring young women who live 'in a state of exquisite feeling', sexually aroused by powerful dreams.[22] Dreams perform many different functions in texts; in these novels they permit an indulgence of sensuousness without reflection or judgement. In *The Heavenly Twins*, of course, the end consequence of Edith's dream is her syphilitic baby and her own descent into insanity.

Elizabeth Bowen, in an introduction to a reprint of Sheridan Le Fanu's *Uncle Silas*, suggests that:

> *Uncle Silas* is, as a novel, Irish in two other ways: it is sexless and it shows a sublimated infantilism. It may, for all I know, bristle with symbolism; but I speak of the story, not of its implications – in the *story*, no force from any one of the main characters runs into the channel of sexual feeling.[23]

Bowen, in her own fiction a mistress of indirection, knows quite well, of course, how the novel bristles with sexuality, but in distinguishing between the story and implications she executes a divorce which everything in the text militates against. Maud's dream of her father's face 'sometimes white and sharp as ivory, sometimes all hanging in cadaverous folds, always with the same unnatural expression of diabolical fury' connects the sexuality and infantilism.[24] Only in her dreams can Maud accuse her father of terrorizing her, and only in fiction is there an acknowledgement that illicit intergenerational passions can fracture the home.

I began by suggesting that novelists have as much problem representing bodies and sexuality as famine and dispossession. One reason for this may be that the two had become intimately associated in discursive constructions of nineteenth-century Ireland. Feminists in Britain, many of whom offered powerful critiques of the family as a British institution, identified it as a site of resistance in Ireland.[25] In particular, they drew on the work of the Poor Law Commission to suggest that Irish chastity and domesticity were undermined by poverty and misgovernment. 'The admirable tales of Banim and Carleton have, I trust, paved the way for the success of the TRUE STORIES of the Irish Peasantry told to the Poor-Law Commissioners', announces Christian Johnstone. Johnstone and successive apologists for the Irish peasantry contributed to the production of a moral climate in which unruly, illegitimate sexuality became unrepresentable. Frances Power Cobbe offers a powerful image of this unspeakability: 'There is a peculiarly ferocious scream, really worthy of wild beasts, practised among these wretched girls whenever a mutiny takes place. It is called the poor-house scream.'[26] In contrast to this scream novelists increasingly present a chasm of silence on the subject of sexuality.

The turn to melodrama or sensation allows the juxtaposition, as opposed to reconciliation, of violently disparate material. If the black prophet's murder is insufficiently motivated or explained then so is the behaviour of Sally's 'unnatural' mother, and so is the famine, but these things are not made to stand for one another. Sensational plots also require an interrogation of the borders of sanity and insanity, sometimes the terrain of dreams. At the height of sensation fiction's popularity, which was also the period when feminists were campaigning for repeal of the Contagious Diseases Acts, Frances Browne's novel, *The Hidden Sin* (which starts, like *The Black Prophet*, with an old Irish murder for money) situates insanity precisely as a colonial legacy:

'Yermiska was a Tartar Moslema, accustomed to think of revenge, but never of revolt or disobedience; and the night before her marriage she deliberately drank a potion...How, or of what that draught was compounded, the Powers of Darkness best know; but the Princess declared, and time has proved her statement true, that it would transmit hereditary and irremediable madness to the utmost generation of her descendants.

'You look incredulous, my friend. There are secrets in nature for which the boasted science of Europe has neither name nor place...That knowledge, like all the deeper and higher sorts, has no written records. It cannot be found in books; they contain but the husks and rinds of learning, being meant for the common eye and mind. It exists, nevertheless, among primitive and unlettered races; the African slave and the Hindoo pariah have visited the sins of the fathers upon the Anglo-Saxon families by means similar to those which the unwilling bride employed against mine.'[27]

D. A. Miller, in his study of Wilkie Collins and other Victorian English novelists, suggests that the point of the nineteenth-century novel 'is to confirm the novel-reader in his identity as "liberal subject", a term with which I allude not just to the subject ... but also to, broadly speaking, the political regime that sets store by this subject'.[28] In his chapter on Collins, Miller suggests that what is sensational about the sensation novel is the somatic experience of sensation in reading it, and that these sensations, the ones felt on the pulses of the reader's body, help to disavow the text's apparent interpretations of its own sensationalism. 'Reader, if you have shuddered at the excesses into which he plunged, examine your own heart ...' begins the final paragraph of *The Collegians*, confident that the reader has been physically, sensibly and sensationally, as well as morally and mentally moved by the events.[29] One might argue that in asking the reader to identify, however provisionally, with Eily's seducer and murderer Griffin acknowledges a failure to identify with Eily and her class. On the other hand, a recognition of the power of sexual passions casts a melancholy and sinister hue on the rational domesticity of the Dalys, whose expression is as much the childbed death as the family breakfast feast.

At the close of the century Horace Plunkett was to express his concern that excessive sexual surveillance was driving people to emigration: 'In some parishes the Sunday cyclist will observe that strange phenomenon of a normally light-hearted peasantry marshalled in male and female groups along the road, eyeing one another in dull wonderment across the forbidden space.'[30] If some novels sought to represent this bleakness, other chose to intervene and breach the space by concentrating on fantasy rather than realities.

10

Tantalized by Progress

Christopher Morash

Oh! Ireland – oh! my country, wilt thou not
>ADVANCE?
Wilt thou not share the world's progressive lot,
>ADVANCE?
Must seasons change, and countless years roll on,
And thou remain a darksome Ajalon?
And never see the crescent moon of Hope
>ADVANCE?
'Tis time thine heart and eye had wider scope –
>ADVANCE![1]

'The torture of Tantalus'[2] was how William Drennan, jun, described the view of 'the world's progressive lot' from Famine Ireland: close enough to see the parade of progress, but not close enough to join the march. For those Irish men and women who were attempting to formulate a coherent definition of Irish nationality and culture during the middle years of the nineteenth century, this tantalized posture led to some excruciating ideological gymnastics. In the case of John Mitchel, it was to produce a group of texts which have been among the most important in shaping subsequent understandings of the Famine,[3] and which, at the same time, bear a strange affinity with that textual constellation which includes Nietzsche and Foucault.

'The History of England', Macaulay had declared in an 1835 essay, 'is emphatically the history of progress.' Over the course of seven centuries, he wrote, the English had become 'the greatest and most highly civilized people that ever the world saw'.[4] Continuously subjected to this Anglocentric imperial narrative of history as progress, the Irish nationalist intelligentsia of the 1840s found themselves struggling within a web of contradictions. Were they to claim – against the undeniable evidence of the emaciated thousands who were struggling to the poor houses – that Ireland was participating in that progress of which England boasted so loudly, they would have been denying the very thing which differentiated them from their colonizers, and which proved the failure of the colonial administration: to pronounce that 'the history of Ireland is the history of progress' would have been to admit

114

the success of the Union. However, to distance Ireland from the entire complex of concepts that went into the mid-nineteenth-century formulation of the idea of progress would have been to deny that Ireland had a right to the political liberty which was the index of social progress.

This complex and ambivalent relation of Irish nationalism to the idea of progress was given a focus in 1851 by two events: the Great Exhibition, which ran at Crystal Palace in London from May until October; and the release in June of preliminary figures from the decennial Irish Census, which gave statistical confirmation of the horrific scale of the Famine. In many ways, it is difficult to imagine two events which illuminate the contradictions of progress more vividly. 'The objects on display at the Exhibition were symbols of visible progress,' writes Asa Briggs. 'The concrete and the abstract were both stressed, the materialism and the spirit that lay behind it.'[5] While reports of starvation continued to come in from Mayo and Clare in the spring of 1851, and while Irish emigration reached unprecedented levels, in London progress was no mere idea; it was tangible, and, it seemed, irrefutable. Nor did the contrast between England and Ireland in 1851 escape notice. Thackeray, for instance, writing in *Punch* could think of few things more humorous than an Irishman marvelling at the sights of the Crystal Palace:

> With conscious proide
> I stud insoide
> And look'd the World's Great Fair in,
> > Until me sight
> > Was dazzled quite,
> And I couldn't see for staring.[6]

For Irish nationalists of the period, the disjunction between the Famine and the Great Exhibition was anything but funny. The *Nation* of 10 May 1851 reported on the Crystal Palace extravaganza in a curious article entitled 'Dives and Lazarus'. Poised uncomfortably between desire and parody, the piece is indicative of the alienation which the Great Exhibition must have produced among the Irish nationalist intelligentsia:

> The Universe seems to halt in its career of progress and action, and, passing in review the relics of the past, and the novel marvels of the present, to enumerate the conquests which intellect has achieved over the laws of physical nature ... in this the grand climacteric of Time. ... it inaugurates the supremacy of the accumulated thought and travail of the whole family of our kind, from the dawn of Creation to the fullness of this hour.
>
> For all lands, save Ireland, it typifies this sublime result.
>
> Here there is an Exhibition which might well startle the nations. A country, the richest in material wealth of all the ocean's isles, a

sea-guarded garden, pines and faints in the throes of hunger, in the shame
and torture of tyranny.[7]

Had the first paragraph of this piece been published in a popular English
journal of the time – the *Illustrated London News*, for instance – it would
have appeared in no way unusual with its confidence in 'the career of
progress' of 'the whole family of our kind' at what is unquestionably the
'grand climacteric of Time'. In the *Nation*, however, the confidence is so
strident, the language so sumptuous, that it borders on parody. The tension
in the first paragraph becomes more apparent when the text asks what
Ireland has to 'exhibit'. The disjunction between a description of Ireland
'in the throes of hunger', and the Edenic evocation of Ireland as a 'sea-
guarded garden' – a phrase that suggests nothing so much as one of the
best-known paeans to England, the 'sceptred isle'[8] speech from *Richard II* –
aggravates the unresolved tension still further. In the description of Ireland
as 'A country ... richest in material wealth of all the ocean's isles', there is a
yearning to have Ireland included in 'the fullness of this hour' which chaffs
against a contradictory impulse to use the poverty of Ireland as a means of
differentiating it from England and the Empire. Unable to claim for Ireland
a place in the modern world of progress and prosperity, Ireland's poverty
and consequent lack of participation in the grand march of progress become
for the cultural nationalist an unwilling but potent emblem of difference.

To a certain extent, this badge of difference was forced upon nationalists
by the degree to which the idea of progress, stated so triumphantly by the
Great Exhibition, was claimed as the exclusive preserve of supporters of
Empire. In a piece on the Great Exhibition entitled 'The Day After the
Storm' which appeared in the unionist *Dublin University Magazine* in July
of 1851, the writer argues that 'the electric telegraph, the extension of
railways and the wonderful improvements that have been made in steam
navigation, have done more to further the amalgamation of England and
Ireland, than all the legislative enactments of the last half century'.[9] The
acceleration in communications and travel which was to facilitate the unity
of mankind could, it seems, equally facilitate the Union of England and
Ireland. This message was restated in monumental terms in 1853 when
Ireland was granted its own Great Exhibition, held in the Royal Dublin
Society buildings in Ballsbridge. The lavish catalogue, describing the linen,
wrought ironwork, furniture, and floor coverings which made up the Exhibition, includes a 'prayer' that 'this undertaking may be made the means of
cementing more closely the bond of union between the two countries,
making England and Ireland more thoroughly and essentially ONE'.[10]
Even the *Nation* was swept along by the spectacle with which the doctrines
of empire and progress were presented, devoting pages to the Exhibition's
wonders, and offering only the faintest criticism of the organizing commit-

tee, who, the newspaper opined, 'have done all that lay in their power to make it [the Exhibition] anything but Irish'.[11] The implicit definition of 'Irish' here is a negative one – not connected with industrial progress.

And yet, while Irish nationalist texts of the Famine era are unable to use the language of progress unproblematically, they are equally bound by the narrative of history as progress. Responding to the release of the preliminary figures for the 1851 Census, the *Nation* ran an editorial entitled 'The History of Ten Years':

> 1841–1851! Those ten short years have seen more grievous and over-whelming changes in Ireland than befall to other countries in the course of centuries. Down the long files of figures on the census Table is indexed one of the most mournful histories the eye of GOD has ever rested upon. Within ten years the world has advanced greatly toward its goal – noble thoughts and actions keeping apt harmony with the music of the spher-es.... But Ireland has struggled and starved for ten years.... Of all the wide world, ours is the only country we know of that, during this decade, has retrograded in the scale of national strength and liberty.[12]

The difficulty faced by nationalists who would have used Ireland's destitu-tion as a sign of difference is registered in the inability to step outside of a progressive historical metanarrative. 'The world has advanced greatly toward its goal,' writes the author, suggesting an implicit acceptance of a progressive teleology, in which the natural state of society is one of improve-ment, and stagnation is aberrant, in need of explanation or expiration. The writer even goes so far as to equate the relatively recent idea that society is continually expanding with a pre-Renaissance image of the elemental, 'the music of the spheres'.

Even more importantly, both the aim and the engine of this elemental, progressive teleology is 'national strength' and 'liberty'. 'Barbarism', de-clared the *Irishman* in 1849, 'is the paradise of exclusiveness...civilization is the requisite for, as it is the creation of, Democracy. And hence, in this world of progress, exclusiveness naturally had its stronghold in the past, as Democracy will have its domain in the future.'[13] To be debarred from 'this world of progress' was to be side-stepped by the inevitable march from barbarism into a new civilization which belonged to the middle classes. For the bourgeois nationalists of Young Ireland, this was little short of catastrophic. 'The Europe-wide spirit of progress', claimed the first edition of the *Irishman*, 'has struck deep roots amongst...the accomplished profes-sional man – the enthusiastic student – the independent burgher – the sturdy farmer – the intelligent artisan – those are a nation's middle classes, whose enlightenment makes them formidable.' Hence, for the Irish middle classes of mid-century, 'comprehending almost all our intelligent, and therefore dangerous Nationalists',[14] the idea of progress was absolutely necessary; but it was also, at the same time, almost unusable.

'The age we live in is a busy age in which knowledge is rapidly advancing towards perfection,' wrote Jeremy Bentham in his anonymous *Fragment on Government* of 1776. 'In the natural world, in particular, everything teems with discovery and improvement.'[15] Nature, Bentham went on to argue, had placed humanity under 'the governance of two sovereign masters, *pain* and *pleasure*'; to impose any other governor upon humanity was to risk progress itself, as it interfered with the individual's quest for happiness, the great Benthamite engine of progress. With events such as the passing of the Reform Bill of 1832 and the publication of Alex de Tocqueville's *Democracy in America* later in the decade, the discursive links between progress and democracy multiplied, so that by the 1840s it would not be too severe a generalization to say that, for many, democratic self-determination could be understood as simultaneously cause and effect of a reified progress.

Hence, a nationalist movement which was also a liberation movement was compelled to participate in the discourse of progress, even when that discourse was so deeply implicated in the project of imperialism. 'It appears certain that the Governments of all civilized European nations are advancing', writes the *Irishman*, in 1849, 'to the principles and the spirit of Democracy.' Again, however, the writer is forced to contrast all other 'civilized European nations' with Ireland. 'Let us bethink ourselves', the article continues, 'that as long as we submit to the oppression, or are duped by the false pretences of tyranny, we are a drag upon the progress of humanity, and civilisation.'[16] The language of 'oppression' and 'tyranny' may be orthodox nationalist liberation rhetoric, but the historical narrative on which it is predicated is the Benthamite version of the idea of progress in which each free individual's struggle for happiness cumulatively produces 'the greatest good for the greatest number',[17] thereby contributing to 'the progress of humanity'.

If the picture of the discursive relations between Irish nationalists and the idea of progress emerges here as contradictory and tortured, the populism of the Irish nationalist press in the 1840s adds a further level of contradiction. While nationalist writers consistently excoriated the imperial government for the lack of relief given to Ireland during the Famine, the free-market economic policies which forbade interference in the markets were based on the same Enlightenment principles of individual free will which formed the basis of the argument for democracy. 'The free exercise [of trade]', Adam Smith had written in the same year as Bentham's *Fragment on Government*, 'is not only the best palliative of the inconveniences of a dearth, but the best preventative of that calamity.'[18] The 'free exercise' of trade and the free exercise of democratic will were part of the same Enlightenment discursive formation, in so far as both found in a reified rational freedom the simultaneous cause and effect of history as progress. Hence, from nationalists like Daniel O'Connell, whose ideas were, as Jacqueline Hill has argued, 'a genuine outgrowth of the Enlightenment',[19] to the more militant Young Irelanders, most of the Irish nationalist intelligentsia of the 1840s found themselves enmeshed within the same Enlightenment discourses of individual liberty which were telling the starving poor that 'it is no man's business to provide for another'.[20] On the other hand, to accept the alternative of imperial government intervention in the economy was to accept a measure which 'treats Ireland as a part of the empire', as the *Nation* ruefully recognized when faced with Lord George Bentinck's proposal to build Irish railways as a Famine relief project. 'If carried out it will save her people and make her the wealthiest appanage of British Imperialism.'[21]

MITCHEL'S REFUSAL

It is in this context – where the concept of individual freedom necessary to all shades of nationalist ideology was claimed by imperialist discourses, events, and policies – that the textual strategies of John Mitchel take shape. Unlike many of his contemporaries, who attempted to work within the terms of the dominant post-Enlightenment discourses of freedom, Mitchel recognized discourse itself as a site of struggle. In many ways, Mitchel and his contemporaries are all victims of what Foucault calls 'the "blackmail" of the Enlightenment': the 'simplistic and authoritarian alternative' of either 'accepting the Enlightenment and remaining within the tradition of rationalism', or its equally coercive opposite, 'criticiz[ing] the Enlightenment and then try[ing] to escape from its principles of rationality'.[22] What makes Mitchel different from so many of his contemporaries is that he chose the latter strategy: he refused Enlightenment.

Mitchel's anti-Enlightenment writing of the Famine cannot be located in a single text; instead, we need to look to a sequence of texts which were rewritten over three decades. Trained as a lawyer, Mitchel was working in Banbridge, County Down, when he began to write for the *Nation* during its first year of publication in 1843. By 1845 he was co-editor of the newspaper, a post he held until December of 1847, when the differences between Mitchel and nationalist colleagues such as Charles Gavan Duffy became too great, and he left to found his own *United Irishman* early in 1848. He edited the *United Irishman* until May of 1848, when the newspaper was closed by the imperial authorities, and Mitchel was charged, tried, and deported for the crime of 'treason felony'. It was during these years as a journalist that Mitchel developed Thomas Davis's suggestion that history should 'explain the past, justify the present, and caution the future',[23] writing a number of the passages which he was to incorporate into his longer texts over the next twenty-five years. More importantly, it was during this period that Mitchel sharpened the rhetorical edges of the prose style which was to radicalize the nationalist historical project.

Mitchel assembled these pieces of fugitive journalism for the first time in the 'Introductory Narrative of Events in Ireland' with which he prefaces his *Jail Journal* of 1854. He was later to expand his 'Narrative' in *The Last Conquest of Ireland (Perhaps)* (1861), and again in 1868, when it was rewritten as the final seven chapters of his two-volume *History of Ireland from the Treaty of Limerick to the Present Time*. What unites the latter two texts with the 'Introductory Narrative' of the *Jail Journal* is the point at which they bring the history of Ireland to a close. Even though Mitchel's *Last Conquest* was written ten years after the Famine, and his *History of Ireland* was written seven years after that, neither account brings Irish history further than 1851 in any serious way; indeed, in all of his texts, the treatment of the period after Mitchel's deportation in May of 1848 is cursory.

The contrast between the detail which Mitchel lavishes on events of the five years prior to 1848 and his attenuated version of events after 1848 produces at least three important effects for the reader. By ending the history of Ireland with Mitchel's removal from Ireland, Mitchel's texts establish such a high degree of identification between the individual and the nation that the two become interchangeable. 'The general history of a nation may fitly preface the personal memoranda of a solitary captive,' declares Mitchel; 'for it was strictly and logically a *consequence* of the dreary story here epitomized, that I came to be a prisoner, and to sit writing and musing so many months in a lonely cell.'[24] 'Mitchel's wrongs are Ireland's wrongs,' David Lloyd notes of this passage, 'and justice for the one is justice for the other.' One of the cornerstones of the cultural nationalist ideology, as Lloyd argues, is the identification of the individual with the nation, in which there is 'a repetition in the individual of the national spirit which in himself he represents'.[25] At this basic level, Mitchel's termination of Irish history in 1848 has a purely ideological function, creating a structural equivalence between author and nation. Mitchel's history is Ireland's history; Ireland's history is Mitchel's history.

Equally important, however, is the effect which Mitchel's narrative has on the shape of Irish history. A reader encountering the *Jail Journal* or the *Last Conquest of Ireland* would find that Irish history after 1848 enters a state of suspended animation – suspended in the midst of the Famine. For those readers who were part of the great tide of emigration which dates from the Famine period (and there were many such, for Mitchel's works went through a number of popular American editions),[26] Mitchel's abruptly terminated history of Ireland would duplicate the experience of emigration. This, too, has an ideological function, in so far as the incomplete narrative acts in a

Brechtian fashion as a powerful incitement for the reader to support action in the world outside of the text, action which will bring about the narrative closure the text refuses. History as unfinished business, like Robert Emmet's unwritten epitaph,[27] challenges its readers to write their own ending.

As well as performing these ideological functions, Mitchel's structuring of Irish historical narrative acts as a repudiation of the progressive metanarrative found in novels such as Anthony Trollope's *Castle Richmond*, in which history moves beyond the abyss of the 1840s to scenes of 'Ireland in her prosperity'. Trollope's *Castle Richmond* and other similar nineteenth-century Famine novels (including Margaret Brew's *Castle Cloyne*, or Annie Keary's *Castle Daly*) are Comedies, in the sense in which Hayden White uses the word 'Comic' to describe Hegel's concept of history: 'based ultimately on his belief in the right of life over death; "life" guaranteed to Hegel the possibility of an ever more adequate form of social life throughout the historical future'.[28] As Herbert Butterfield writes of the equally 'Comic' 'whig interpretation of history': 'provided disaster is not utterly irretrievable . . . the whig historian looking back upon the catastrophe can see only the acquired advantages and happy readjustments'.[29] 'We have gained', Sir Charles Trevelyan wrote in 1848, 'both by what has been unlearned and by what has been learned during the last two years.' If Trevelyan's Famine is *All's Well that Ends Well*, Mitchel's is *King Lear*; in Mitchel's writing, the Famine is Tragic. By locating the Famine as an end to history, Mitchel balances the reader on the edge of an incomplete transitional state, where, as in all tragedies, there is a sense that 'time is the devourer of life, the mouth of hell at the previous moment, when the potential passes forever into the actual'.[30]

The title of Mitchel's book-length account of the Famine, *The Last Conquest of Ireland (Perhaps)*, suggests the sense of incompletion which his narrative enacts. Does 'last' mean 'final', 'most recent', or both? Perhaps. It ends with these words:

> The subjection of Ireland is now probably assured until some external shock shall break up that monstrous commercial firm, the British Empire . . . its cup of abomination is not yet running over. . . . So long as this hatred and horror shall last – so long as our island refuses to become, like Scotland, a contented province of the enemy, Ireland is not finally subdued. The passionate aspiration for Irish nationhood will outlive the British Empire.[31]

In so structuring his history of Ireland, Mitchel is locating his text in a moment suspended by 'hatred and horror' between a recent past of 'subjection' and a future of 'passionate aspiration'. Both past and future are incomplete, and neither possess the finally of the 'perfection' which the whig historian saw as history's aim. History in such a text is not linear; there is no progression or even retrogression. There is simply a continuous present, the 'now' of writing. Similarly, in his *Jail Journal*, where the solitary Mitchel in his cell is removed from all but the most remote indicators of change in the outside world, the existence of the text as a negation of the progress of history is even more pronounced. 'Prison writing', notes Ioan Davies, 'is self-reflexive',[32] and the *Jail Journal*, once its introductory historical narrative is finished, turns inward to 'imagination and memory'.[33] In both the *Last Conquest* and the *Jail Journal*, there is an erasure of the 'pastness' of the text, thereby inscribing it in the present of his readers; the Famine not only *existed*, it continues to exist every time his texts are read. In Mitchel's writing, the Famine is now.

In bringing the past events of the 1840s into the present of his readers, Mitchel is in effect deferring the past, with the consequence that 'the past' in Mitchel's histories is a period before the writing of history. 'The past' is bardic, a time before the written word – and 'before British civilization overtook us'.[34] In certain respects, this historical narrative of the idealized pre-colonial past as perfected future was the common property of Young Ireland, and, indeed, could be said to be the aspect of the movement which differentiated it from O'Connell's whig pragmatism, which, as Lloyd notes, 'left him more than willing to abandon Gaelic culture and language for the sake of material progress'.[35] From Thomas Davis's influential essays on the need to revive the Irish language to the antiquarian images of round towers and warrior heroes which fill the poems of writers like Thomas D'Arcy McGee, the spirit of the essential Irish nation was located by cultural nationalists in a period before colonization. This retrospective idealization leads the cultural nationalist to equate the invading English with modernity, in spite of the fact that the first 'conquest' of Ireland took place in the twelfth century. Like the economic theories of James Fintan Lalor,[36] based on the premiss that 'a productive and prosperous husbandry is the sole groundwork of a solid social economy',[37] the Irish cultural nationalist project for Ireland appeals to an idealized pre-industrial society as an economic utopia.

There is a passage in Mitchel's *Last Conquest of Ireland (Perhaps)* which can be read as a troubled apotheosis of this rural ideal. It begins with a long aerial sweep along the western seaboard of Ireland:

The Western and South-western coast, from Derry round to Cork, is surely the most varied and beautiful coast in all the world. Great harbours, backed by noble ranges of mountains, open all round the Western coast of Munster, till you come to the Shannon's mouth: there is a fine navigable river opening up the most bounteously fertile land in the island – Limerick and Tipperary. North of the Shannon, huge cliff-walls, rising eight hundred feet sheer out of the deep water, broken by chasms and pierced by sea-caves, 'with high embowed roof', like the choir of a cath-edral . . .

The sweeping, bird's-eye perspective then carries on northward up the coast beyond this untenanted Eden, through 'the dreariest region of moor and mountain that is to be found within the five ends of Ireland' in Donegal, past the primeval evidence of the first human settlement, 'a cluster of ragged-looking, windowless hovels, whose inhabitants seem to have gathered them-selves from the wastes', arriving at last in Glenties, where Mitchel locates his heart of darkness:

> Rearing its accursed gables and pinnacles of Tudor barbarism, and staring boldly with its detestable mullioned windows, as if to mock those wretches who still cling to liberty and mud cabins – seeming to them, in their perennial half-starvation, like a Temple erected to the Fates, or like the fortress of Giant Despair, whereinto he draws them one by one, and devours them there: – the Poor-house.[38]

'Create the husbandman,' wrote James Fintan Lalor in 1847, 'and you create the mechanic, the artisan, the manufacturer, the merchant.'[39] Mitchel's aerial sweep over Famine Ireland, by contrast, while it begins with the eulogy to Ireland's natural resources so typical of nationalist writers of the period, reduces 'the husbandman', base of the economic structure and repository of the national spirit, to a few straggling 'wretches', who 'seem to have gathered themselves from the wastes', clinging to 'liberty and mud cabins'. 'Liberty' here becomes the equivalent of 'mud cabins' in a distinctly Carlylean undermining of the reified status of liberty. Yet, even more horrific than this Eden turned wasteland is 'the fortress of Giant Despair' which presides over it – the Poor-house. In Mitchel's writing of the Famine, true horror lies not in cholera, typhus, or starvation, but in the increased amount of government control which they occasioned.

In the passage above, the transition from pure landscape, to an area inhabited by small farmers 'in their perennial half-starvation', to the 'Tudor barbarism' of the Poor-house is more than just a complete reversal of the narrative of history as progress. In Mitchel's text, the Poor-house becomes the single object capable of standing as a symbol of Famine Ireland, for it is the apex of the development of the 'English civilization' which he sees as bringing about the last conquest of Ireland (perhaps): 'The thing was done by a process of "relieving" and "ameliorating"; – for, in the nineteenth century, civilized governments always proceed upon the most benevolent motives.'[40] The 'acid disdain' which Malcolm Brown notes in passages such as this is more than just what he calls 'the age-old dialogue between bureau-cracy and starvation'.[41] Mitchel is here writing about what Foucault has called 'The Great Confinement', the Enlightenment need to incarcerate the Other of the emerging bourgeois society. 'The house of confinement in the classical age', writes Foucault, 'constitutes the densest symbol of that "police" which conceived of itself as the civil equivalent of religion for the edification of a perfect city.'[42] If we recall Foucault's argument that public institutions such as the asylum, the prison, and the poorhouse arose out of a desire to be able to see and categorize those on the margins of society (comparable to the scientific desire to see and categorize the extremes of the natural world), it is possible to understand Mitchel's identification of the Poor-house and all that it represents as his discursive enemy. 'And, for the "institutions of the country",' Mitchel announces, 'I loathe and despise them; we are sickening and dying of these institutions, fast; they are consuming us like a plague, degrading us to paupers in mind, body, and estate...from the top-most crown jewel to the meanest detective's notebook.' For Mitchel, the 'institutions' which had been established by the state, ostensibly for the prevention of suffering, were in fact instruments of imperial hegemony. Later in *The Last Conquest*, when bringing his account of the Famine to a close, he writes: 'No sack of Magdeburg, or ravage of the Palatinate ever approached in horror and desolation to the slaughters done in Ireland by mere official red tape and stationery, and the principles of political economy.'[43]

While a certain mistrust of 'political economy' was part of the Young Ireland idealization of a pre-mercantile economy born of alienation from the idea of progress, Mitchel's use of the phrase goes beyond mere critique. 'The English', exclaims Mitchel in his *Jail Journal*, 'could afford to cry out "Free Trade!" "True principles of political economy!" and-so-forth, taking care only to prevent any interference by law or otherwise, with the satisfactory state of things they had established.'[44] In Mitchel's texts, the name of a realm of knowledge is purely a signifier of colonial hegemony, its genealogy in the discourse of science subjugated to its instrumental role in the present exercise of power. He accomplishes this reversal by undermining at the level of language the discourse of political economy, particularly in its free-market and Malthusian forms, subjecting its terminology to a series of satiric inversions.

11

The Politics of Poetic Form

Clair Wills

Is it that to refer, however obliquely,
Is to refer?[1]

IN what ways do the formal dynamics of a poem shape its ideology? How
do poetic styles have political meanings? We are used to at least two
principal arguments about the nature of the relationship between poetry
and politics. On the one hand there is the model of committed or engaged
literature, or literature with a specific political purpose, which is not usually
associated with a distinctively 'literary' poetic form since this sets it apart
from the mass of the reading public. On the other hand there is the
paradigm of literature whose politics lies precisely in the fact that it is
without purpose in the political world. In Northern Ireland these seemingly
opposed views are inflected in a very particular manner, partly because of
an aesthetic or cultural interpretation of the nature of the political sphere,
which leads to an emphasis on cultural politics and on the poet's role in
giving voice to, or representing, his or her community. In a certain sense
engaged literature is thus deemed to be that which is rooted in a particular
community (and therefore authenticated through experience), but also that
which, through its formal qualities, refuses to be reduced to the level of
propaganda for one side or the other. The opposition between the drive
towards poetic responsibility to the political situation, and the desire for
poetic freedom lies at the root of almost all discussions of Northern Irish
poetry. In *The Government of the Tongue* Seamus Heaney articulates a now
well-established tension. He suggests that in choosing to write the poet is
'arrogating to [himself] the right to take refuge in form'.[2] Noting the
dangers of solipsism, Heaney's conscience is none the less allayed by his
conviction of the 'redemptive' qualities of art. As he comments in his
reappraisal of Kavanagh's work, that quality of 'redemption' arises from
the authenticity of the poet's experience as it is captured in poetry and
given form:

> I have learned to value this poetry of inner freedom very highly. It is an
> example of self-conquest, a style discovered to express this poet's unique

125

response to his universal ordinariness, a way of re-establishing the authenticity of personal experience and surviving as a credible being.[3]

Without this quality of authenticity or sincerity the private lyric cannot hope to find a voice beyond its own individual concerns, and the implication is that herein 'irresponsibility' lies.

This ideal of authenticity is undercut in the poetry of Paul Muldoon, Medbh McGuckian, and Tom Paulin. In their work private or personal discourse, the discourse of the family and the small community, are associated with the obscure and enigmatic, rather than with truth value and authenticity. Discomfort with the ideal of poetic sincerity is perhaps clearest in Muldoon's work (and this is signalled in his interest in Byron, who made a career out of 'insincerity'). Yet I will argue that Muldoon's suspicion of the value of 'experience' is merely one sign of a more general condition in contemporary Northern Irish poetry. For example, despite McGuckian's ostensible commitment to the representation of her personal life, we might note the teasing play with the idea of privacy, the double selves, and ever-disappearing centre of her work. So far from 're-establishing the authenticity of personal experience', McGuckian's poetry puts into question the very possibility of knowing, far less of communicating, such experience. Though perhaps less apparent the rejection of the ideal of romantic authenticity and rootedness has also been of fundamental importance in Paulin's more recent work; as I will argue, it is related to his desire to find an alternative to traditional post-Romantic aesthetics, which he sees as bound to a conservative political ideology. For all three poets, the private sphere is not the place of truth and generalizable individual experience, but is continually displaced, found to be empty, or its contents to be of little significance. The idea of poetic form as refuge or resolution is thus totally inadequate to an understanding of this work; the private space of the lyric is parodied, through the mechanism of impenetrability, and at the same time instability of poetic reference ensures that the lyric is open to public and political meanings.

In this essay I will examine in some detail contemporary debates about the relationship between poetry and politics in Ireland, and specifically the perceived function of 'mythic' or 'tribal' thought in political consciousness. I shall argue that obliqueness carries a particular weight in the work of the three poets and that this has to be understood in part in relation to general arguments about postmodern form. However, in the context of Northern Irish culture and politics, such obliqueness and obscurity has a very particular function in questioning the validity of established definitions of the public sphere – how poetry should speak for a community and thus how it can speak to a political situation.

POSTMODERNISM AND 'OBSCURITY'

This study examines the work of a group of contemporary Northern Irish writers whose writing careers have shadowed and been shadowed by the political situation in Northern Ireland during the last twenty or more years. Their work is shadowed too by the debate over the relationship between 'private' lyricism and 'public' and political statement. In this the younger writers differ from poets such as John Montague, Michael Longley, James Simmons, and Seamus Heaney who were established writers before the onset of the recent violence, and it may therefore be possible to discern in their work a different aesthetic and political response to the Troubles and the perceived need for writers to address them. If not an ideology these poets broadly share a common historical experience. Paul Muldoon and Medbh McGuckian were contemporaries at Queen's University, Belfast; they became students at the beginning of the Civil Rights protests in the late 1960s in Northern Ireland. Academically, they followed a similar path, studying English, and, significantly, studying under Seamus Heaney among others, who was at that time a lecturer in English at Queen's.[4] Tom Paulin's biography differs significantly from that of his contemporaries, and this is the first of many points at which I shall note a contrast in the tradition from which Paulin springs, as well as in his aesthetic and political beliefs – differences which serve to render the similarities between his work and that of his contemporaries all the more striking. Unlike the other poets I focus on, Paulin's background is Protestant; moreover he left Belfast in 1967 to take a degree in English at Hull University, and subsequently a further degree at Oxford, though he has always maintained strong personal and political links with Northern Ireland.

Beyond biographical considerations, however, there are stylistic and formal links between the work of these ostensibly very different poets. Increasingly their poetry is characterized by a certain codedness and obscurity of reference, although the type of interpretative difficulty which the poetry affords also differs in significant ways (and very rarely does the poetry seem to suggest the impossibility or undesirability of critical interpretation – quite the reverse, as I shall argue, it invites it). But does this obscurity or privacy of reference suggest a lack of responsibility towards the larger political situation? On the level of reception it must be conceded that, whereas Paulin's poetry is read (and often condemned) as fiercely committed and public poetry, readers and critics of Muldoon's work, and more particularly of McGuckian's, have often found it hard to disentangle a meaning for the poems which goes beyond private or enigmatic reference. (Responses to Muldoon's work tend to focus not on the obscurity of the public statement, but on the characteristically enigmatic refusal to take up any one public position.)

McGuckian's work in particular has called forth a variety of strategies in critics and readers for attempting to hold the poetry down to a meaning, or to open the meaning out into general significance. The dense syntax of the poems is peppered with seemingly logical grammatical markers which should add up to a narrative. But words such as 'like' and 'as' take on an almost parodic role as otherwise logical grammatical constructions are undermined by the randomness of the images. Strange shifting metaphors and circular syntax encourage the diffusion of meaning rather than the pursuit of conclusions. This uncertainty with regard to meaning has given rise to denunciations of the poems as nothing more than a metaphorical game, and one reviewer has characterized the technique as one 'which connects nothing with nothing'.[5] This reaction springs in part from the seeming chaos of the images which seem impossible to fix to a particular referent, as in these lines from 'Rowing', which gather together a seemingly capricious and subjective collection of associations:

Where
My hand is, there is the pain that wires
Its sour honey through my flush,
As an ear-ring grows precocious in the vellum
Of a head, with all its sutures
In the offing, or the sand unhindered
Thickening with marble dust.[6]

This arbitrariness with regard to meaning is deceptive (and this poem in particular is illuminated by a careful reading of the volume *Venus and the Rain* as a whole), but the very resistance to interpretation evokes the desire to crack the code and to lay the matter open. Knowing full well that the scattered fragments of narrative will not add up, the reader still feels compelled to construct a coherent story.[7] That story has been interpreted primarily as a representation of the 'feminine' sphere: the complexities of women's experience of sexuality and childbirth, the opposing claims of the self as woman and the self as writer, and the intricacies of familial relationships. Yet this intimate sphere is never separated from the public, political world, a linkage which is drawn formally as well as thematically. Moreover, in tension with this perceived aim to express the inner self of the woman lies McGuckian's sustained exploration of the legacy of post-Romantic poetry. She carries out a formal and symbolic dialogue with (predominantly male) Romantic and modern poets such as Coleridge, Byron, Rilke, Mandelstam, and Tsvetaeva.

In contrast, Muldoon's poems reveal none of the surface syntactical confusion of McGuckian's work. In the main he uses metaphors taken from everyday life: clichés, and the language of the media. But underneath the surface simplicity, as he says of Robert Frost, 'all kinds of complex things are happening'.[8] In contrast to McGuckian, in Muldoon's work it is not the images, but the grammar which will not fit into a coherent narrative. Interpretation is complicated in his poems not by a mass of shifting images, but by riddles, ironies, word play, and a seemingly hermetic system of mythic and symbolic reference. Muldoon's fondness for tracing duplicitous, ambiguous narratives, in which several histories are held in tandem, has often been noted. In his early poems Muldoon creates the sense of parallel narratives, or narratives whose significance lies elsewhere than in the evident tale by means of a duplicitous use of tense. So in the poem 'Mules' the contradictory tenses of the final stanza suggest two planes of time, one earthly, one heavenly, on which the events might be taking place:

> We might yet claim that it sprang from earth
> Were it not for the afterbirth
> Trailed like some fine, silk parachute,
> That we would know from what heights it fell.[9]

The uncertainty of reference is created in the longer poems, such as 'The More a Man Has the More a Man Wants', by an extended use of such techniques. The poem switches between styles, languages, places, and story-lines with no warning.[10] The creation of narrative out of discrete yet interconnecting units, found materials, and quotations from literary and non-literary texts has been the mark of Muldoon's poetry since 'Immram', and in *Madoc – A Mystery* this hybrid eclecticism seems to have reached its apotheosis. The poem has accordingly been read as an exemplary postmodern work: 'in true postmodernist fashion, its aim is to deconstruct our presumptive desire for a grand, unifying "metanarrative".'[11] In part this association of Muldoon's repertoire of styles with postmodernity arises from the poet's own engagement with contemporary literary theory (and in this sense the postmodern does become thematized in the work), an interest, more or less hostile, which he shares with Tom Paulin.

Paulin is well known for his espousal of a public and political poetry, and yet his most recent work reveals an increasing tendency towards hermeticism, and private or enigmatic reference. While Muldoon's concerns about the referential qualities of poetic language remain distanced, mediated through the frame of the poetic and historical characters which populate his poems, Paulin engages with the relation between textual and extra-textual realities directly and personally:

> We'd hid from your tribe
> and disappeared from ourselves
> (I've heard *n'y a pas de hors-texte*

and guess Universal Man's
a simple fold in all our knowledge
*comme un tout petit pli
de lin ou de toile*).[12]

The difficulty of interpreting Paulin's work arises less from the instability of the writerly persona than from the kinds of knowledge the poetry takes for granted, such as, in this poem, an acquaintance with the ideas of Derrida and Paul de Man, as well as a keen ear for verbal play. 'Universal Man' suggests not only Paul the Man, but also the Enlightment ideals of free and common citizenship. Such techniques are used to almost bewildering effect in 'The Caravans on Lüneberg Heath' which like Muldoon's long poems undermine the traditional expectations of narrative and story-telling in the constant cutting back and forth between characters, moments of history, and levels of significance.

So how are we to interpret the significance of this aesthetics of the obscure and enigmatic, this elevation of parody and verbal play? Critical responses divide primarily into two groups; those who interpret the poetic techniques in terms of an international (or European and American) postmodern condition, and those who situate the poetry's problematics of address in the context of specifically Irish debates about the nature of community and identity. While each approach enables certain fruitful poetic and political comparisons to be made, neither can fully account for the status or significance of these poetic strategies.

To take the formalist explanation first, it is not difficult to isolate a series of stylistic techniques in the poetry which have become standard markers of the postmodern. Altogether the juxtaposition of different styles and forms, the parodic reintroduction of traditional literary materials, semantic indeterminacy, and enigmatic statement have been heralded as the radical new forms of British poetry. Indeed both 'obliqueness' and 'relativism' were judged by Blake Morrison and Andrew Motion to be the defining characteristics of contemporary poetry in their Penguin anthology.[13] Moreover they suggest that the increasing hegemony of such stylistic devices springs first of all from the turn away from the self-enclosed nature of the Movement lyric which took place in Northern Irish writing, and they instance particularly the Heaney of *North*. The implication is that the traditional lyric is inadequate to a new social and political reality, and that such obliqueness is the only way to deal with the changed situation in the North in the 1970s. Since obliqueness is clearly valorized by the editors it could be interpreted as a positive symptom of the effects of the political on poetry (as opposed, for example, to Fredric Jameson's negative symptomology of LANGUAGE poetry as the cultural logic of late capitalism).[14] But while it may be able to point to reasons for the emergence of a postmodern formalism, such a reading is unable to offer any more cogent analysis of the work's relationship to the political sphere.

The link drawn by Morrison and Motion between 'post-modernist "secrecy"' and the long poem is expanded in an essay on James Fenton and Paul Muldoon by Alan Robinson. Robinson associates the deconstruction of narrative figurative strategies, which frustrate the reader's expectations of formal coherence, with an increased obscurity or privacy of reference which he deems characteristic of postmodern poetry's drive to mock 'the seriousness of the High Modernist rage for order, which desired to elevate the imaginative structures of art to a socially redemptive role in an era of cultural disintegration'.[15] In this reading the difficulty and obscurity of reference appears to preclude a public or political dimension to the poetry, since public statements are veiled behind a system of symbolic correspondences, and references to public events are subordinated almost entirely to the private narrative the poems tell. The function and purpose of the poetic form thus becomes 'delight in deconstructive rationale'. Central to Robinson's thesis is the claim that what he terms 'unrecognized allusions' and hidden sources do not aid the reader in interpreting the poem, indeed that interpretation is rendered obsolete by the poem's style. Yet this ignores the contradictory messages sent by the obscure and enigmatic style. On the one hand the verbal slipperiness seems designed to undermine the referential aspects of language and to suggest that language escapes the control of both writer and reader, and on the other such techniques necessitate considerable work from the reader in uncovering this very message. In many cases it is only by exposing the hidden references, for example to Paul de Man in Paulin's 'Universal Man', that the escape of meaning can be interpreted for what it is, rather than simple meaninglessness. Far from celebrating semantic irreducibility, the poems in fact ask to be unveiled and interpreted in order that the rationale behind the use of a particular style may be understood. And as a corollary to this, control of meaning remains very much in the hands of the writer, at least as far as his or her project is concerned. Robinson implicitly acknowledges this fact when he associates postmodern narrative techniques with privacy and secrecy (in other words with personal ownership, a form of public concealment in which the data may be available but not their meaning).

In part this misinterpretation of the significance of poetic form stems from a structural difficulty related to the question of audience. The poet's public role, his or her ability to make public statements, depends of course on the public's consciousness of those statements. Neither Muldoon nor McGuckian are generally read or critically received as poets who are attempting to engage their audiences in a political manner, and Paulin's political stance is repeatedly caricatured in critical reception. While this may be explained as the poetry's unsuccessful completion of the writer's intention (so one might ask, does a poem work if McGuckian describes it as dealing with a particular historical or political situation but none of her readers are aware of this level of reference?), it also bears on the nature of the contemporary readership. On the one hand the poets write for an audience highly educated in the poetic tradition, alert to the significance of poetic forms and to literary echoes and allusions. Both Muldoon and McGuckian have spent several years as Writers in Residence at universities in Northern Ireland, England, and the United States, and Paulin teaches in a university English department. Clearly much of the success of their styles depends on an academic readership. Yet their work is also directed towards an Irish readership, and situating it within the context of the contemporary Irish community may offer alternative ways of interpreting the significance of its poetic strategies. One study which has profitably addressed this issue is Dillon Johnston's discussion of contemporary work in *Irish Poetry After Joyce*. As Johnston points out, much contemporary poetry reveals in its strategies of address an understanding of the breakdown of any 'unity of culture' of the Irish audience, a breakdown which suggests the inadequacy of traditional modes of public address:

> To the fluidity of the culture itself we can add a second factor to account for the Irish poet's unstable relation to his audience. The Irish audience is itself unstable and fractured synchronically as the tradition is broken diachronically.[16]

The importance of Johnston's argument lies precisely in this linkage between the poet's stance towards tradition, and his or her relation to an audience. Yet strangely this most contextual of interpretations ends by recapitulating the abstract and formalist readings of the significance of linguistic play and obscurity as part of a generalized postmodernism. For the diverse nature of the contemporary Irish audience is associated with what are deemed to be postmodern developments in the social sphere; the heterogeneous nature of the Irish community is interpreted as both symptom and cause of transformations in the structure of society which seem finally to transcend the debilitating division between 'traditional' and 'modern' Ireland. The title of Johnston's essay, 'Toward "A Broader and More Comprehensive Irish Identity"' is taken from the New Ireland Forum Report of 1984, and it reveals the importance to this strand of thinking of recent debates on the nature of tradition and the need to reconfigure notions of Irish identity in the political realm. Journals such as the *Crane Bag* and the *Irish Review* have entertained arguments for both 'tradition' and 'modernity' in the realm of culture, as well as attempts to transcend the antagonism between the two which seems to have stamped discussions of Irish identity.[17] Seamus Deane clearly delineates the major paradigms of these discussions in his article 'Remembering the Irish Future', where he isolates two characteristic modes of figuring and conceptualizing Irish identity which he calls 'Enlightenment' and 'Romantic', or following William James, the 'tough' and 'tender' minded.[18] As we shall see, the perceived need to overcome the division between Enlightened and Romantic formulations of Irish identity (all too often confounded with quite other distinctions, for example between modernity and tradition, or even Protestantism and Catholicism) has adversely determined the shape of discussions of the relationship between literature and politics in Ireland.

Questions about the nature of Irish literary history are fundamentally imbricated with the debates about Irish social and political historiography, and more particularly with the 'school' of historiography known as revisionism.[19] The overcoming of the opposition between tradition and modernity in contemporary literature is read as the aesthetic counterpart of the new-found faith in 'Varieties of Irishness',[20] which, translated from a historical to a political axis, suggests the resistance to both 'orthodox' nationalist and Unionist positions in favour of a new construction of community which is the mark of the New Ireland Forum. It becomes increasingly clear that this emphasis on new configurations of culture and community constitutes a reflection in the Irish political realm of arguments about postmodernism in the realm of international aesthetics. Both rely on a valorization of the dissolution of tradition and its 'pieties', consonant with the breakup of 'unity of culture', and the consequent reconstruction of the past, and its child, the contemporary community. So, for example, the philosopher Richard Kearney argues for a postmodernist re-evaluation of myth with reference to Marcuse's dictum that authentic utopias must be grounded in recollection, which facilitates interpretation of the past as an enabling force for the future. The reconsideration of Irish identity thus involves the reinterpretation of tradition and myth as ambivalent concepts: 'What is required is a radical interrogation of those mythic sedimentations from our *past* and those mythic aspirations for our *future*, which challenge our *present* sense of ourselves, which disclose other possibilities of being.'[21]

Unsurprisingly, given the uncanny mirroring of formalist and contextual interpretations here, there are both political and poetic difficulties with this reading of poetic strategies as a representation of a more comprehensive Irish identity. Naturally I do not wish to question the necessity and importance of the construction of a heterogeneous Irish community in terms of race, religion, class, and gender. However, the emphasis on the need to overcome the division between Enlightenment and Romantic conceptions of identity suggests that such labels are indeed accurate designations of the two forces in Irish history. In this reading nationalist sentiments are rejected as mythic 'pieties', romantic tribal affiliations which, while perhaps necessary or 'natural', require a healthy dose of rationalism in order to be rendered acceptable, while nationalist history is similarly designated both mythic and homogeneous. But such a construction ignores not only the traditional, customary, and mythic elements within Unionism, but also the many diverse and radical strands within the concept of tradition itself. As Luke Gibbons points out, the association of traditional or pre-modern culture with 'stagnation and conservatism' discounts the fractured legacy of Ireland's colonial history, which, in a sense, anticipates the fragmentation of modernism before the fact.[22] Moreover, the assumption that modern nationalism is primarily an irrational and atavistic force denies the Enlightenment values of universal citizenship, political legitimacy, representation, and so forth, on which the very concept of the modern nation in part depends.[23] Indeed it is precisely this interpenetration of 'tribal' and 'civic' values which concerns Tom Paulin in *Liberty Tree* and *Fivemiletown*, as he traces the subsequent history in Ireland of the Enlightenment ideals of the French Revolution and the United Irishmen.

Poetically, the difficulty with both the postmodernist and 'Irish identity' readings of the significance of poetic form is that the poetry is thereby reduced either to merely symptomatic or reactive status. The form of the work is deemed to arise out of a particular set of social co-ordinates, but its function is considered to be a reflection in the realm of the aesthetic of an image of future possibilities in the social arena. While I would wish to deny neither the importance of supranational stylistic movements on Irish poetry, nor the fact that contemporary poetry in Ireland is indeed engaged in representing alternative constructions of community and identity, I would argue that the poetry, rather than being simply a symptom or reflection of the social, is actually engaged in an intervention in public or political discourse, in its alteration of the relationship between public and private discourses. I mean the distinction between public and private here to suggest the most basic distinction between the arena of public affairs, civic society and the public communications of the media, and private life as it is most generally understood, i.e those experiences and events which lie outside the knowledge and discussion of the wider community (but which, of course, is also socially constructed). Readings of Muldoon and McGuckian which emphasize the complexity of poetic address fail to account for the genuinely political aspects of their work, interpreting it as a representation of complexities in the public realm. However, both poets refuse the accepted definitions of public and political statement which have governed debates in Northern Ireland, and in so doing they create new ways of linking private life and public assertion, despite the fact that neither poet is generally considered to be a writer of political statement. Responses to Paulin's work are reductive in an antithetical way – he is characteristically read as a self-consciously public poet and the ways in which he problematizes conventional notions of the public arena are ignored. All feel the need to reconfigure the relationship between public and private languages.

12

'In the Midst of All this Dross': Establishing the Grounds of Dissent

Richard Kirkland

THE COUNTRY

A few miles outside Belfast at Cultra Manor in County Down can be found the Ulster Folk and Transport Museum: a curious recreation of Ulster society in microcosm. Buildings, selected not for their authentic localized distinctiveness but because of their assumed mundane generality, have been pillaged jackdaw-like from across the nine counties and carefully rebuilt following the shape of a 'typical' Ulster town and its rural hinterland.[1] Entering this unnamed settlement is therefore to experience a keen sense of otherness within the specificity of place as, inevitably, the desire to 'recognize' the area as *authentic* contradicts its standing as museum – its own self-conscious fictionality.

The venture becomes impossibly ironic; in the face of hard physical evidence (the museum takes pride in pointing out that each individual stone from each individual building is carefully catalogued to ensure absolute exactness in reconstruction), the visitor must *imagine* authenticity, agree to be temporarily displaced in order to experience the enrichment of heritage. The artefacts encountered, not just houses and buildings but also spades, kettles and other general agricultural and domestic equipment, are frozen at around the turn of the nineteenth century and have to speak (loudly) for themselves. They must tell their own story, and in this way subtend social division through the processes of assumed communal inheritance.

It is then appropriate that we are given very little information about each building. As the visitor walks around the museum – the exhibits are widely scattered – we must 'discover' them for ourselves. In this there is a certain self-gratifying labour as history is stumbled across almost by chance. The town does not display its own arbitrary narrative but contains it, the 'tourist' (more often than not an inhabitant of Ulster) becomes the active half of the

135

reaction, and if he or she fails to read the signs they are the ones found wanting. Such a concept cannot hope to fulfil the contradictory, although much desired, state of a 'living museum' but instead stands unwittingly as a metaphor for the act of rebeginning in narrative. Qualities of the physical, the spatial, are promoted above the temporal and the historical and yet firmly anchored at a safe distance from the present. Resolution is placed off-stage – perhaps the town will continue to grow until it envelops the settlements on which it parasitically draws – but simultaneity across a community and across time is foregrounded as a curiously self-fulfilling prophecy.

Although the museum cannot recreate the typicality for which it strives, there is in its own history as a Northern Irish state-funded institution a more reassuring and familiar story. Founded in 1958 through an Act of Parliament and subsequently expanded by further Acts relating to financial provision in 1964 and 1967, its creation was indicative of a confidence in the regional status of Northern Ireland within the United Kingdom. This was a confidence strengthened by the failure of the IRA's border campaign to gain widespread support amongst the Catholic minority[2] and, as Sabine Wichert has noted, there was 'a clear indication that the old controversies were taking a rest, or even becoming traditions, less and less relevant in the increasing relative prosperity of the later 1950s'.[3] This transformation bore its own resonances for a museum which could encourage such a sense of tradition while containing it within carefully defined geographic and temporal limits and yet this ossification – from lived political culture to self-conscious inheritance – would also cause problems for the museum's social function in the less confident seventies.

Not that there was any freedom of choice for the early Board of Trustees. The unusual legislation that had founded the museum in the initial Act had outlined its statutory obligations: the Folk Museum must explore and demonstrate 'the way of life, past and present, and the traditions of the people'.[4] It has been within this concept of a notionally plural tradition that the museum has differentiated itself from similar projects elsewhere; its role becoming one not simply of embodiment or representation but of mediation and education. George Thompson, the first Director of the Museum, was aware of this dilemma, perceiving that 'Ulster may be seen as one of the least fertile areas in Western Europe in terms of Folk Museum growth'.[5] Unlike similar projects in Wales and Scandinavia, the museum could not be seen as 'a manifestation of a strong sense of national or cultural identity';[6] rather it was initiated as a way of neutralizing distinctive or even dangerous local cultural activity by a process of rendering such tendencies within a paradigm of tradition.

The underwritten concept behind this project can be defined therefore in Phillipe Hoyau's[7] terms as 'ethno-history', a focus on the details of everyday life which 'derives less from a will to preserve and value a "monumental" and academic past than from the promotion of new values articulated on a largely transformed conception of inheritance and tradition'. The emphasis on a rural, countrified version of history is clearly central to this movement. Political division can be veiled within a *new* discourse which celebrates the vernacular imagination as a form of collective and non-academic identification and through which the inhabitant of Northern Ireland can display his or her best self to the world. In 1971, George Thompson illustrated the museum's belief in this project through an extended article on the development of the museum[8] and its focus on 'practical methods consistent with the prevailing social situation':

> It is, then, in the history of day-to-day life which has, more often than not, followed its course in spite of political manoeuvring than because of it, that the personality of the community and its people is to be found.... The Ulsterman must be made much more aware of a heritage which transcends factional divisions, and that awareness must be developed beyond the level of conscious effort; it should be instinctive, for a sense of cultural identity is a basic, deep-rooted need in the human individual.[9]

How a project as artificial as a museum is able to instil an 'instinctive' cultural identity is an issue the article does not address, and yet it is correct to see the museum's strategy, especially after the beginning of the current period of social violence, as formative rather than confirmative. Tradition, envisaged by a later Director of the Museum as 'a means of admitting cultural performances based on precedents coming down to the present from the nearer or more distant past',[10] in turn is perceived as an inheritance that must be obtained, to paraphrase T. S. Eliot, by great labour. In this way the concept of tradition could be saved from those forces of atavism, whether from the loyalist or nationalist communities, that had been seen to hijack it for violent ends and precedents. If history was now in some way a dangerous and betraying concept, then tradition could become a redemptive force reminding 'Ulstermen' just what they had in common.

In many ways such a perception places an intolerable pressure on the actual visitor who through self-conscious effort must strain for the instinctive recognition demanded by Thompson which will validate their own sense of belonging. Walking around the buildings and trying to feel some instinctive bond with them, he or she is caught within the disabling semantics inherent to the process of defining that which is to be considered 'real' and that which is evidently artificial. For this reason then it is not too fanciful to argue that the museum offers its vision of the past as somehow more 'real' than the outside world and concomitantly suggests that it is the present society of sectarian fracture which is now somehow false, somehow imposed. Operating at the level of conscious effort, yet straining for an instinctive recognition, the subject is defined in relation to the object-symbol and as such it is not inappropriate to read the Folk Museum as a postmodern event in its accordance with Jean Baudrillard's theory of the simulacrum and its ultimate divorce from the realm of the actual.[11] In the commodification of the traditional object-symbol – exemplified for Baudrillard by 'tools, furniture, even the house' – traces of 'a real relation or of a lived situation' inherent to those objects are destroyed by the act of consumption.[12] The object 'must become sign; that is, in some way it must become external to a relation that it now only signifies'. While the museum wishes to preserve above all else the lived values and relations inherent to the artefacts it displays, the new context of display as a consumed object ironically erases any sense of this original value; the objects can only signify something that was once assumed to exist. With this process the new frame of reference – the museum's relationship to the 'real' Ulster – can only confer meaning on the symbol-objects that it displays by an eternal play of difference. The materiality of those artefacts is both proclaimed and questioned as 'human relations tend to be consumed in and through objects, which become the necessary mediation and, rapidly, the substitutive sign, *the alibi*, of the relation'.[13]

It is in the inevitable interpretative vacuum left by this process that tradition asserts itself. If it is the role of the museum as simulacrum to replace and *determine* the real, if, in other words, the flow of meaning is running in the opposite direction envisaged by the initial Act of Parliament, then similarly it is the role of tradition (and with it, its less respectable alter-ego, nostalgia) to mediate this new relationship in terms of strategic contemporary needs located in the present. This point is fundamental to a reading of the museum as an aspect of ethno-history which, as Hoyau insists, is able to 'adjust ethnological and historical research to the ideological demands of the time . . . and above all rationalize nostalgias, offering them "real" contents. By revaluing "poor" forms of knowledge and despised objects, ethno-history affirms its spirit of openness, and at the same time makes its appeal to as widespread an audience as possible.'[14] This democratic appeal is in itself symptomatic of a nervous condition. In the act of giving nostalgia a physical legitimacy its efficacy as a lived system of values is simultaneously denied as its new-found dominance signals an insecurity in that very realm of the real that it seeks to support; as Baudrillard has noted, 'When the real is no longer what it used to be, nostalgia assumes its full meaning'.[15] With this awareness nostalgia is rendered as a proactive force operating in the dimensions of the present moment and forming a dialectical relationship with a perceived crisis in human relations as they, in turn, negotiate a connection with the objects of the past. As Baudrillard develops his thesis: 'There is a proliferation of myths of origin and signs of reality. . . . There is an escalation of the true, of the lived experience; a resurrection of the figurative where the object and subject have disappeared. And there is a panic-stricken production of the real and the referential, above and parallel to the panic of material production.'[16]

Such recourse to the concrete actualities of production to effect a displacement of history – which in turn becomes synonymous with betrayal – can be read as one of the dominating tropes in recent Northern Irish culture and constitutes perhaps one of the more obvious 'morbid symptoms' that Gramsci perceived as part of life in the interregnum.[17] While, in his model, the 'old' is dying, its symbiotic relationship with the as yet uncreated 'new' necessitates that it lingers on with a stubborn irascibility. For all the brave statements of support for the poor despised forms of knowledge the museum is protecting, its actual function can be understood as an attempt to subtend a received sense of history as official state gravitas by artifically aspirating a much older ideology: nature as redemptive force. Physical images of origin and unity can foreclose history by an appeal to timelessness *and* placelessness against which it offers only the assurance of the physical and material. For this reason the artefacts in the museum do not stand in the present moment of time but must be encountered on more-or-less arbitrary terms at a date which is vague and yet securely pre-partition. Any attempt on the part of the visitor to gain a more certain historical fix is not only frustrated but should be seen as strictly contrary to the spirit of the institution. On entering the replica of the Northern Bank building, the observant will notice a calendar displaying bank holidays for the year 1920, a short distance away a gravestone proclaims someone's death in 1922. In the desire to represent the typical Ulster, the museum effortlessly enters the vacuum of interregnum and indeterminacy: a permanent monument to the perceived betrayal of the Ulster people by an illogical and sundered sense of inevitable narrative development.

With this awareness, it is hard to avoid the irony which clings to these images of transposed permanence, especially when the artefact under examination owes its existence to those forces of schismatic breakdown that the museum is usually silent about. For this reason, perhaps the most incongruous exhibit within the anonymous country town which forms the main part of the museum is the presence of a full terrace of high density housing from the Sandy Row area of Belfast.[18] In what sense can they still be perceived as 'part' of Belfast itself? The visitor from the city must fit them into a narrative of Belfast which, crucially, places dislocation at its locus. As Patrick Wright has stated in relation to the housing of Hackney in London, the preservationist attitude that deems such objects worthy of retention has

...a more subjective side as well, involving as it does a contemporary *orientation* towards the past rather than just the survival of old things. As so few guide-books ever recognize, this is not merely a matter of noticing

old objects situated in a self-evident reality: the present meaning of historical traces such as these is only to be grasped if one takes account of the
doubletake or second glance in which they are recognized. The ordinary or
habitual perspectives are jarred as the old declares itself in the midst of all
this dross.[19]

Wright's recognition that in the socially determined present self-evidently
'old' artefacts are granted a value above and beyond their actual historical
worth orientates the preservationist drive embodied by the museum's strategies towards a specific articulation of needs, desires and contemporary
absences. To 'read' the history of a settlement is therefore an interpretative
skill dependent on a shifting, negotiated, identification with the community
which is to be recognized; a circular argument which avoids problematic
issues of communal loyalty by saturating the merely old (and unpleasant at
that) with arbitrary narrative meaning. The 'cottages' of Sandy Row speak
to us and proclaim the primacy of the physical actuality over the assumed
strangeness of history written as a discourse of social breakdown. Culture,
henceforward defined as 'everyday life',[20] celebrates the material over the
temporal and disguises its own displacement (which is all the more notice-
able in the now ruralized locale of the Sandy Row terrace) through a reliance
on the fixed essence of the 'old': a space that can only exist a safe distance
from the present.

It is then sadly appropriate to note that, in line with the political developments of Northern Ireland since that founding 1958 Act, the museum does
not democratize history but instead seeks to erase it by foregrounding the
politics of identity as central through the process of grounding, an occurrence defined by David Lloyd as 'the act of fostering, by which a people
"separated from their forefathers" are...given back an alternative yet
equally arbitrary and fictive paternity renaturalized through the metaphor
of grounding: through its rootedness to the primary soil'.[21] With this,
Northern Ireland, a construct which of course had temporariness needled
into its very existence,[22] is displaced by the (ironically) Tudor-established
nine-county Ulster in an attempt to perceive the past as established touchstone rather than as a narrative of schism and fracture. The difficulties of
this, as I have demonstrated, are manifold but were ably encapsulated by
John Hewitt who voiced unease after a visit to the museum in the poem
'Cultra Manor: The Ulster Folk Museum':

What they need now, somewhere about here,
is a field for the faction fights.[23]

There is, of course, nothing anomalous about the role of the museum in this
regard. In offering symbols of embodiment and representation, its perception

of identity is one that has also nourished a number of pervasive literary strategies in the North. To escape the tautology of a betraying language the writer who seeks (and of course will inevitably achieve) transcendence through the efficacy of location must also negotiate an embodying role within an assumed community and landscape. To speak legitimately about the area delimited the writer must, paradoxically, be typically of it and yet be privileged in being able to effect the transcendence of its typicality in order to demonstrate it, like the museum, to the public. It is here that the function of the writer as paradigmatic becomes significant. To navigate a route through often arbitrary shifts in narrative, the concept of intentionality rewrites the text as autobiography so that closure can only be achieved when it aspires to express, in the absence of political discourse, the fulfilment of the human subject. The achievement of the text becomes the physical actuality of the text and the unseen labour behind its production. In *Ian Paisley My Father* (1988), Rhonda Paisley addresses these issues directly through a text which manifests an extraordinarily personal meditative philosophy. To reclaim her father as the true leader of a lost tribe in the face of previous biographical attacks,[24] Rhonda Paisley's revisionist urge incorporates the personal reminiscence, the accusation of betrayal by the outsider, and, most importantly, the constant restatement of the Ulster narrative as a justifying litany:

> For a child, things of great consequence always have a beginning and an end. 'The troubles' began, to my mind as a child, one morning when I learnt that the Rt Hon. Bill Craig, then Minister of Home Affairs, had been sacked by the Northern Irish Prime Minister, Captain Terence O'Neill. It was the late '60s and O'Neill, a liberal Unionist, had been pursuing a policy of appeasement with the Roman Catholics. . . . That day for me was when 'the troubles' began. Regrettably, my childhood brought no memory which signalled an end to this event of such consequence.[25]

Here, as elsewhere in the book, Rhonda Paisley's style evokes irresistibly the Protestant confessional novel of nineteenth-century England, so that, at times, she can sound like an Ulster Unionist version of Esther Summerson. In the muddle of a narrative which has a clear beginning but no perceivable end (again a parallel with the labyrinthine plot structure of *Bleak House* is possible), she seeks to perfect the individual life as one dedicated firstly to her father and secondly to God; a work of justification which promotes the quotidian aspect of Ian Paisley's life[26] over the failed and increasingly schismatic political vision. With this, the fluid prose she adopts seeks a point in space which is securely pre-twentieth century and rooted in a common inheritance of Protestant political values unified around the totality of the islands. As the tension between this pre-lapsarian technique and the betraying history from which it seeks to remove itself grows greater, Rhonda

Paisley can only bear witness to the individual leader as a man for all time;
an absolute entity whom the reader must necessarily acknowledge as such or
be condemned as a sceptical 'outsider' (possibly the most extreme label of
condemnation Northern Irish culture can envisage). Again, theoretical
explanations become undesirable and are foreclosed by the pervasive
influence of the primary soil:

> To know a person, that is to know them genuinely and not just be
> acquainted with them, you must understand their heart. It is a process
> which takes time. To know Ulster and comprehend the situation here you
> must understand the beat of the land and the rhythm of its music. It is a
> process which takes time. Outsiders do not usually give the time. . . . Often
> I have sat alone on a hillside close to the beach which I love to walk along
> and tried to take in, to absorb into my being the beauty of this land. . . . It
> permeates my blood and the bond created can never be broken. The
> rhythm of the land will be part of my pulse forever. Its influence cannot
> be taken away – it is too late for that.[27]

By reading such a declaration as coherent with nationalist discourses, one can
argue that such rootedness is placed in doubt simply through it being given a
voice. *Ian Paisley My Father* acknowledges failure and despair through its
declarative tone. Its status as text is forced to make conscious the relationship
between object and subject that ideally its author would subtend under a
universal paternalism. With this Rhonda Paisley inhabits a landscape where it
is perpetually 'too late' to initiate a political strategy. The land is given a voice
as disillusionment with Westminster becomes overwhelming yet the history of
betrayal by England,[28] which her brand of Loyalism proclaims, becomes
endlessly cyclical. Through the course of *Ian Paisley My Father* the imaginative sweep of the vision gestures towards the final betrayal of the Ulster
Protestant as a political subject, a goad to the imagined concept of a British
nation-state which has long since lost interest. This messianic concept of final
destruction leaves the text, and possibly the Democratic Unionist philosophy
it embodies, faltering on the final precipice of history and calling sado-
masochistically for the final act of humiliation which will free it. Seemingly
this humiliation will always come but it can never be enough. The politics of
despair are always inarticulate and offer only the sign, the analogy (Ian
Paisley as Moses) and the eternal opposition of the outsider as a theoretical
framework. Despite Rhonda Paisley's stated wish to demythologize her father
he is displaced through the work as an endlessly metaphoric figure embodying
the feeling of the land and the 'common man in the street' through the silence
of his rhetorical and figurative tropes.

It is in this way that Rhonda Paisley's unwilling commodification of
seemingly natural impulses and emotions defines her position within disab-

ling semantic arguments and oppositions. In a later article for the *Irish Times*, 'A Struggle about Identity, Loyalty, Government and, above all, Territory',[29] the function of the Union and with it the possibility of democratic exchange is located at the centre of the now familiar disjunct between nature and culture:

> We have been fed in our state schools the English version of our Irish history. We have been called British first and Irish as a sub-title, a geographic addition. We have been weaned from an organic and beautiful Ulster heritage and fed the synthetic, over-ripe (or half-rotten) heritage of a British empire that is no more and which also was broken by betrayal on betrayal. Now we are chained and fettered by direct rule. . . . To be a part of Ulster is not to be a geographical term nor a subtitle. It is an inheritance. It pulses through the landscape and the veins, we are born to it.

Read alongside *Ian Paisley My Father* such statements provoke certain questions about the author's belief in the desirability of the state democracy to which the rest of the article nominally adheres. Coherent with her previous views on the essentially problematic nature of any artefact marked by artificiality, the article's lines of enquiry are a logical extension of the issues that play through the representational contradictions of the Folk Museum as outlined by Thompson. Finding in Ulster an 'organic' inheritance and sentimental connection to the land, the politics of betrayal by the British Empire become simultaneously the politics of artificiality. Any attempt to separate the idea of representation from that of embodiment, or indeed any attempt to privilege culture over heritage as a lived system of values is rendered, by an intriguing twist, un-Irish and alien. To return to *Ian Paisley My Father*, it is through this instinctive connection of inheritance that totalitarianism enters the social framework of values as the only natural and intuitive response to betrayal.[30]

Of course neither Rhonda Paisley's *Irish Times* article nor *Ian Paisley My Father* should be perceived as unusual in their reliance on grounding to circumvent political stasis. Indeed, while her particular political philosophy prompts her ambiguous stance towards any form of social settlement not predicated on an organic connection, the issues of embodiment and representation with which she is engaged have had a distorting effect across many aspects of Northern Irish culture. Such arguments have often been identified in relation to writers such as John Montague or Seamus Heaney who have consciously felt able – although not always comfortably – to draw on a tradition of rural, Gaelic poetry in their work,[31] and have thus been able to accept the mantle of 'singer' appropriate to their community. Yet it is in the areas of instability, the torn, divided city or the fractured, displaced tradition, where these aesthetic manoeuvres become most fascinating. John

Hewitt, famously of 'Planter stock',[32] spent a long and uncertain writing career agonizing over the politics of identity from a historical position which needed constant examination, constant rebeginning:

> To return for only a moment to this question of 'rootedness'. I do not mean that a writer ought to live and die in the house of his fathers. What I do mean is that he ought to feel that he belongs to a recognizable focus in place and time. How he assures himself of that feeling is his own affair. But I believe that he must have it. And with it he must have *ancestors*. Not just of the blood, but of the emotions, of the quality and slant of mind. He must know where he comes from and where he is: otherwise how can he tell where he wishes to go? The overtones and implications of this would, however, lead us beyond the limits of these pages and must be left over for another more spacious occasion.[33]

That 'another more spacious occasion' was never found was perhaps not a coincidence. The terms invoked here form an inadequate point of beginning but are significant in that they illustrate the particular type of impasse into which Hewitt's epistemology was inexorably heading. Realizing both the potency and despair implicit in the concept of a received history, Hewitt reinterpreted narratives of possession as formulated through the region and was prepared to apply European models of regionalism to Northern Ireland as a specifically mythological system. As the ineffable statement 'how he assures himself of that feeling is his own affair' indicates, this is predicated on an individualism too vague to be supportable and, again like the strategies of Ulster Folk and Transport Museum, the subject is left having to be already inherently part of the system in order to identify with it. His later short essay, 'Regionalism: The Last Chance' (1947) polemically restated this difficulty and emphasized the centrality of narrative development to his vision through a belief in pre-lapsarian wholeness:

> Threatened by over-centralization, already half subdued by a century of increasing standardization in material things, rapidly losing his individual responses in the hurricanes of propaganda, political, commercial, ideological, western man gropes instinctively for the security of a sheltering rock. Many in these islands seek among the rubble of once valid religions for that shelter. Some believe that a wise psychology, aware of many-faceted human nature, will serve. Others, that in achieving a proper relationship with organic nature they may be saved.... One other approach remains, to my mind more urgent and no less valuable because it does not exclude any of the foregoing, rather, indeed, would provide circumstances to which they might be more readily applicable; one which, although it begins with the individual, must immediately pass beyond the

individual and react upon the community – another word which to live must become flesh. This word is regionalism.[34]

As the reference to 'these islands' suggests, Hewitt's regionalism was not necessarily a direct attempt at changing the constitutional position or existence of Northern Ireland as a political entity. As the examples of successful regionalism he later cites[35] demonstrate, the concept becomes at best a way of decentralizing small amounts of power to the provinces. Indeed he goes on to admit that regionalism can only benefit Ulster if it remains, in turn, part of a larger association, his preference being for a federated British Isles. The precarious post-war political situation of Northern Ireland makes such reasoning understandable yet, even then, there is something too comfortable in Hewitt's belief in a pre-twentieth-century individualism which returns, before the 'hurricanes', to a myth of first beginnings pure and unalloyed. As a narrative which seeks to undercut the primary narratives of Irish or Ulster nationalism, it offers a resolution which is predicated on the reconciliation of previous individual liberty with a form of communal association. Hewitt's methodology is here on uncertain ground; while the polemical drive of his prose and his seamless syntactical shifts between the (assumedly) individual 'I' and the communal 'we' indicates a paucity of any theoretical basis for an application of regionalism to Ulster,[36] it becomes clear that the work stands as an angry cry from the provinces desperate to find significance amongst the atavisms of a failed political concept.

In this way, to return to the work of Lloyd, Hewitt's regionalism becomes interesting not through the political initiative it spectacularly failed to deliver, but through the way it allowed him to imagine a community based not on history but along aesthetic and geographical guidelines. It was a myth which idealistically claimed individual loyalty through the tropes of rootedness to the primary soil of Ulster[37] as a 'natural', organic allegiance, and by so doing placed centrally the artist as crucial arbiter of communal judgement:

But if the approach were merely to be on the economic level a long period of time must inevitably elapse before an *emotional unity* could emerge. To quote Mumford further: the 'process begins rather with a dynamic emotional urge, springing out of a sense of frustration on one hand and a renewed vision of life on the other. Only at a later stage does the movement achieve a rationale, a systematic and economic basis. Regionalism, as one French observer points out, begins with *a revival of poetry and language*: it ends with plans for the economic invigoration of regional agriculture and industry, with proposals for a more autonomous political life, with an effort to build up local centres of learning and culture.' [Emphases added.][38]

By subscribing so closely to Mumford's thesis, Hewitt allows the problematic relationship between the individual – who after all is central to his beliefs – and the communal 'emotional unity' to be reconciled only through the paradigmatic figure of the artist: an ideology which accords at least as well with the nationalist thinking of the nineteenth-century Young Ireland journal the *Nation*[39] as it does to any of the regionalist thought to which he more obviously subscribes. The writer becomes saturated with meaning and must mediate the relationship between the individual and the territory in such a way as to propose language as a force of unification rather than division. While Yeats, in obviously differing circumstances, was capable of occasionally fulfilling these conditions on his own eclectic terms, it was a task beyond Hewitt's more limited intellectual grasp or affiliations. By never clearly recognizing which community he was serving[40] or writing for, the absolute concept of Hewitt's Ulster regionalism was always open to the misreadings and political appropriations that its ambiguity sought to foreclose. As his contemporary Roy McFadden noted, 'I suspected that the Ulster Regionalist idea could be used to provide a cultural mask for political unionism or a kind of local counter-nationalism. I was also troubled by Hewitt's use of the word "Ulster", which he did not clearly define.'[41] Hewitt had moved from a period of studying the works of C. G. Jung during the forties,[42] a move which suggests a further Yeatsian trope in the opportunity it afforded him to find a personal myth again predicated on the individual subject. Certainly it is significant that this interest waned when he became fully conscious of the regionalist agenda. Whatever regionalism might have been in Northern Ireland, it seems clear that for Hewitt at least it was a mode of evasion: a way of posing delusory ethical debates on the question of bourgeois identity in his work while avoiding any attempt to address political or *territorial* schism.

As has often been the case in Northern Irish culture, it has been within the structures of the aesthetic artefact itself that such practices have been most effectively interrogated. In John Montague's 1961 collection *Poisoned Lands and Other Poems*,[43] the poem 'Regionalism, Or Portrait of the Artist as a Model Farmer'[44] effectively condemned regionalism as provincial, nativist and insular. While this critique was one Montague would later modify after his collaboration with Hewitt on 'The Planter and the Gael' Arts Council tour of 1970, his accusations were well aimed and clearly had Hewitt – and through him Kavanagh – specifically in mind:

> Wild provincials
> Muttering into microphones
> Declare that art
> Springs only from the native part;
> That like a potato it best grows

Planted deep in local rows: ...
Shield from all might harm her,
Foreign beetles and exotic weeds,
Complicated continental breeds:
And when my baby tuber
To its might has grown
I shall come into my provincial own
And mutter deep
In my living sleep
Of the tradition that I keep.
My tiny spud will comfort me
In my fierce anonymity.

Although the nature of this satire allowed Montague to construct himself in opposition as a sophisticated internationalist, the poem's presence within a collection which sought to identify those symptoms which had 'poisoned' Ulster indicates a more serious critique. As Montague recognized, for Hewitt the conflation of regionalism and formal poetic achievement became a way of containing and controlling dangerous passions; the literary equivalent of the 'little towns to garrison/the heaving country' which appear in his poem 'The Colony'.[45] As a reading of this poem indicates, Hewitt's poetry through this period is obsessed with the concept of the enemy both as external force and internal temptation. Desperate to protect a notional selfhood from the corrupting influence of passion, even his interest in Jung, to which I have already referred, can be seen, not as an exploration, but as a schematicization of troubling impulses and desires into a readily understandable epistemological framework. The pattern of his intellectual life that begins to emerge is one in which methodology seeks to restrict the chaos of sensory impression. In opposition to the Joycean model of aesthetic detachment invoked by Montague's title, Hewitt as 'model farmer' seeks to cultivate, contain and catalogue the discordant and anomalous voices which continually interrupt his work, disrupt the steady flow of his neo-dialectic method and escape into print.

Read in this way, Hewitt's writings appear as nothing less than wagers with heterogeneity: if his analytic method cannot prevail, sensory impression and prejudicial emotion will inevitably break through. Moreover, there is evidence that Hewitt was aware of this dilemma. An interesting, although little cited, sonnet 'Aquarium'[46] takes as its theme agency and representation and notes, with some exasperation, that 'the old obsessive search/for binding epithet' will lead to nothing 'riper' than '*striped* Perch/or *pink-finned* Rudd'. The aquarium itself represents a 'challenge to my verbalizing mind' although does not entail 'the risks of dialogue' as the fish who inhabit it are merely subjects to be represented. As Hewitt perceives the danger and inevitable confrontation of agency the poem's thematic concern oddly resembles Paul Muldoon's later 'Chinook' which similarly seeks to contain within a metaphor the disruptive energies of language: 'I was micro-tagging Chinook salmon/on the Qu'Apelle/river'.[47] The analogy is telling. In its reluctance to enter language, to give voice to the 'dumb' fish, 'Aquarium' recognizes that all such codification can be seen as fundamentally reductive and aesthetically inadequate: 'to drag my leaky net to land' is not to bring to a successful conclusion a well-turned sonnet but to sense impending despair.

The neo-Georgian forms and belief in regionalism which haunt much of Hewitt's work can be seen then as self-conscious admissions of defeat; methods of strategic containment and a buttress against the centripetal energies of modernism and the formal chaos which can follow. While Montague's critique of regionalism and formal insularity is important if only because there was little effective criticism of regionalism as a political or aesthetic practice at this time, it required Seamus Heaney, responding to Hewitt's regionalism and to 'Portrait of the Artist as a Model Farmer', to suggest through a poetic dialectical method the ultimate universalism of a carefully applied regionalist agenda in his poem 'The Seed Cutters':[48]

> ... The tuck and frill
> Of leaf-sprout is on the seed potatoes
> Buried under that straw. With time to kill
> They are taking their time. Each sharp knife goes
> Lazily halving each root that falls apart
> In the palm of the hand: a milky gleam,
> And, at the centre, a dark watermark.
> O calendar customs! Under the broom
> Yellowing over them, compose the frieze
> With all of us there, our anonymities.

The seed cutters' dissection of the seed potatoes as locations of meaning – the point at which growth will begin – ultimately reinvigorates the 'anonymity' that Montague condemns through his 'spud' in the final word of 'Portrait of the Artist as a Model Farmer'. With this 'The Seed Cutters' moves from an image of communal anonymity to a parable of the literary self-conscious that can transform the 'wild' provincial stance offered by Montague into a repetitive, calendrical, aesthetic practice. However, this is not to suggest that Heaney's covert defence of regionalism entailed that he would fall back to the overtly deterministic strictures of 'Regionalism: The Last Chance'. While in the later essay 'The Regional Forecast',[49] Heaney acknowledges the importance of regional cultural activity as a precursor to political identity in a way which accords with Hewitt's previously stated arguments, he is concomitantly aware that 'it is necessary to beware of too easy an assumption that the breaking of political bonds necessarily and successfully issues in the forging of a new literary idiom'.[50] By drawing attention to the conflict of interests between 'the imaginative and activist wings' of regional development, Heaney seeks to disentangle those impulses that Hewitt had deliberately unified through a belief in an 'idealized past'.[51] Heaney's regionalism then stops short of Hewitt's call for a 'more autonomous political life' perhaps because it would be through such a manoeuvre that Ulster would dissociate itself from the rest of Heaney's imaginative hinterland. Instead he is content to perceive the phenomenon as a means of raising 'our subcultural status to cultural power'; a strategy that can continue to contain and demonstrate the subversive discourses of Irish nationalism that other Heaney poems (collected alongside 'The Seed Cutters' in *North*) express.

It is through these attacks that the limits of 'Regionalism: The Last Chance' are contextualized. As Montague reads the concept as cravenly provincial, so Heaney, like McFadden before him, finds in its polemic bluster a covert expression of unionism. With this, the essay stands as testament to an ideology which was essentially despairing of history and the political subject and which sought to foreclose such forces within the landscape and within silence. As a poet, however, it allowed Hewitt to grant contemporary significance to his own essential instincts which lay in the foundation of a writing coterie as social force[52] – an obsession which haunts writing in Belfast and Derry even now. In his later years the recognition Hewitt sought as paternal head of such a movement was finally fulfilled and his memory exists as a mythological phenomenon; the benign protector of a poetic tradition in Ulster at a time when it was near total eradication.[53]

13

Subalternity and Gender: Problems of Postcolonial Irishness

Colin Graham

Floozy, Skivvy, Whore is my name and symbol of my identity.

Which brings me in passing to the
question of Irish women's place
within but without culture and
identity
Transparent floating capacious signifier,
from what place can I speak?
Confined 'by the waters of Babalong'
in sink, sewer, bidet, jacuzzi, in a
flowing babel of other-determined
myths, symbols, images, can I speak
myself at all?[1]

What Ailbhe Smyth calls 'the question of Irish women's place within but without culture and identity' certainly constitutes a 'running sore on the body politic of Ireland'.[2] The position of women in Irish society, bound to constitutional and institutionally religious issues of abortion, contraception and divorce, has invoked serious examination of how gender and femininity relate to the notion of an Irish identity. And it has been the specifics of the category of 'Irish' which have necessitated a debate which can envisage alternative placings 'within but without culture and identity' in an Irish context – Irishness, variously understood, may encapsulate or expunge the female, denying or seeking to define and legitimize what the 'Irish woman' may be.

It is inevitable, indeed crucial, that developments in understanding, argument and resistance which unfold from the domain of constitutional and activist politics are given parallel expression in reading cultural texts which both absorb and deny the changes in how gender is understood in Ireland. As Smyth suggests, the 'change' is still very much a flux, a debate without resolution, in which the relationship between gender issues and the potential solidities of 'Irishness' have yet to settle. There is therefore an opportunity to interrogate how gender might be read in or against Irishness. Below I attempt to set out one prospect for rethought notions of the conflux of gender and Ireland by scrutinizing the difficulties and potentialities of the socio-cultural and postcolonial category of the 'subaltern' in Irish cultural criticism, focusing in particular on how ideas of subalternity can be applied to gender issues in the Irish context. The aim here is to move towards an understanding of the subaltern which can be specific to the constitutive fabric of Irish cultures, which can retain a theoretical rigour and radicalism, and which can place 'gender' within a theoretical framework capable of accounting for alterations in the prioritization and submergence of gender issues within Irish societies.

The 'subaltern' in contemporary critical theorization usually functions as a description of 'oppressed groups within society'. I begin my discussion of the relevance of the notion of the subaltern as a marker of gender in Irish culture by noting the transformation of the meaning of the term subaltern from its original use in the writings of Gramsci to its more recent provenance in postcolonial criticism. From this analysis I move on to look at competing ways in which the subaltern could be and has been used in relation to gender and Irish culture. And out of the problems and debates of this discussion I attempt the beginnings of an alternative construction of the gendered-subaltern suitable to the complexities of the Irish postcolonial situation.
[...]
The category of the subaltern within contemporary cultural theory has two important sources. The origins of the term as a means to understanding the position and possible coherence of oppressed groups are found in the writings of the Italian Marxist thinker Antonio Gramsci, especially the 'Notes on Italian history' in his *Prison Notebooks*. For Gramsci, the subalterns are a diverse collection of social groups subject to the rule of dominant classes and the State. Gramsci's main concerns in the 'Notes on Italian history' were the methodological processes involved in writing the history of these groups; he set out a six-point plan in which he stressed that the subaltern has a 'fragmented and episodic'[3] history, that the subaltern groups are disunified and that, despite their definition *as* subaltern, they are *affiliated* to 'dominant political formations'.[4] Importantly, Gramsci notes that the subaltern groups 'cannot unite until they are able to become a "state"':[5] an unlikely prospect in Gramscian analysis given the nature of the dominance of the ruling classes, but nevertheless an essential defining feature of these groups – they aim for 'integral autonomy', unity and dominance.[6] The subaltern classes, then, in a Gramscian critique, will be counter-hegemonic, seeking not only to destabilize the dominant ideology but to take over its position. This is a crucial distinction between subversity from below which

seeks only to subvert, and that which seeks to topple and replace 'the
dominant'. (I will return to this in a moment specifically in the context of
recent Irish cultural criticism and gender issues.) Gramsci's notion of the
subaltern as a collection of groups with a shared oppression is then vitally
underlain by the knowledge that the subalterns are not willing participants
in their social and political position – they seek to 'rise' out of their status,
and they do so, as Gramsci says, by 'active or passive affiliation' to dominant formations in order 'to influence the programmes of these formations
[and . . .] to press claims of their own'.[7]

This Gramscian definition is central to, and yet significantly distorted by,
the second source of the usage of the term 'subaltern' in contemporary
vocabularies which derives, broadly speaking, from postcolonial criticism
and most specifically from the work of the Subaltern Studies group of
historians in India.[8] Subaltern Studies take the methodological challenge
of Gramsci's project to write what the editor of the first six volumes of
Subaltern Studies, Ranajit Guha, calls the 'politics of the people',[9] which he
considers to have been previously omitted from Indian history.

Subaltern Studies have had two important effects on thinking concerning
the category of the subaltern which need to be understood in order to read
the subaltern into an Irish context. Firstly, and almost despite themselves,
they have expanded the remit of the term 'subaltern' beyond the confines
of a solely class-based Marxist critique. While the initial volumes of
Subaltern Studies concentrate almost solely on peasant insurgency, trade
unionism and the working-classes, there is a perceptible widening of focus
in the later volumes, which is perhaps traceable to the intervention in Vol.
IV of the feminist cultural critic Gayatri Chakravorty Spivak.[10] Spivak's
deliberate reading 'against the grain of [Subaltern Studies'] theoretical self-
representation'[11] is remarkable in itself, but in tactical terms it seems to have
opened the project to allow the inclusion of, for example, feminist and ethnic
critiques of the 'dominant', and thus by implication to have expanded the
idea of the subaltern to include oppressed and marginal groups of many
types within society. This expansion of the term has been increased by the
concentration in postcolonial cultural and literary criticism on the conflux of
discourses of gender, nationalism, colonialism and postcolonialism, in which
the subalternity of women is reassessed, revised, and often complexly
affirmed.[12]

The second major effect of the Subaltern Studies project arises in its
originary moments and from its frustration with the historical narrative
and political formation of the Indian nation. Subaltern Studies identifies
postcolonial India, *apropos* its *nationality* and its state apparatuses, as 'the
ideological product of British rule in India'.[13] Thus, no longer can the
postcolonial nation be regarded as a triumph of the labours of an oppressed
people – rather it is an aping and repetition of the colonial structures which it

displaced, and a continuum of oppression for subaltern groups despite the narrative of liberation and freedom by which the postcolonial nation justifies its existence. This reverberates into postcolonial cultural studies in an increasing acknowledgement that the concept of the nation, while a necessary part of the colonial/postcolonial teleology, is in itself an over-homogenizing, oppressive ideology which elides the multiplicity of subaltern classes and groups and acts to maintain their subaltern status.

It is important to note at this point the distinction between Gramsci's understanding of the subaltern and that of Subaltern Studies and a vast body of postcolonial criticism. Gramsci stresses that the subaltern is linked, 'actively or passively', to the dominant structures which seek to maintain the subaltern *as subaltern* – for Gramsci, the subaltern seeks to become part of the dominant structures, to gain power, to form a 'State' – thus the subaltern, while defined by its subordinate relationship to the dominant, is not 'innocent' of the processes of domination. In Subaltern Studies and particularly in postcolonial criticism there is tendency to read into the category of the 'subaltern' an ethics of oppression, which can be seen to be doubly justified by an ethics of a postcolonialism which purports to speak for victims – the subaltern thus becomes made subaltern by colonialism and by postcolonial nationalism. The result is often a cultural criticism which makes the subaltern a theoretical site of disempowered purity – social groupings apparently so subsumed by colonialism, capitalism and nationalist ideology and practice, that their oppression leaves them unsullied by these dominances. In other words, the subaltern can become prioritized, even utopianized, in critical discourses, functioning eventually as a refuge for cultural and political authenticity. This necessarily reads against Gramsci's notion of 'affiliation' between subaltern groups and their dominants which sets up a more complex, almost complicitous, system of socio-political stratification – Gramsci effectively denies the ideological sanctity of the 'subaltern' which is apparent in later re-readings.

Bearing these distinctions and tendencies in mind, how will the contemporary conceptual bases of the subaltern read when they are then translated into the context of Irish cultural and gender criticism? From the context of the notion of the 'subaltern' in contemporary cultural criticism it is clear that the term brings with it a particular type of postcolonial thinking – one which is aware of the failure of nationalism in the postcolonial world, and one which highlights the hierarchical nature of social, cultural and gender relations. Additionally, it is obvious that the questions which are raised by the use of subalternity as a critique will concern the relationships between nationalism and feminism, nation and gender, questions which have been confronted in recent years in Ireland.

The question of how Ireland is read in postcolonial cultural criticism is an obvious framework for this discussion, but the arguments necessary for establishing a postcolonial vocabulary for Irish culture are too broad for inclusion here. I wish instead to focus on how Irish culture has ordered the politics of gender within the narratives of the nation, and to see how the subaltern has been and could be placed in an Irish gender/nation debate.

A broad consensual view can be discerned among critics and writers who deal with gender and nationalist (and indeed unionist) ideology in Ireland, suggesting that nationalism and unionism encompass gender in their theoretical constructions and social workings in patriarchal, controlling ways, creating metaphors and cultural discourses which Gerardine Meaney says exhibit 'for Irishwomen the sign of their invisibility'.[14] The recognition of the enforced silence of women and their simultaneous importance as a representational category integral to a dominant discourse is common to both Irish and postcolonial feminist thinking. For example, in an essay entitled 'Identity and its discontents: women and the nation', Deniz Kandiyoti sees the concept of nation, indeed the whole discourse of cultural difference, as an assertion of 'control over women'.[15] Nationalism, says Kandiyoti, '[exerts] pressure on women to articulate their gender interests within the terms of reference set by nationalist discourse'.[16] Gender then becomes subaltern to dominant nationalism, being forced, in Gramsci's configuration, into 'affiliation' in order to press its claims. The subaltern/dominant relationship of gender/nation is further illuminated by Radhakrishnan, who notes that:

> the politics of nationalism become the binding and overarching umbrella that subsumes other and different political temporalities [...The] ideology of nationalist politics... acts as the normative mode of *the political as such* ...Consequently, the woman's question (...or the subaltern question)... is constrained to take on a nationalist expression as a prerequisite for being considered 'political'.[17]

The resonances of such critiques hardly need to be laboured in the Irish context, where the liberative doctrine of nationalism became the nation-state's constitutional discrimination and where, in the Republic, the woman as 'revolutionary' transmuted into what Eamon de Valera, when Prime Minister, fetished in his St Patrick's Day broadcast of 1943 as the 'laughter of comely maidens', an image ironically appropriate for its linguistically-silenced subject.[18] Nationalism, in this configuration, is complicit in assuming and enforcing the subaltern status of women and other marginalized groups.

Recently, however, the turn against the 'overarching umbrella' of Irish nationalism and its end-product state has been challenged in ways which directly impinge upon reading the category of the (gendered-)subaltern into Irish culture. Both David Lloyd and Carol Coulter have dissented from what Lloyd describes as the 'anti-nationalist prejudice', which they see as a critical 'distaste' for nationalism, pervasive both in Ireland and beyond. Lloyd and Coulter both imply that this turn against nationalism, promoted by the liberal West, deliberately detaches nationalism from any radical forces or histories it might claim – and both Lloyd and Coulter seek to counter this by re-inscribing nationalism as a subversive force in cultural theory, stressing its anti-colonial energies as resources still available for radicalism.

For Lloyd anti-nationalism is a modern trait, what he has described as a 'traditional metropolitan antagonism towards anti-colonial movements',[19] a convenient liberalized veneer under which, Lloyd suggests, resides a continuing Eurocentric disabling of peripheral politicization. Lloyd thus prioritizes the anti-colonial nature of nationalism and insists that solidarity within oppressed societies reveals what he suggests is a common experience of domination among those oppressed.[20] This describes a particular kind of subaltern position – one which has changed from the Gramscian 'fragmented and episodic' to a more coherent collective experience which initiates collective action (bringing feminists and socialists into common bonds with nationalists – thus Countess Markievicz, Sinn Féiner and first woman to win a seat in Westminster, becomes a useful and important figure for Lloyd). Thus in his article 'Nationalisms against the state: towards a critique of the anti-nationalist prejudice', Lloyd interestingly turns away from Gramsci, continuing his reading of 'Gramsci's portrayal of the subaltern group's history against itself' which is apparent in *Anomalous States*.[21]

The collective, rather than dispersed, experience of subalternity which arises from Lloyd's critique is not merely a conglomeration of feminism, socialism and nationalism – rather nationalism is acknowledged as the ideological gel of these subaltern movements (a notion which ironically already recognizes the fact that nationalism later enacts a transformation into the oppressive constitutional State). Lloyd's version of nationalism *as* subaltern thus relies upon a de-hyphenation of the nation-state. Nationalism cannot be continually thought of as teleologically intended for Statehood; rather it is preserved as an insurgent force – nationalism, in Lloyd's terms, has an 'excess' over the nation, containing groups, notions and individuals which deny the nation's push to homogeneity.

It becomes increasingly obvious why Lloyd must reject Gramsci, since, as pointed out above, Gramsci's version of the subaltern is defined by its desire to form the State. Lloyd's attempted subalternization of nationalism is reliant upon understanding nationalism as *always insurgent* but never hegemonous, a notion with intensely problematic connotations to which I will return in a moment.

Lloyd's re-assessment of the subaltern nature of nationalism may well have had an influence on (since early versions of it are cited in) Carol Coulter's contribution to the 'Undercurrents' series, *The Hidden Tradition: Feminism, Women & Nationalism in Ireland*.[22] Coulter follows Lloyd's initial

reaction against the 'commonplace [notion] in modern debate in Ireland
... that nationalism and feminism are opposites',[23] and partially echoes
Lloyd in identifying this binarism as a metropolitan construction acting as
a cover for another agenda.[24] Coulter argues that there is a 'tradition of
women's involvement in nationalist struggle',[25] and that this calls for a
revaluation of the relationship between nationalism and feminism. And
like Lloyd's, Coulter's critical rhetoric relies on a crucial distinction between,
rather than a Gramscian mergence of, the nation and the state – thus it is, for
Coulter, the 'patriarchal state' and not nationalism which 'closed off',[26] the
political activity of women in Ireland (though Coulter interestingly goes on
to argue for a constant level of such activity despite the State).

Lloyd's use of nationalism as an ideologically active site for the meeting of
various subalternities translates into Coulter's idea of nationalism as a
'unifying ideology ... subversive of all authority'.[27] Nationalism is then
prioritized as always subaltern, always insurgent, and thus inherently
compatible with the claims of women within the State, and of subaltern
groups in general. There are various problems with re-assessments of the
putatively subaltern status of nationalism such as Lloyd's and Coulter's, and
it is in discussing these that I hope to move towards an alternatively pos-
itioned use of subalternity and gender in the Irish context.

Firstly, there is the basic assumption that nationalism can be viewed as
orientated only towards subversion and not towards power and homogeneity. While this can explain the inclusion of feminists in insurgent nationalist
movements, it contorts the ideology of nationalism by separating it from and
fetishizing the concept of the State, and ignores Gramsci's implicit insistence
that a subaltern force such as anti-colonial nationalism was always aimed at
becoming the State. Indeed Gramsci's belief that subaltern groups 'affiliate'
themselves to dominant groups can be adapted to suggest that nationalism succeeded precisely because it imitated so exactly the State which pre-
ceded it.

The prioritization of nationalism and subalternity as always insurgent
leads to a second problem. If nationalism is subaltern only when it is
unsuccessful (still insurgent, rather than in the process of forming the
State), then there is a serious intellectual danger of celebrating the subalternity of subaltern groups. Ethically-endowing the position of the subaltern
can lead to a revelling in the insurgency of nationalism or feminism which
easily slides into a continuous and necessary restatement of their oppressed
position. Indeed it forms an academic subject which would be lost were it to
progress.

In such a scenario, where the subaltern becomes the object of study
because it is always in unsuccessful revolution, the subaltern becomes the
site of cultural integrity and authenticity, filled with an ethically-charged
identity which paradoxically relies on what Spivak calls the 'monolithic and

anonymous [subject]-in-revolution'.[28] Subalternity, decried as a politically unjust status by those who speak about it, will simultaneously function as an invocation of an unspoilt consciousness, pure because disempowered. Spivak notes the danger, in talking of the subaltern, of 'a nostalgia for lost origins [which] can be detrimental to the exploration of social realities within the critique of imperialism'.[29] Lloyd's reading of street ballads,[30] his notion of the people as 'excess'[31] over the nation (so that any denigration of nationalism leaves the 'people' untouched) and Coulter's emphasis on 'tradition' as an historical and conceptual link between women and the nation,[32] all seem to me to be perilously close to such a nostalgic purification of the subaltern as a political residue.

Re-inventing nationalism as subaltern has a third problem which directly concerns how gender can be read into the subaltern category. In Lloyd's and Coulter's works there is an implicit acknowledgement of the fact that nationalism, even when it was subversive and subaltern, still ordered and dominated women's movements – that gender became an exigent aspect of nationalist subversion. This ensures that 'women' will always remain submerged by nationalism no matter how much gender plays a part in nationalism, and that this will be the case even when nationalism is frozen in its pre-Statehood embodiment. The 'commonality' of oppression which Lloyd sees as the means of coalescing subaltern groups in fact works as a hegemonous stratification within the whole collection of subaltern groups – women's movements are continually subsumed within nationalist movements and resetting nationalism as an always-subaltern force condemns the 'woman-as-subaltern' to a perpetual existence under the 'overarching umbrella' of nationalism. As Spivak points out, the notion of the subaltern already runs the risk of being a 'global laundry list with "woman" as a pious term' – and she criticizes the *Subaltern Studies* historians for 'emptying' women of meaning. Insisting on nationalism as always-subaltern seems to flirt with confirming this discrimination and repeating such a semiotic disappearance.

How, then, as a result of this critique of the reassessment of nationalism and subalternity, can we posit an alternatively configured concept of the subaltern? How can we read gender as subaltern in the Irish context without allowing the 'nation' to dictate our discourse? If the re-ordering of the subaltern under 'nationalism' is to be resisted, and the stress on the ethical value of the subaltern to be treated warily, then the writings of Gayatri Chakravorty Spivak become a vital reference point.

In her essay 'Can the subaltern speak?' Spivak points out that the 'colonized subaltern subject is always irretrievably heterogeneous'.[33] In the heterogeneity which Spivak identifies we should recognize the need to allow discourses within the subaltern category to collide as well as collude, to be in conflict with each other, and thus to be closer to Gramsci's original definition of the subaltern. Spivak criticizes the Subaltern Studies historians for 're-naming' sexual difference as class or caste-solidarity:[34] in the Irish context such transmutations of gender in the name of nationalism should also be resisted and gender allowed to exist within, outside and in opposition to the State *and* the nation.

Spivak's most important comments on the subaltern are in relation to the construction of the subaltern as a site of subversive 'consciousness': she says 'the subaltern's view, will, presence, can be no more than a theoretical fiction to entitle the project of reading'.[35] This is intended partly to warn the academic against privileging a notion of the subaltern as a coherent site of insurgency made exigent by a need to find a place of political incorruption. Lloyd's use of a notional 'experience' in his idea of 'a common *experience* of domination' seems liable to fall into this 'fiction', positing the intellectual as what Spivak ironically describes as 'the absent non-representer who lets the oppressed speak for themselves'.[36] Spivak's comments point to a specific danger in an Irish context: a complex, contorted intellectual nativism, rehearsing the idioms and rejuvenating the discourses of an essentialist Irishness which is always oppressed, and yet is itself oppressive of the heterogeneity with which it is confronted.

Spivak's alternative methodology is summed up in the following, challenging remark: 'what I find useful is the sustained and developing work on the *mechanics* of the constitution of the Other; we can use it to much greater analytic and interventionist advantage than invocations of the *authenticity* of the Other'.[37] Emphasizing the mechanics of the ordering of subaltern/dominant relations rather than searching for an authentic site of pure insurgency is the starting point of reading the gendered-subaltern.

The analysis of the subaltern, and its relationship with gender in both postcolonial and more specifically Irish critical contexts, which I have so far undertaken implies a way of reading Ireland and Irish culture which recognizes that gender will exist 'inside' nation in an Irish context, but which will deny the necessity of the domination or stratification of gender by nation. In order to make more specific the power relations involved in the notion of the gendered-subaltern in Irish postcolonial terms, I wish now to examine a text in which the relationship between gender and nation in Ireland is specifically contemplated and to suggest that in order to maintain the theoretical ideal that subalternities are best seen to be complexly affiliative rather than merely commonly oppressed, we must be aware that even where nation acknowledges gender as subaltern such recognitions will retrace themselves into hierarchized relationships.

[. . .]

So how do we progress to a notion of subalternity which views the subaltern as a cross-hatched collection of discourses in which the subcategories of the subaltern are not given a fixed or over-determined status?

Ailbhe Smyth's 'The Floozie in the Jacuzzi', an extraordinary and multifarious examination of the meeting points of 'Irishness' and femininity offers a series of contemplations on the subject:

> The ex-colonized oppressors colonize. (Habit of centuries.) They don't listen. Theirs is the Republic, the Power and the Discourse.[38]

> Dual struggle with the imprint of colonially-induced dependence and patriarchally-imposed otherness struggling to extricate ourselves from the simultaneous web that binds us into the pattern of non-entity ... The problem is not how to negotiate entry inside, into a tradition, culture, discourse which designates the Other as necessary alien, necessarily *outside*.[39]

Smyth acknowledges the potential dual history of oppression in subaltern groups in Ireland – 'woman' and 'Irish', Smyth acknowledges, implies a 'dual struggle'. What Smyth lucidly denies is the necessity, plausibility and wisdom of combining these struggles, since to struggle to be Irish is, for Irish women, to risk attempting acceptance where 'she' can only ever be 'Other', and to fall back into the belief in dual subalternities working harmoniously in their perpetual subalternity.

The extent to which the subaltern can 'contain' gender, in an Irish and a wider postcolonial context, only becomes clear when gender and nation are both seen as potentially subversive *and* affiliative, existing variously in the subaltern matrix of empowerment, disempowerment, confrontation and hierarchization. Such a model may then be able to explain the contradictions of gender, its roles in and outside nationalism, without resort to the ethics of authenticity and without surrendering a critique of nationalism's homogeneity.

In order to produce a full cultural critique of gender and subalternity in the Irish context, a wider notion of the postcolonial status of Ireland is vital. But my discussion of the position and nature of the subaltern should have made clear that gender will have a vital role to play in opening up postcolonial and subaltern critical discourses in the Irish context. Ireland's ambiguous postcolonial status allows it to move as a signifier in postcolonial criticism. The category of the subaltern, which Spivak notes already has a degree of fluidity even in Subaltern Studies,[40] is notably unfixed if we return to Gramsci's stress on affiliation. Disagreements about the status of gender in the Irish context show that gender in Ireland, because it is figuratively central to nationalist ideologies and yet subversive of them, will enable a critique of subalternity, nationalism, colonialism and postcolonialism which will unveil the mechanics of their constitution of the gendered Other. It is its ability to be a precise and rigorous theoretical lever upon entrenched discourses that makes the gendered-subaltern an important notion in cultural criticism, and gives it the potential to reformulate debates on gender and Ireland.

14

The Spirit of the Nation

David Lloyd

According to Young Ireland doctrine, the struggle to revive a sense of the continuity of Irish cultural history with its obscured origins both prefigures and helps to produce the political integration that is actually lacking. The assertion of a distinct identity for the nation-state on the basis of a supposedly lost unity is an essential element of European nationalism in the early and mid-nineteenth century. Nationalism emerges as a political doctrine in this period to unify and legitimate the nation-state after the overthrow of arbitrary monarchic states, whose unity had been territorially defined and symbolized in the figure of the monarch.[1] Nationalism must accordingly be understood in relation to a nineteenth-century political theory that conceives the state itself to be the historical expression of the fundamental unity of any people, transcending the specific social conflicts that threaten to disintegrate civil society.[2]

In British political theory, which initially centres on the notion of the constitution rather than on that of the state, a development can be traced in which the largely static model of the constitution, conceived in the eighteenth century as a system of checks and balances, gives way to an evolutionary model, in which the reconciliation of opposing social forces produces an ever higher and more integrated realization of the essential spirit manifested in the English people. It is to this notion of the constitution that unionist ideologists appeal.[3] It is equally striking that in Young Ireland writings, including even those of John Mitchel, this model of the British constitution is accepted as accurate and even admired, although, for reasons that will be discussed, it must necessarily be rejected as an option for Ireland. Beneath the superficial appearance of antagonism and incoherence on the part of England lies a deeper coherence, a reconciliation of conflicting interests into mutual necessity. Despite the antipathy to political economy that is found everywhere in nationalist writings, it is clear that what Young Ireland admires in the British constitution is the apparent political coherence of a vigorous economy.[4]

The anomalous condition of Ireland, however, precludes the kind of integration promised by either British political economy or British political theory. Split between a rural subsistence economy, which largely pre-exists both the use of money and the exchange of commodities, and a maritime economy, whose principal function is the mediation of the export of agricultural produce and of capital in the form of the absentees' rent, Ireland is marked by a literal and irreversible deterritorialization of all its resources and a part of its people.[5] Among those who experience this deterritorialization most acutely both in culture and in economic and social position are the intelligentsia, whose class position leaves them deracinated with regard to rural and Gaelic Ireland and only awkwardly recentred with regard to the Empire, on whose political power they are socially, economically, and often culturally parasitic but from whose centre they are nonetheless excluded. Theoretically, the solution to Ireland's economic predicament has already been given: to recentre that economy within an Ireland that has regained the power to regulate its own commercial laws and practices. In practice, however, the strategy must be quite different and must effectively reverse the political resolution of economic conflict provided for in the British constitution. Recognizing their inevitable alienation from the population as a whole, the nationalist intelligentsia seeks to project the image of a spiritual Ireland that pre-exists its actual economic destitution and political divisions, incorporating the entire Irish people in the fundamental sameness of their identity and the fundamental identity of their primary political interest, that is, a self-governing Ireland. Political reconciliation here must precede economic revival.

[. . .]

The necessity of commencing by affirming the ground for its own political and national identity differentiates Irish nationalism not only from British political thought but also from that of the revolutionary constitutional republics, France and America, which are to some extent its sources of inspiration. The revolutionary success of these nations defines in advance their political cohesion, which is only then enshrined in the constitution. Unlike them, Ireland seeks to define and constitute its nationhood precisely out of the actual or threatened loss of its identity. Despite frequent appeals to the example of the 'giant nation' that 'sprang from the waters of the Atlantic', Ireland's situation is more closely analogous to that of its European counterparts, Germany and Italy, and its version of nationalism is more closely related to theirs.[6]

Lacking as these 'nations' do the *de facto* political identity forged by France and America in their military struggles against monarchy, their primary appeal is to a prior cultural unity on which basis the *right* to self-determination can be formulated. The distinguishing features of these nationalisms can be located in the fact that, as Eugene Kamenka neatly expresses it, 'self-government requires a community that is to be the self'.[7] The 'self' of the nation is, in the first instance, discerned in the language that provides the objective basis for cultural unity. Mazzini, leader of the Young

Italy movement after which the Young Irelanders were dubbed, puts the point unambiguously in terms that foreshadow the future expansionism of Italian nationalism: 'Your country is one and indivisible. As the members of a family cannot rejoice if one of their number is far away, snatched from the affection of his brothers, so you should have no joy or repose as long as a portion of the territory upon which the language is spoken is separated from the Nation.'[8] For Mazzini, language defines the 'natural divisions' of the 'Countries of the People', whose 'innate spontaneous tendencies... will replace the arbitrary divisions sanctioned by bad governments'.[9]

The full complexity of an argument that relates the 'innate spontaneous tendencies' of a people to their language – thus baldly stated by Mazzini – was initially developed by the German post-Kantians, in particular by J. G. Fichte in his *Addresses to the German Nation*.[10] These addresses, delivered in 1808 after the defeat of the Prussians by the French, are concerned to provide the basis for a German national resurgence by locating the constitutive principles of the German people beyond actual political divisions. Fichte's argument opens with the idea that the defeat of the Germans has come about as the inevitable consequence of their spiritual contamination by French influences, which are, in the fullest sense, foreign to the essence of the Germanic peoples. If a large part of this argument is directed against the contamination of the German language by the introduction of French vocabulary, this is precisely because in the German language lies the essence of the German nation:

> To begin with and before all things: the first, original, and truly natural boundaries of States are beyond doubt their internal boundaries. Those who speak the same language are joined to each other by a multitude of invisible bonds by nature herself, long before any human art begins; they understand each other and have the power of continuing to make themselves understood more and more clearly; they belong together and are by nature one and an inseparable whole.[11]

The burden of Fichte's argument here is not simply that where a language is *actually* spoken there exists a community with the right to consider itself a nation. More important than that almost contingent circumstance is the notion that the language of a nation is a continuing and developing entity.[12] The defining characteristic of the German peoples, as opposed to the French, according to Fichte, is that the former have continued to use their original language and in so doing have remained in touch with the living stream of an original language, whereas the latter have exchanged their living Teutonic language for a dead Latin one: 'They get symbols which for them are neither immediately clear nor able to stimulate life, but which must seem to them entirely as arbitrary as the sensuous part of the language.

For them this advent of history, and nothing but history, as expositor, makes the language dead and closed in respect of its whole sphere of imagery, and its continuous onward flow is broken off.'[13] Ultimately, Fichte's argument leads him to distinguish 'German' from non-German not on the sole basis of language and race, but on the basis of the acceptance or not of the will to secure 'the eternal development of this spirituality by freedom' as opposed to 'stagnation, retrogression, and the round dance'.[14] It nevertheless supplies the rationale for a quite exclusive set of national discriminations.

Most important for Fichte is that the evolution of an original language is seen as reconcilable with its remaining 'nature's one, same, living power of speech', developing, in a manner reminiscent of Coleridge's philosophical method, in 'a continuous transition without a leap'.[15] That reminiscence is no accident, for Fichte is concerned to demonstrate the continuity between philosophical concepts and the sensuous base of the language as a life-giving interchange between the sensuous designation and supersensuous 'extended use of the sign', between perception and the conceptual metaphors that arise from and return on it through 'another, direct, and living relation to his sensuous instrument'.[16] Fichte's insistence on the *living* nature of an original language is bound up in a reversible analogy between the 'immediate' relations of body to spirit, perception to apperception, and those between the sensuous and supersensuous elements of the language.[17] The entry of the arbitrary into the language thus attaints the very life of the language. A similar analogy applies to the relation of the language to the nation, the former becoming the spirit, the latter the body. 'Foreign' influence thus becomes an encroachment of death into the spirit, and the foreign qualities of the French nation are represented not only in the mechanical forms of their bureaucracy, but in the very fact of their dependence on a 'dead' language and on the philosophy that arises therefrom, of 'fixed forms' and 'alienation from originality'.[18]

The necessity of developing another unifying principle to replace the system of arbitrary monarchy thus involves the sense of a transition from a model of the state as an aggregate of members whose unity is centred on an *arbitrary* monarch (which Fichte would define as a 'dead' form) to the model of a living, evolving body that contains within itself the principle of its own continuing unity just as the body contains a spirit that constantly shapes its 'members' into a living unity. The 'spirit of the nation' can be identified with its language, since that language, in the speech of the individual as in the continuous relations that bind together a linguistic community actually and historically, can be taken to represent ideally the medium through which those unifications are enacted. By the time that Mazzini was writing, in the 1840s and 1850s, it was almost axiomatic that, as Wilhelm von Humboldt had put it in 1822: 'Language is the external manifestation, as it were, of the spirit of a nation. Its language is its spirit and its spirit is its language; one can hardly think of them as sufficiently identical.'[19]

The fundamental problem that an identification of the 'spirit of the nation' with the national language would present for Irish Romantic nationalism is quite apparent. Not only were there already two language communities in Ireland, the Irish and the English, but the former of these, in which it would have been most consistent to locate the defining spirit of the Irish nation, had already ceased by 1800 to be the dominant language of culture or even, for that matter, the principal language of the majority.[20] Thomas Davis, one of the principal members of the Young Ireland group, registered in an article in the *Nation* of 1843 the fact that only 'about half of the people west of a line drawn from Derry to Waterford speak Irish habitually', though it was still common 'in some of the mountain tracts east of that line'.[21] The loss that the decline of Irish involves was expressed by Davis in terms that at once suggest the parallels between Irish and German nationalistic theories and the necessary differences:

The language, which grows up with a people, is conformed to their organs, descriptive of their climate, constitution, and manners, mingled inseparably with their history and their soil, fitted beyond any other language to express their prevalent thoughts in the most natural and efficient way.

To impose another language on such a people is to send their history adrift among the accidents of translation – 'tis to tear their identity from all places – 'tis to substitute arbitrary signs for picturesque and suggestive names – 'tis to cut off the entail of feeling, and separate the people from their forefathers by a deep gulf – 'tis to corrupt their very organs, and abridge their power of expression.[22]

The burden of Davis's article is an exhortation to the middle classes in particular (for whom, he claims, it was 'a sign of vulgarity to learn Irish') to relearn their native language. What German nationalists feared in prospect – the increasing contamination of their national language by that of a politically and commercially more powerful nation – had in Ireland already occurred, virtually irreversibly. The power of Davis's rhetoric at this juncture registers the multiple deterritorializations that, he is aware, afflict the nationalist intellectual all the more consciously than the middle-class merchant who willingly abandons the Gaelic language for the commerically more functional English. Already by virtue of class and education, the nationalist is contaminated by the English language and culture. He is triply dislocated in his own nation: his language is no longer fitted to the land to which his identity would be bound; the signs that he receives in place of the fitting names are arbitrary, devoid, like the commodities which flood the economy, of any natural relation to Irish ground; and in consequence, he is cut off from any lived relation to the history and traditions of the nation. Perhaps most significantly, given the political aims of nationalism, he is deprived of voice at the same moment that he ceases to be 'representative' of the Irish people: his 'power of expression' is 'abridged'. Whether 'set adrift among the accidents of translation' or occupied in the business of relearning a lost, or, as in many cases, never-possessed tongue, the Irish nationalist is in the position of Fichte's 'foreigner', dependent on the dead letter of history rather than that continuous correspondence with the past which the 'living stream' of an original language provides.

The loss of the national language is one aspect of, and may stand as symbolic of, a whole set of discontinuities that cut the Irish people off from the 'entail of feeling'. The actual disunity of the nation, which permits England to oppress it, is replicated in the ignorance of the Irish concerning their own past as well as their present: 'For centuries the Irish were paupers and serfs, because they were ignorant and divided.'[23] Faced with ignorance and division and with the necessity of looking to history for the establishment of his identity, the Irish nationalist – in a move that replicates that of the conservative on the opposite wing – has deliberate recourse to history and to research to furnish both the image and the very process of unification. Where the German nationalist's identity is guaranteed by his language, revitalized by the philological tracing of the sensuous origins of his super-sensuous ideas, the Irish nationalist revitalizes a relation to history that might have represented only death and division, finding in it both the lesson and the promise of unity. Charles Gavan Duffy summed the case up retrospectively: 'Rightly understood, the history of Ireland abounded in noble lessons, and had the unity and purpose of an epic poem. . . . The true lesson they [the national annals] taught was that Irishmen were enslaved because they were divided.'[24]

The notion of a continuity that has only to be sought to become live underlies Duffy's conception of history as a mere lifting of the veil from the past. The counterpart to that assertion of the continuity which research restores is an education through which the people are to be restored to their past. The slogan that formed the banner above the *Nation*'s leaders each week perfectly encapsulated the complex of ideas that the organic metaphor is able to hold together: 'To create and foster public opinion in Ireland and make it racy of the soil.' The concept of the Irish *race* is thus to be grafted to its *roots* in sensuous contact with the land, through which it imbibes the particular *taste* of its spirit. And if the ambition of the nationalist is to create nationalist opinion, he will achieve it as a re-creation, fostering the seed that is an *a priori* presence in the soil of Ireland.

This belief in the possibility of forging through research of whatever kind the unity of the nation, historically and politically, points to the curious formal coherence between nationalist and unionist thinking. The reasons for that coherence are perhaps already apparent: quite as much as the unionists, the middle-class Young Irelanders lacked, in consequence of the historical conditions of their existence, any 'organic' connections (to borrow Gramsci's formulation) with the people in whose name they claimed to speak. In consequence, both parties invoke an alternative concept of organicism that rewrites actual discontinuity as merely a moment in the continuously evolving narrative of the Empire or the nation. Ironically, their mutual preoccupation with historical research aims to transcend the effects of that history, and their politics becomes in turn most ideologically effective where it seeks to belie actual political differences. Such a move was required if either party were to claim to speak in the name of an integrated Ireland, since the very existence of each was in effect the product of the social and cultural fragmentation induced by imperialism. The subsequent course of Irish history leaves little doubt that their thinking was instrumental in forging a modern Irish 'national consciousness'. What remains to be seen, however, is the extent to which, necessarily, that consciousness was *ethically* and *aesthetically* constituted at the expense of historical political consciousness and at the cost of denying the full subjective and cultural dislocations undergone by a colonized people.

THE ETHICS AND AESTHETICS OF NATIONALISM

Despite all the *Nation's* efforts to 'create and foster' popular unity in Ireland in the 1840s, the rebellion of 1848 was abortive, which only demonstrated once again the total lack of unity in Ireland and the total failure of the Young Irelanders to achieve popular support. But contemporary and modern criticisms of this failure and of the general ignorance of the Young Irelanders of the Irish language, which is intimately bound up in that failure, themselves fail to observe that it is precisely on a sense of separation that nationalism is founded.[25] The isolation of the Young Irelanders with regard to the Irish people repeats the discontinuities in Irish history and political life that bring about the constitutive drive of nationalism toward the production of images of unity. The instinctive distaste of the bourgeois for the civil disorder represented by the sporadic and loosely organized tactics of the Ribbonmen terrorist groups – 'the most important underlying fact of Irish internal history up to the days of the Fenians and the Land League', according to at least one historian[26] – finds its ideological rationale in the double meaning of the notion of principle which supports the ideal of union. If on the one hand the notion can be defined in terms of the first and formative principles of Romantic epistemology, it has on the other hand a set of ethical implications, which tend in the end to ossify into 'fixed moral principles'. The appeal to the concept of growth as opposed to cultivation in the moral sphere is an apt indication of the intimate linking of moral and formative notions of principle at the heart of nationalist thinking, a linking which becomes more important the further the nationalist is perceived to be isolated in his society. For that linking of the two senses of principle enables an account of the relation of the individual to society that can be theorized in terms of union rather than antagonism:

> Dis-union was the fixed character of their [Gaelic] nationality, made up of a cluster of clans. It is the evil which appertains to all localism, like a cholera house beyond the gates of a city. Centralization in great crises, is more favourable to union than localism; but union in its keeping degenerates into uniformity, and thence to slavery. It is the problem of the human race to reconcile individual liberty and association; a problem which all nations think they have solved at some period of their history, our own among the rest.[27]

Morality thus enters the nationalist ideology as an ethical injunction where it is conceived that the freedom and full identity of the individual are achieved only when he is immersed in the greater life that is the nation. The problem of democratic nationalism is, as Mazzini argued in terms reminiscent of the *Nation* writer just quoted, 'to find a centre for all the many interests' and 'to prevent the clash of individualities'. Its exponents are accordingly 'driven to the sphere of *principles*',[28] to an education that will cultivate in the individual those moral principles that are the repetition in the finite individual of the eternal principles of the divine essence of life, or, on yet another level, a repetition in the individual of the national spirit, which in himself he represents. The whole man, the man of integrity, becomes thus the man who is integrated with and reproduces the spirit of his nation.

Robert Emmet's famous appeal for the suspension of his epitaph until his country 'takes her place among the nations of the earth' stands as the classic statement of the Romantic Irish nationalist insofar as the question of the individual's true meaning is bound up with the nation's assumption of its own identity and both are cast in the future tense.[29] It is exactly in becoming – in the strictly Coleridgean sense of the term – a *symbol*, which 'while it enunciates the whole, abides itself as a living part of the Unity, of which it is the representative',[30] that the martyr is transformed simultaneously into a 'confessor': by his absolute identity with the fullness of meaning that the spiritual nation embodies he invokes the realization of that identity by the members of a nation that is yet to be. If such a demand necessarily involves what is in political terms a potentially disastrous process of 'ironing out the contradictions and inconsistencies for which the present tense would furnish all too much evidence',[31] such a sacrificing of the real in the name of the ideal is exactly what characterizes the ideology of nationalism, seeking in its past the original principles for the form of the nation's future evolution.

In such a manner the self-appointed martyrs of nationalism participate in that process by which 'the future shall realize the promise of the past', their actual present becoming a mere parenthesis whose meaning is given and assimilated by the origin and goal of the nation. Through his association in the continual labour of creating the nation to which he is bound and called, the nationalist transcends the potentially divisive effects of his presence as an individual subject and re-enters the continuous stream which, we have seen, provides Romantic thought with the analogy by which it can produce a method that is unifying in effect at all its stages. History accordingly ceases to be political insofar as it ceases to register struggle and conflict and becomes a process that produces a unity that transcends actual division. The spirit of the nation, hypostatized against the alienation of a middle-class intelligentsia, theoretically encompasses all classes insofar as it is always identical to itself. Anti-progressive in its ethical and economic prescriptions for Ireland as it perhaps had to be, Young Ireland's ideology appears even more profoundly conservative when compared with the quite similar postulates of racial identity issuing from its unionist contemporaries. That conservatism is prescribed by the aestheticization of history and politics, which rapidly comes to supply the pivot of nationalist thinking. Culture comes to represent the site of unity elsewhere denied by historical facts.

The figure of the martyr, his identity totally immersed in the spirit of the nation, forms the ideal paradigm of the individual's relation to the nation. But what the martyrs provide are only the moments of intensity, the 'burning symbols', to use Pearse's expression, in which the national spirit is most clearly manifested. In the absence of a constitutional incarnation of that spirit, the continuity that links those moments must be supplied from elsewhere. Literature in the broadest sense is already devoted to rememoration as the medium through which a knowledge of the past of the nation is conveyed and preserved for future restoration. More than that, its instrumental function as the medium of the spiritual nation comes to establish literature as the very form of the national constitution:

> One of the grand social bonds which England – in fact, every other nation but ours – possesses, is the existence of some *institution* or *idea* towards the completion of which all have toiled in common, which comprehends all, and renders them respectable in each other's eyes. Thus her *history* knits together all ranks and sects in England. . . . Each has erected a story of the constitution. They value each other, and acknowledge a connection. There are bright spots in our history; but of how few is the story common! and the contemplation of it, *as a whole*, does not tend to harmony, unless the conviction of past error produces wisdom for the future. We have no

institution or idea that has been produced by all. We must look to the present or future for the foundation of concord and nationality. We must set ourselves to erect some such institution or idea. A national literature is in its very essence amalgamating, and may eventually become the great temple of concord.[32]

In this sense 'literature is practical ... and the writer is a man of action',[33] participating in the construction of the nation within which he will be 'comprehended'. The mutual interdependence of writer and nation in nationalist theory was succinctly expressed by the *Nation* critic D. F. McCarthy: 'A great literature ... was either the creation or the creator of a great people.'[34] The ambivalence of that formulation indicates exactly the problem with which the Irish nationalist is confronted when appealing to literature as a national institution. If the function of literature is to form and unite a people not yet in existence, how will a writer of sufficient stature arise, given that it is from the people he must arise if he is to express the spirit of the nation?

The problem is one that has in various ways confronted all nation-states on their assumption of a distinct identity and that has been resolved theoretically in equally various ways. The most apposite parallel to the Irish context would be the deliberate attempts in Germany to construct a literary language through the combined efforts of translation from other languages and research into medieval Germanic poetry in a tradition that stretches from Luther's translation of the Bible to the researches of scholars such as Karl Simrock and the brothers Grimm in the nineteenth century.[35] Allusion to the German tradition, however, reminds one forcibly of the 'anomaly' of the Irish situation, in which the virtual loss of the Irish language causes a twofold break in the continuity of that process. In the first place, simple ignorance of Gaelic tradition permitted the assumption – rooted in centuries of indifference on the part of the English-speaking community – that that tradition could not itself constitute a national literature, that it was too primitive and unsophisticated to do so. 'There are', remarks Thomas Davis with something of the tone of a mason assessing the monumental work to be performed, 'great gaps in Irish song to be filled up', gaps which he attributes to 'ignorance, disorder, and every kind of oppression'.[36] In the second place, even the use of the rubble of Gaelic tradition for the foundations of the institution of national literature will have to be permitted by research and translation. Unlike the German nationalist, who can conceive translation of foreign material to be assimilation and research to be revivifying, the Irish nationalist's work of research and translation is determined by a gap and is involved in an assimilation of the native to the foreign, Irish into English, thus incurring the risk of being 'set adrift among the accidents of translation'.

The theoretical resolution of these difficulties entails an almost exact repetition of the forms of the nationalist recourse to history, elaborated this time in the idea of the 'ballad'. If the national literature is to be 'the very flowering of the soul' of the nation,[37] rather than an institution arbitrarily imposed upon it, it will, like the nationalist himself, need to be made 'racy of the soil' and absorb the spirit of the people. That spirit is to be found in the ballad. By the time D. F. McCarthy had assembled his *Book of Irish Ballads* in 1846, the idea that ballads represented the original and primitive poetry of a people was a critical commonplace. McCarthy's introduction to the anthology, however, recasts this notion in order to appropriate it to specifically Irish concerns. His belief that 'Hesiod and Homer built their beautiful and majestic structures on the original ballads that were probably floating among the people' leads him to a formulation of the need for a ballad poetry in Ireland to form the basis of a literature that, deriving from such ballads, will be equally filled with the 'distinct character and peculiar charm' of Irish genius.[38] What is of most importance to McCarthy is the belief that contact with the Irish spirit, which a knowledge of ballads provides, will give back a distinctive character to an Irish literature which must perforce be written in English:

> To those among us, and to the generations who are yet to be among us, whose mother tongue is, and of necessity must be, the English and not the Irish, the establishing of this fact is of the utmost importance, and of the greatest consolation: – that we can be thoroughly Irish in our writings without ceasing to be English; that we can be faithful to the land of our birth without being unfaithful to that literature which has been 'the nursing mother of our minds', that we can develop the intellectual resources of our country, and establish for ourselves a distinct and separate existence in the world of letters, without depriving ourselves of the widely-diffused and genius-consecrated language of England, are facts that I conceive cannot be too widely disseminated.[39]

Thus through a thorough knowledge of the *spirit* of the Irish ballad, translation in the widest sense becomes assimilation, and the language which might have been the badge of conquest is reinfused as a national as well as an individual 'mother tongue'.

A parallel argument in an anonymous *Nation* article on Barrett Browning and Tennyson clarifies even further the historical principles involved and the kind of demands made on the Irish writer by the nationalist. Lamenting the fact that 'the healthy growth of an Irish literature' has been 'thwarted and impeded' by English domination, the writer continues with a sketch of the ideal evolution of a literature:

The different stages of social development have their distinct characters written in the development of mind. First there is the ballad, simple, direct, and unadorned; then lyric poetry, the epic, the drama, history, philosophy, each growing naturally out of the other. So are all great national literatures built; . . . so must it be here, if we are ever to have a literature of our own.[40]

This being the natural course of development, the very fact that English literature is 'the nursing mother of our minds' constitutes an impediment to a healthy growth, introducing the refinements of a fully developed national literature to force the growth of a plant whose first shoots are scarcely apparent. The remedy is already familiar:

The philosophical tone of a high civilization does not suit us; we have our history to make, and our writings must help us make it. We want strength, earnestness, passion, the song and ballad, all that fires and nerves the minds of men. Perfection in this is to be attained, not by studying English co[n]temporary poets, but by becoming saturated as it were with Irish feeling, by learning the Irish language, sympathizing in every beat of an Irish peasant's pulse, by being filled with knowledge of Ireland's past and of boundless hope in her future.[41]

Once again the nationalist is called to identify totally with the nation, evacuating himself of the subjectivism of an English civilization in order to be 'saturated' and 'filled' with the Irish spirit, his present only part of an unbroken arc stretching from past to future. That spiritual identification serves to conceal – or to suture, as one's point of view may be – the gap that drives one artificially to 'make' a history, whether national or literary.

The demand made by *Nation* writers such as Davis and McCarthy for the full-scale production of ballad poetry is not, then, simply a call to the work of propaganda through direct statement and appeal, a kind of 'poster art', as Padraic Fallon has suggested. This aim might have been most effectively attained through precisely the sort of street ballad that the *Nation* writers despised as an Anglo-Gaelic hybrid.[42] Far more important than the present for the nationalist is the future, and in calling the Irish to the labour of ballad writing, the Young Irelander is looking to lay the foundations of a national literature that is yet to be. The lack of individuality in the ballads published in the nationalist journals, and reprinted in the enormously successful anthology entitled deliberately *The Spirit of the Nation*, is thus a part of the programme rather than a failing.[43] Total immersion of the writer's identity in that of the nation was seen as the first condition of a process that sought to fabricate a foreshortened literary history in which the development that had hitherto been thwarted might speedily be made up. For if, in the first stage of that missed development, the ballad would have been the anonymous voice of the people, in the attempt to forge the trace of a never-existent literary history an *impersonal* balladry becomes the necessary first step. The spirit of the nation may thus manifest itself uncontaminated by a subjectivism which would be the mark of English civilization and be kept pure for future emergence in a fuller growth of the literary tradition. And, implicitly, the more intense the production of ballads, the more rapidly can the gaps be filled in and this primitive or 'minor' stage be transcended.

Accordingly, the programme of Young Ireland comes to replicate the very aesthetic history that legitimates the subordination of the Celtic races. The absence of a 'fully formed' literature becomes the index of a low level of historical development in both the political and the cultural sphere, while the production of a literature that will mediate the image of transcendental Irish unity becomes the remedy for the political divisions consequent on underdevelopment. That literature, which projects a transcendent space of quite literal reconciliation, is envisaged as attaining mediating power by its capacity to replicate the original identity of the Irish race. In turn, that capacity depends upon insisting that the nationalist writer be totally identified, as an individual, with the spirit of the nation, which lacks any other form of representation. Thus what is, for a nation with a political state constituted independently of its cultural identity, merely a means to legitimation becomes in the context of nationalism an instrument of political action. In consequence, the political instrumentality of the aesthetic sphere, which is dissembled by its major theorists, is highlighted by a nationalism that otherwise accepts the logic of the forms of thought that legitimate domination. It is the failing of Irish nationalism never to have questioned the idealism of identity thinking, which, even in its resistance to imperialism, links it closely to imperialist ideology. If an explanation for this phenomenon is required, it may be found in the fact that Irish nationalism, in its early theory as in its later practices, has always sought to be an instrument of bourgeois hegemony.

Summaries and Notes

1. CLAIRE CONNOLLY, INTRODUCTION: IRELAND IN THEORY

1. Éilís Ní Dhuibhne, *The Dancers Dancing* (Dublin, 1999), p. 1.
2. Ibid., pp. 2–3.
3. Jim Smyth, 'Introduction: the 1798 Rebellion in its Eighteenth-Century Contexts', in Jim Smyth (ed.), *Revolution, Counter-Revolution and Union: Ireland in the 1790s* (Cambridge, 2000), pp. 1–20 (p. 18).
4. For a chronology and interpretation see Linda Connolly, *The Irish Women's Movement* (Basingstoke, 2001).
5. See Chrystel Hug, *The Politics of Sexual Morality in Ireland* (Basingstoke, 1999).
6. *Irelantis: Paper Collages by Seán Hillen* (Dublin, 1999). See www.irelantis.com – the official Irelantis website; and www.seanhillen.com for other instances of the artist's work.
7. Rosita Boland, 'Hillen's Hinde-sight', *The Irish Times*, 9 October 1999.
8. Lance Pettitt, *Screening Ireland: Film and Television Representation* (Manchester, 2000), p. 65.
9. See essay 6 in this Reader; also Luke Gibbons, 'Romanticism, Realism, and Irish Cinema', in Kevin Rockett, Luke Gibbons and John Hill (eds), *Cinema and Ireland* (London and Sydney, 1987), pp. 194–257 (p. 200).
10. Luke Clancy, 'Constructing Ireland', *The Irish Times*, 13 January 1998.
11. For analyses see Luke Gibbons, 'Synge, Country and Western: The Myth of the West in Irish and American Culture', in *Transformations in Irish Culture* (Cork, 1996), pp. 23–36; Shaun Richards, 'Breaking the "Cracked Mirror": Binary Oppositions in the Culture of Contemporary Ireland', in Colin Graham and Richard Kirkland (eds), *Ireland and Cultural Theory: The Mechanics of Authenticity* (Basingstoke, 1999), pp. 99–118.
12. Ní Dhuibhne, *The Dancers Dancing*, p. 6
13. James Joyce, 'The Dead', *Dubliners*, ed. Jeri Johnson (Oxford, 2000), p. 148.
14. Joyce, 'The Dead', p. 149
15. Fintan O'Toole, 'Introducing Irelantis', *Irelantis: Paper Collages by Seán Hillen* (Dublin, 1999), p. 4.
16. Kya de Longchamps, Review of *Irelantis, The Irish Examiner*, 13 November 1999.
17. Conn O'Donovan, Review of *Irelantis, CIRCA*, 91 (2000), 49–51.
18. Jean Baudrillard, *Simulations*, trans. Paul Foss, Paul Patton and Philip Beitchman (New York, 1983), p. 12.
19. Ibid., p. 12.
20. Martin McDonagh, *Plays 1: A Skull in Connemara* (London, 1999), p. 67.

173

21. Graham Linehan and Arthur Matthews, 'Grant Unto Him Eternal Rest', *Father Ted: The Complete Scripts* (London, 1999), p. 90.

2. SEAMUS DEANE, 'HEROIC STYLES: THE TRADITION OF AN IDEA'

(From *Ireland's Field Day* [London, 1985], pp. 45–58.)

Summary

This essay can be read as one of the inaugurating moments of the Field Day project. Field Day originated as a theatre group in Derry in the 1980s. Its directors (who included Brian Friel, Seamus Heaney and Tom Paulin, as well as Deane himself) wished to find cultural forms adequate to the crisis in Northern Ireland. They issued pamphlets such as this one, first published in 1984. Deane identifies 'romantic' and 'realist' ways of reading Ireland, approaches which he links with W. B. Yeats and James Joyce respectively. Arguing that both procedures are stymied when faced with the seemingly intractable violence in the North of Ireland, Deane calls for a move beyond these 'hot' and 'cold' rhetorics. The essay is pioneering in its close attention to the style in which debates about Ireland were conducted.

Notes

1. The phrase is from the penultimate sentence of *Castle Rackrent* (1800):

   It is a problem difficult of solution to determine, whether an Union will hasten or retard the amelioration of this country. The few gentlemen of education who now reside in this country will resort to England: they are few, but they are in nothing inferior to men of the same rank in Great Britain. The best that can happen will be the introduction of British manufacturers in their places.

   On Maria Edgeworth's reluctance to accept fully the idea of an Irish Catholic gentleman, see the comments by Stephen Gwynn in *Irish Literature and Drama in the English Language: A Short History* (London, 1936), pp. 54–6.
2. James Joyce, *The Critical Writings*, ed. E. Mason and R. Ellmann (New York, 1964), pp. 204–5.
3. Ibid., pp. 162–3.
4. Ibid., p. 198. On his use of this incident in *Finnegans Wake*, see John Garvin, *James Joyce's Disunited Kingdom and the Irish Dimension* (Dublin, 1976), pp. 163–9.
5. Joyce, *Critical Writings*, p. 221.
6. Ibid., p. 157.
7. The *Athenaeum*, 4 July 1919, p. 552.

3. ANGELA BOURKE, 'THE VIRTUAL REALITY OF IRISH FAIRY LEGEND'

(From *Éire-Ireland*, 36 [1991], 7–25.)

Summary

A rereading of fairy legend that develops a distinctive theory of oral tradition in its changing cultural contexts. Situating story-telling within historical, comparative and critical frameworks, the essay undoes any opposition between 'tradition' and 'modernity' by depicting a cultural form that exists in dynamic relation to technological innovations. Bourke finds in virtual reality a fitting contemporary model for understanding fairy legend.

Notes

1. An earlier version of this paper was delivered as the 1996 Vernam Hull Memorial Lecture at Harvard University. I am grateful to Harvard's Department of Celtic Languages and Literatures for the invitation, and to Professor Art Cosgrove, President, University College Dublin, for a discretionary research grant which enabled me to prepare it for publication.
2. The best collection of transcribed and translated Irish-language texts is Seán Ó hEochaidh, Máire Mac Néill and Séamas Ó Catháin, *Síscéalta ó Thír Chonaill/ Fairy Legends from Donegal* (Dublin, 1977). For discussion see Peter Narváez (ed.), *The Good People: New Fairylore Essays* (New York, 1991), esp. (for the English-language tradition), Patricia Lysaght, 'Fairylore from the Midlands of Ireland' in Narváez (ed.), *The Good People: New Fairylore Essays*, pp. 22–46. Closely similar traditions are found in Scotland: clergyman Robert Kirk's *The Secret Common-Wealth of Elves, Fauns and Fairies* was written more than 300 years ago; Walter Scott, *The Minstrelsy of the Scottish Border* (London, 1869), includes an essay, 'On the Fairies of Popular Superstition' (*The Minstrelsy of the Scottish Border*, pp. 439–73), and the periodical *Tocher* contains many modern examples. For North American reflexes see Barbara Rieti, *Strange Terrain: The Fairy World in Newfoundland* (St John's, Canada, 1991).
3. For the use of Basil Bernstein's work on linguistic codes in cultural analysis see Mary Douglas, *Natural Symbols: Explorations in Cosmology* [1970] (Harmondsworth, 1973), pp. 41–8 and passim; Walter Ong, *Orality and Literacy: The Technologizing of the Word* (London, 1982), p. 106; Robert Wuthnow, *Meaning and Moral Order: Explorations in Cultural Analysis* (Berkeley, CA, 1987), pp. 190–1, 205.
4. 'The fairy tales were a matter of entertainment. And I think again it was really to scare young people...' Peter Flanagan, Co. Fermanagh, 1977, quoted in Henry Glassie (ed.), *The Penguin Book of Irish Folktales* (London, 1985), p. 166.
5. Angela Bourke, 'Reading A Woman's Death: Colonial Text and Oral Tradition in Nineteenth-Century Ireland', *Feminist Studies*, 21, 3 (Fall 1995), 553–86 (p. 583); cf. Luke Gibbons, *Transformations in Irish Culture* (Cork, 1996), pp. 153–5.
6. James H. Delargy, *The Gaelic Story-teller* (Chicago, 1969; from *Proc. Brit. Acad.*, 31 [1945], 177–221), pp. 6–7.
7. Quoted in James H. Delargy, Editorial note, *Béaloideas*, 4 (1933–4), 87.
8. See Bo Almqvist, 'Irish Migratory Legends on the Supernatural: Sources, Studies and Problems', *Béaloideas*, 59 (1991), 1–43.
9. Frank Kinahan, *Yeats, Folklore, and Occultism: Contexts of the Early Work and Thought* (Boston, 1988), pp. 41–84.
10. Angela Bourke, 'Fairies and Anorexia: Nuala Ní Dhomhnaill's "Amazing Grass"', *Proceedings of the Harvard Celtic Colloquium*, XIII (1993) [1995],

25–38; Angela Bourke, 'Silence in Two Languages: Nuala Ní Dhomhnaill and the Unspeakable' unpublished keynote lecture, Seventh Annual Graduate Irish Studies Conference, 'Briseadh Amach / Breaking the Hermeneutic Seal', Boston College and Harvard University, 19 March 1993.

11. Narváez (ed.), *The Good People: New Fairylore Essays*, pp. 336, 360–1; Angela Bourke, 'Hunting out the Fairies: E. F. Benson, Oscar Wilde, and the Burning of Bridget Cleary' in Jerusha Hull McCormack (ed.), *Wilde the Irishman* (New Haven, CT, 1998). The expressions 'in the fairies' and 'away with the fairies' can be used as euphemisms for a wide range of refusals or failures to conform to prescribed norms. My essay, 'Hunting out the Fairies', traces analogies between the Oscar Wilde scandal of 1895 and the contemporary case of Bridget Cleary, burned to death in County Tipperary as a fairy changeling. [See Bourke's book *The Burning of Bridget Cleary* (London, 1999).]

12. Henry Glassie, *Passing the Time in Ballymenone: Culture and History of an Ulster Community* (Philadelphia, 1982), p. 546.

13. See, for example, ibid., p. 151.

14. Séamas Ó Catháin (coll., ed. and trans.), *Scéalta Chois Cladaigh / Stories of Sea and Shore* (Dublin, 1983), pp. 51–2; 54–5.

15. Lysaght, 'Fairylore from the Midlands of Ireland', pp. 36–8; Rieti, *Strange Terrain: The Fairy World in Newfoundland*, pp. 2, 104.

16. Sean O'Sullivan, *Legends from Ireland* (London, 1977).

17. Ibid., pp. 64–6, recorded 22 September 1938 in Carna, Co. Galway, from Éamon a Búrc, then aged 72.

18. Rieti, *Strange Terrain: The Fairy World in Newfoundland*, pp. 15–19.

19. Jan Brunvand, *The Vanishing Hitchhiker: American Urban Legends and their Meanings* (New York, 1981), p. 26.

20. See, for example, Declan Kiberd, *Inventing Ireland: The Literature of the Modern Nation* (London, 1995), p. 2.

21. Yi-Fu Tuan, *Space and Place: The Perspective of Experience* (Minneapolis, 1977), p. 6.

22. Ong, *Orality and Literacy: The Technologizing of the Word*, p. 34.

23. For protective codes in folk culture, see Joan N. Radner (ed.), *Feminist Messages: Coding in Women's Folk Culture* (Chicago, 1993).

24. See Albert B. Lord, *The Singer of Tales* (Cambridge, MA, 1960).

25. Conrad Arensberg, *The Irish Countryman* (Garden City, NY, 1968 [1937]), pp. 166, 188.

26. Mary Douglas, *Purity and Danger: An Analysis of Concepts of Pollution and Taboo* (Harmondsworth, 1970 [1966]).

27. Robert Wuthnow, *Meaning and Moral Order: Explorations in Cultural Analysis* (Berkeley, CA, 1987), p. 70.

28. See Gearóid Ó Crualaoich, 'The Primacy of Form: A "Folk Ideology" in De Valera's Politics' in John P. Caroll and John A. Murphy (eds), *De Valera and His Times* (Cork, 1983), pp. 47–61 (pp. 48, 50).

29. American greeting-cards for St Patrick's Day are a case in point, and the use of Ireland, rather than the Deep South, as setting for the sequel to *Gone With the Wind* is perhaps another. The same thinking may also explain what is to me the breathtakingly offensive chapter title, 'The Bog Irish' in Mary Douglas's otherwise admirable and elegant *Natural Symbols: Explorations in Cosmology* (Harmondsworth, 1973 [1970]).

30. See, for example, Jim McLaughlin, *Travellers and Ireland: Whose History? Whose Country?* (Cork, 1995).

31. Ó Crualaoich, 'The Primacy of Form: A "Folk Ideology" in De Valera's Politics' in Caroll and Murphy (eds), *De Valera and His Times*, pp. 47–61 (pp. 48, 50); Diarmuid Ó Giolláin, 'An Béaloideas agus an Stát', *Béaloideas*, 57 (1989) 151–63.
32. Bourke, 'Reading A Woman's Death: Colonial Text and Oral Tradition in Nineteenth-Century Ireland'.
33. Claude Lévi-Strauss, *The Savage Mind (La Pensée Sauvage)* (London, 1966 [1962]), p. 3.
34. Ibid., p. 9.
35. B. Toelken, *The Dynamics of Folklore* (Boston, 1979), p. 95.
36. Ibid., p. 96.
37. Ong, *Orality and Literacy: The Technologizing of the Word*, p. 33.
38. See Lord, *The Singer of Tales*, pp. 124–38; Ong, *Orality and Literacy: The Technologizing of the Word*, pp. 31–6.
39. Delargy, *The Gaelic Story-teller*, p. 10.
40. The *Fontana Dictionary of Modern Thought*, published in 1977, shows how far we have moved, counselling that 'the neutral term *store* is to be preferred to *memory* to avoid the danger of anthropomorphizing computers' (p. 603). Rather than turning our computers into people, however, we have tended during this period, as social satirists keep telling us, to turn ourselves into machines.
41. Frances A. Yates, *The Art of Memory* (Chicago and London, 1966).
42. Lord, *The Singer of Tales*, pp. 3, 279.
43. Ong, *Orality and Literacy: The Technologizing of the Word*, pp. 135–8.
44. Angela Partridge, *Caoineadh na dTrí Muire: Téama na Páise i bhFilíocht Bhéil na Gaeilge* (Dublin, 1983) pp. 140–2; cf. Fintan Vallely, 'The Bucks of Montrose', *Graph*, Second series, Issue 1 (1995), 42–51.
45. Wlad Godzich, *The Culture of Literacy* (Cambridge, MA, 1994), p. 11.
46. In Walter Benjamin, *Illuminations*, ed. and introd. Hannah Arendt (New York, 1968), p. 83.
47. Dónal Ó Drisceoil, *Censorship in Ireland, 1939–1945: Neutrality, Politics and Society* (Cork, 1996).
48. Peadar Ó Ceannabháin (ed.), *Éamon a Búrc: Scéalta* (Dublin, 1983), p. 17.
49. Paul Theroux shows this contrast vividly in a series of train-travel books, notably *The Great Railway Bazaar* (1975).
50. See, for example, Wolfgang Schivelbusch's *The Railway Journey: The Industrialization of Time and Space in the 19th Century* (Berkeley, CA, 1987), p. 189, for a discussion of how railroad travel affected reading and verbal exchange in the nineteenth century.
51. Cormac Ó Gráda, *Ireland: A New Economic History 1780–1939* (Oxford, 1994), pp. 240–1.
52. Ó Gráda, *Ireland: A New Economic History 1780–1939*, p. 241.
53. Bourke, 'Reading A Woman's Death: Colonial Text and Oral Tradition in Nineteenth-Century Ireland'.
54. Godzich, *The Culture of Literacy*.
55. Ó Ceannabháin (ed.), *Éamon a Búrc: Scéalta*, p. 17, and personal communication with the author. Ó Ceannabháin mentions the storyteller's absorbed interest in the radio news in 1938, when radios were still relatively rare in the west of Ireland.
56. Ó Ceannabháin (ed.), *Éamon a Búrc: Scéalta*, pp. 25–8.
57. Liam Mac Coisdeala, 'In Memoriam. Éamonn (Liam) a Búrc (Aill na Brón, Cárna, Co. na Gaillimhe)', *Béaloideas*, 12 (1942), 210–14; Liam Mac Coisdeala, 'Im' Bhailitheoir Béaloideasa', *Béaloideas*, 16 (1946), 141–71. Liam Mac Coisdeala

died, aged 89, on 10 April 1996 as this paper was being written. *Ar dheis Dé go raibh a anam*.

58. Kevin O'Nolan (ed. and trans.), *Eochair, Mac Rí in Éireann / Eochair, A King's Son in Ireland* (Dublin, 1982); cf. Delargy, *The Gaelic Story-teller*, p. 16.
59. Bourke, 'Fairies and Anorexia: Nuala Ní Dhomhnaill's "Amazing Grass"'.
60. Anglea Bourke, ' "The Fisherman and the Fairy Boat" / "An tIascaire agus an Bád Sí": Temptation and Fidelity in Éamon a Búrc's Sea-Stories', in Séamas Ó Catháin, Dáithí Ó hÓgáin and Patricia Lysaght (eds), *Islanders and Water-Dwellers: Folk Narrative and Folk Belief in the Celtic-Nordic-Baltic Area* (Dublin, 1999).

4. PATRICIA COUGHLAN, ' "BOG QUEENS": THE REPRESENTATION OF WOMEN IN THE POETRY OF JOHN MONTAGUE AND SEAMUS HEANEY'

(From *Gender in Irish Writing*, ed. Toni O'Brien Johnson and David Cairns [Milton Keynes and Philadelphia 1991], pp. 88–111.)

Summary

Written in the early 1990s in response to the figuration of the feminine in the writing of two of Ireland's most celebrated poets, Seamus Heaney and John Montague. Coughlan contends that, rather than simply celebrating the feminine (variously inscribed as muse, mother, territory, nation), the poems fix certain damaging stereotypes in place. That this then enables a dynamic interrogation of Irishness or of political identity does not lessen the debilitating effect of the poems and their regressive sexual politics.

Notes

1. For the debate in feminist anthropology on the applicability of the nature–culture opposition to gender, see Sherry Ortner, 'Is Female to Male as Nature is to Culture?', in M. Rosaldo and L. Lamphere (eds), *Woman, Culture and Society* (Stanford, CA, 1974), pp. 67–88; Penelope Brown and Lydia Jordanova, 'Oppressive Dichotomies: the Nature–Culture Debate', in Cambridge Women's Studies Group (eds), *Women in Society* (London, 1981), pp. 224–41; Carol MacCormack and Marilyn Strathern (eds), *Nature, Culture and Gender* (Cambridge, 1980); and Shirley Ardener (ed.), *Perceiving Women* (London, 1975). On the limitation of woman to domesticity, see Patricia Jagentowicz Mills, *Women, Nature and Psyche* (New Haven, CT and London, 1987); and on Freudian Oedipal dogmatism, Luce Irigaray, *Speculum of the Other Woman*, trans. Gillian C. Gill (Ithaca, NY, 1985). More specifically, I have been helped by John Goodby, whom I wish to thank for kindly showing me his research. Trevor Joyce's discussions with me on theoretical issues and his suggestions about drafts of this paper have been invaluable.
2. The phrase in Heaney's poem 'Punishment' (*North*, p. 38) describing the poet as 'artful voyeur' is only an explicit crystallizing of a very general subject-position in his work, as I shall try to show. Laura Mulvey's classic discussion of the male gaze and the scopic is helpful here ('Visual Pleasure and Narrative Cinema', *Screen*, 16 [1978], 6–18).

3. For baking, see 'Mossbawn 1. Sunlight' (*North*, 8); the ploughing and digging fathers are enlisted in 'Digging' and 'Follower' (*Death of a Naturalist*, 13, 34).

4. This is in contrast with Heaney's deployment of this type, as we shall see. On spousal and maternal versions of Ireland-figures, see Maureen Hawkins (The Dramatic Treatment of Robert Emmet and Sarah Curran', in Seán Gallagher [ed.], *Woman in Irish Legend, Life and Literature* [Gerrards Cross, 1983], pp. 125–36), who finds in the Emmet–Curran plot an instance of the Venus-Adonis or Ishtar-Tammuz myth, in which a son-cum-lover dies seasonally for the Great Goddess who represents natural continuity. See also Clair Wills, 'The Perfect Mother: Authority in the Poetry of Medbh McGuckian', *Text and Context*, 3 (Autumn 1988), 91–111.

5. See J. G. O'Keefe (ed.), *Baile Suibhne* (London, 1913), pp. 61–3, 73–5, 83. I am indebted for useful discussion of this and other Old Irish matters to Máire Herbert.

6. See Alwyn and Brinley Rees, *Celtic Heritage* (London, nd), pp. 73–4; Elliott B. Gose Jr, *The World of the Irish Wonder Tale* (Toronto, 1985), pp. 152–64; and Joseph Campbell, *The Hero with a Thousand Faces* (London, 1975), pp. 103–4. Heaney also mobilizes these associations in his version of old woman and well, 'A Drink of Water' (*Field Work*, p. 16). One ought to point out that in this respect the rewriting of the legendary material is not necessarily faithful to its original: Suibhne's hag of the mill, for instance, has quite a lot to say, and the sovereignty figure in the tale directs operations, in keeping with her divine status, from a position above that of the prince. It might be a mistake to assume that the inherited material itself offers only irremediably disempowering representations of women, however evident such disempowerment is in current masculine *uses* of it.

7. This journey is significantly framed by the haven-like domesticity of the adult poet's marital home, where 'a woman is waiting' (*The Dead Kingdom*, pp. 11, 59, 94, 96).

8. Heaney's sequence 'Clearances' is in a sense also part of this dead-mother literature, with its limitations of caution and distance within the framework of gracefully expressed affection. See, in particular, the endings of poems no. 3 and 4 (*The Haw Lantem*, pp. 27, 28).

9. There is an encyclopaedic mythological literature on this subject, and several recent demystifications of it by feminists. See Mircea Eliade, *Patterns in Comparative Religion* (London, 1958), pp. 418–19, and Campbell, *The Hero*, pp. 102–66, for examples of the former; and Mills, *Women, Nature and Psyche*, pp. 157ff., for some of the latter. There are fairly routine instances of the rendering of the feminine as death-bringer in Montague. In 'O Riada's Farewell' a death-goddess appears in several guises: as 'Miss Death' in evening dress, as a musicianly 'mistress of the bones', and as a wrecker: 'The damp haired / seaweed stained sorceress / marshlight of defeat' (*A Slow Dance*, pp. 59–60). See also his borrowing of Spenser's Mutability goddess: 'dark Lady of Process / our devouring Queen' (*The Dead Kingdom*, pp. 19, 22).

10. The effect is similar to that of some erotic poems in earlier literary tradition, such as Donne's *Elegy XIX*: 'To His Mistress Going to Bed', or *blazon* poems in general. For the general structure of fetishization, see Freud; for an argument linking this with forms of objectivization and dismemberment in colonial discourse, see Homi K. Bhabha, 'The Other Question: Difference, Discrimination and the Discourse of Colonialism', in Francis Barker et al. (eds), *Literature, Politics and Theory* (London, 1986), pp. 148–72.

11. One must point out, however, that John Montague's more recent collection *Mount Eagle* returns dismayingly to the earlier fetishizing perspective in the

voyeuristic 'Sheela na Gig' (p. 31); and when the vocabulary of the earlier well-poems recurs, it is with a far less delicate touch: 'from the spring well / with a brimming bucket; its trembling meniscus, / water's hymen' ('Peninsula', *Mount Eagle* [Oldcastle, Country Meath, 1988], p. 64).

12. See also 'A Meeting', 'Sunset', and 'Waiting' (*The Great Cloak*, pp. 43, 55, 56).

13. Compare 'Harvest' (*Mount Eagle*, p. 43). Heaney also constructs a Ceres-figure, but uses it as an icon of healing fertility in a poem about political murder ('After a killing'; *Field Work* p. 12).

14. See also the following poem, 'Tracks' (*The Great Cloak*, p. 12).

15. See also 'Follower' (*Death of a Naturalist*, p. 24).

16. See Nicholas Roe's argument that this poem reveals what he calls Heaney's 'mythic wish' in an early form. Roe says that the female teacher who explains the natural history of frogs 'appears as external author of guilt – perhaps a sexual awakening –' and represents 'a sort of primary school Eve who bears responsibility for the ... child's lost innocence' ('Wordsworth at the Flax-Dam: An Early Poem by Seamus Heaney', in Michael Allen and Angela Wilcox [eds], *Critical Approaches to Anglo-Irish Literature* [Gerrards Cross, 1989], p. 169).

17. Though, of course, a feminist reader might not be able to avoid giving an ironic *reading* to such a poem: 'I gathered cups ... / And went. But they still kept their ease / Spread out, unbuttoned, grateful, under the trees' (*Door into the Dark*, p. 27). I am grateful to Mary Breen for discussion of the issue of the masculinist representation of domesticity.

18. See Seamus Heaney, *Preoccupations: Selected Prose, 1968–1978* (London, 1980), pp. 57–8, for his own account of his inspiration by Glob. The modern political half of the construct finds perhaps its most popular and familiar expression in the writings of Patrick Pearse.

19. The most sustained account of Heaney's whole bog complex is Jacqueline Genet's, which crisply notices the poems' sexual emphasis and meanings, but foregoes interrogation of them ('Heaney et l'homme des tourbieres' in Genet [ed.], *Studies on Seamus Heaney* [Caen, 1987], pp. 123–47).

20. See Rees and Rees, *Celtic Heritage*; Pamela Berger, *The Goddess Obscured: Transformation of the Grain Protectress from Goddess to Saint* (Boston, 1985). See also Proinsiais Mac Cana, *Celtic Mythology* (London, 1970), pp. 49–50, 85–94: 'the mythological role of love ... is of its nature functional or ritual rather than personal' (p. 85).

21. Neil Corcoran severely understates the case when he says 'the poem has, like "The Wife's Tale", its element of male presumption' (*Seamus Heaney* [London, 1986], p. 58).

22. See Mills, *Women, Nature and Psyche* on the inadequacies of Marcuse's sexual libertarianism in *Eros and Civilization*, which greatly influenced thought in the 1960s. In the Irish context, Haney is also revising the rural vision of Patrick Kavanagh, one of his primary enabling figures, to include sex, but sex neither as ideal romance nor as frustration, its two guises in Kavanagh. The crucial moment in earlier Kavanagh, of critique of the emotional and other deprivation attending Irish rural life, is, however, elided in Heaney.

23. With it may also belong the conjunction in the later 'La Toilette' of dressing, sacredness and language ('But vest yourself / in the word you taught me / and the stuff I love: slub silk') (*Station Island*, p. 14).

24. See 'Freedman' (*North*, 60); 'The Toome Road' (*Field Work*, p. 15), with its British tank crews as 'charioteers'; and also 'Kinship', discussed below.

25. It may be worth remarking that his sense of this identification seems quite different from that in early Irish mythology, in which several female war- and death-divinities appear: the hero or king must couple with them so as to ensure his victory or continued rule, but they – the Morrighan, the Badhbh, and Macha – are actively characterized as speaking figures. The territorial goddesses such as Anu dominated an area but were not especially thought of as murderous. Heaney's version seems a modern and hybrid construct. See Mac Cana, *Celtic Mythology*, pp. 66, 86.

26. See Corcoran, *Seamus Heaney*, pp. 96ff., for an informed and intelligent commentary from a general point of view on these poems. Edna Longley, *Poetry in the Wars* (Newcastle upon Tyne, 1986), pp. 140–69 gives a trenchant discussion which makes some good demystificatory points, but insists on a formalist and depoliticising understanding of poetry which is itself open to question ('Poetry and politics, like church and state, should be separated' [p. 185]). Andrews is sensitive and painstaking, but his formalist approach tends to perpetuate the reification of gender-roles.

27. See Mills, *Women, Nature and Psyche*, pp. 157ff. On Freud, Marcuse and the notion of the 'primal horde': 'Because woman was Eros/Thanatos/Nirvana in "immediate" union she represented the threat of "mere nature" – "the regressive impulse for peace which stood in the way of progress – of Life itself"' (p. 157, quoting Marcuse's *Eros and Civilization* [1972]). One might add that Heaney's repeated meditations on the bog bodies are, of course, not at all concerned to open the enquiry anthropologically towards a rational investigation either of stone age religious and agricultural behaviour, or of Irish politics, but to make 'offerings or images that were emblems' (Heaney interview 1977, quoted in Corcoran, *Seamus Heaney*, p. 96).

28. As Edna Longley has well said: 'Heaney does not distinguish between involuntary and voluntary "martyrdom", and the nature of his "archetype" is such as to subsume the latter within the former' (*Poetry in the Wars*, p. 151).

29. On the irony in the last section of 'Kinship', see Corcoran, *Seamus Heaney*, p. 119, against other commentators who accuse Heaney of a crude nationalism (Longley, *Poetry in the Wars*, pp. 185–210 and Blake Morrison, *Seamus Heaney*, [London, 1982], pp. 68, 81).

30. As Bhabha says: 'Colonial power produces the colonized as a fixed reality which is at once an "other" yet entirely knowable and visible' ('The Other Question', p. 156). On the mirror stage and entry into the symbolic order as a passage beyond dualism, see John P. Mueller and William J. Richardson, *Lacan and Language: A Guide to 'Ecrits'* (New York, 1982), p. 136. I thank Nick Daly for discussion of this point.

31. Irigaray, *Speculum of the Other Woman*, p. 365.

5. SHAUN RICHARDS, 'TO BIND THE NORTHERN TO THE SOUTHERN STARS: FIELD DAY IN DERRY AND DUBLIN'

(From *The Irish Review*, 4 [1988], 52–8.)

Summary

Richards measures the cultural praxis of Field Day against its political and theoretical aims. His desire to relate the twin programmes of the theatre and the pamphlets suggests how quickly the Field Day projects became contested territory and served to initiate new debates. Richards reads theatre space as accommodating an association of the domestic and the political; equally, he argues, attention to the different meanings generated by staging the play in the Guildhall in Derry or the John Player Theatre in Dublin makes audible a clash of these registers. The essay's emphasis on location, performance and audience underpins a close reading of the kind of analysis at that time being advanced by Field Day, leading Richards to insist that a retreat into humanism is inadequate.

6.   LUKE GIBBONS, 'NARRATIVES OF THE NATION: FACT, FICTION AND IRISH CINEMA'

(From *Nationalisms: Visions and Revisions*, ed. Luke Dodd [Dublin, 1999], pp. 66–73.)

Summary

Reviewing the tendency to oppose 'real' to 'mythical' approaches to Irish society and culture, Gibbons performs a strategic revaluation of the meanings of these ideas. The essay discovers a distrust within revisionism of the tendency in Irish historiography (especially in its popular manifestations) to conceive of history as story, exemplified here by Roy Foster. Gibbons understands Foster to be prescribing cool analytic procedures which will remedy the damaging effects of narrative continuity and recover Irish realities; but Gibbons insists that 'reality' is always already structured around stories and that a closer attention to the ways in which these tales have been told represents the way forward.

Notes

1. David Armstrong, cited in Hayden White, 'The Modern Event' in Vivien Sobchack (ed.), *The Persistence of History: Cinema, Television and the Modern Event* (London, 1996), p. 20.
2. 'A Conversation between Eric Foner and John Sayles', in Mark C. Carnes, *Past Imperfect: History According to the Movies* (London, 1996), p. 23.
3. *Far Afield: 1907–1915* (Berkeley, CA, 1994), p. 153.
4. For a valuable discussion of Scott's negotiations of the borders between fiction and history, see Ann Rigney, 'Imminent History, Actual Novels', in her *Imperfect Histories* (Ithaca, NY, 2001).
5. (Review) '*Ivanhoe: A Romance*', *Eclectic Review*, June 1820, 2nd Series, xii, 528, cited in David Brown, *Walter Scott and the Historical Imagination* (London, 1979), p. 181.
6. Lady Morgan, *The Wild Irish Girl* [1806]. 1846 edition (London, 1986), p. 130. The use of the scholarly footnote in the early Irish 'national tales' of Edgeworth, Charles Maturin and Lady Morgan is discussed with appropriate scholarly aplomb in Joep Leerssen's *Remembrance and Imagination: Patterns in the Historical and Literary Representation of Ireland in the Nineteenth Century* (Cork, 1997), ch. 3.
7. For a discussion of the deconstructive effects of the excesses in both Lady Morgan's and Boucicault's pursuit of authenticity, see my 'Romanticism, Realism

and Irish Cinema', in Kevin Rockett, Luke Gibbons and John Hill, *Cinema and Ireland* (London, 1988).
8. The subordination of multiple points of view to an over-arching perspective in *JFK* is well brought out in Robert Brent Toplin, *History by Hollywood: The Use and Abuse of the American Past* (Indiana, 1996), ch. 2.
9. Roy Foster, 'Storylines: Narratives and Nationality in Nineteenth Century Ireland', in Geoffrey Cubitt (ed), *Imagining Nations* (Manchester, 1998), p. 39.

7.   TERRY EAGLETON, 'CHANGING THE QUESTION'

(From *Heathcliff and the Great Hunger: Studies in Irish Culture* [London and New York, 1995], pp. 123–33, 135–6, 137–44.)

Summary

This essay might be understood as putting into practice some of Gibbons's strictures (see previous essay) concerning a close reading of the narratives of Irish history. The essay moves from literature through theory into politics, via a layering of psycho-analytic and materialist concepts. Eagleton examines the many historical anomalies which structure Irish history, especially in its relation to Britain, and uncovers what he calls a grammar of Anglo-Irish relations. He sees Ireland going in advance of Britain as a colonial society precipitated into modernity, and thus already in the nineteenth century an image of what Britain was to become.

Notes

1. Quoted by Lady Ferguson, *Sir Samuel Ferguson in the Ireland of his Day*, vol. 1 (Edinburgh and London, 1896), p. 207.
2. See Terry Eagleton, *The Ideology of the Aesthetic* (Oxford, 1990), Ch. 1.
3. See Conor Cruise O'Brien, 'The Embers of Easter 1916–1966', in Owen Dudley Edwards (ed.), *The Easter Rising* (London, 1968), p. 232.
4. Fredric Jameson, 'Modernism and Imperialism', in Seamus Deane (ed.), *Nationalism, Colonialism and Literature* (Minneapolis, 1990), pp. 50–1.
5. Quoted by Nicolas Mansergh, *The Irish Question 1840–1921* (London, 1965), p. 49.
6. Quoted in Galen Broeker, *Rural Disorder and Police Reform in Ireland, 1812–36* (London and Toronto, 1970), p. I. The most exhaustive treatment of the stereotyping of the Irish, from antiquity to the eighteenth-century stage-Irishman, is Joseph Leerssen, *Mere Irish and Fíor-Ghael* (Amsterdam, 1986).
7. See A. P. W. Malcolmson, *John Foster: The Politics of the Anglo-Irish Ascendancy* (Oxford, 1978), p. 369.
8. Thomas Bartlett, *The Fall and Rise of the Irish Nation* (Dublin, 1992), pp. 36–7.
9. Oliver MacDonagh, 'Ireland and the Union 1801–70', in W. E. Vaughan (ed.), *A New History of Ireland, vol. V: Ireland under the Union 1, 1801–70* (Oxford, 1989), p. liii. MacDonagh comments elsewhere that the Land Acts of the end of the nineteenth century may have been dimly perceived in England as analogous to the Married Woman's Property Acts. See his 'Ambiguity in Nationalism: The Case of Ireland', in Ciaran Brady (ed.), *Interpreting Irish History* (Dublin, 1994), p. 108.

10. Henry Grattan put the point in his own way in a parliamentary speech: 'Identification is a solid and imperial maxim, necessary for the preservation of freedom, necessary for that of empire; but without union of hearts, with a separate Government and without a separate Parliament, identification is extinction, is dishonour, is conquest – not identification' (quoted by W. E. H. Lecky, *Leaders of Public Opinion in Ireland* [London, 1861], p. 143).
11. Quoted by Nicholas Canny, 'Identity Formation in Ireland', in Nicholas Canny and Anthony Pagden (eds), *Colonial Identity in the Atlantic World, 1500–1800* (Princeton, NJ, 1987), p. 200.
12. R. F. Foster, *Paddy And Mr Punch* (London, 1993), p. 91.
13. See Jacques Derrida, *Of Grammatology* (Baltimore and London, 1974), Part 2, ii.
14. For the effect of the Union on Britain, see E. Strauss, *Irish Nationalism and British Democracy* (London, 1951), a rare Marxist study of Ireland. Gearóid Ó Tuathaigh argues that the so-called Irish question in the post-Union period was often enough in Britain 'parabolic' of domestic issues there which could not be so readily discussed as such ('Nineteenth Century Irish Politics: The Case for "Normality"', *Anglo-Irish Studies*, no. 1, 1975).
15. Edmund Curtis, *A History of Ireland* (London 1978), p. 323. For an examination of the equities and inequities of post-Union Ireland, see Oliver MacDonagh, *The Union and its Aftermath* (London, 1977), Ch. 2.
16. See Christopher Clapham, *Third World Politics: An Introduction* (London, 1992), pp. 21f.
17. Quoted by R. B. McDowell, *Ireland in the Age of Imperialism and Revolution* (Oxford, 1979), pp. 686–7.
18. 'Cumulatively, it is perhaps a mass of commonplace, unnoticed discordance of meaning and connotation which has set and still sets Anglo-Irish communication most askew' (MacDonagh, *States of Mind*, p. 13). For an excellent account of Anglo-Irish misunderstandings, see Patrick O'Farrell, *England and Ireland since 1800* (Oxford, 1975).
19. John Stuart Mill, *England and Ireland* (London, 1868), p. 9.
20. See Thomas Bartlett, 'An End to Moral Economy', *Past and Present*, no. 99 (1983). The classic study of the concept is E. P. Thompson, *Customs in Common* (London, 1991), especially Chs 4 and 5.
21. See Sally Warwick-Haller, *William O'Brien and the Irish Land War* (Dublin 1990), p. 24.
22. Quoted by D. George Boyce, *Nationalism in Ireland* (London 1982), p. 213.
23. See J. C. Beckett, *The Making of Modern Ireland 1603–1923* (London 1981), p. 373.
24. See John Stuart Mill, *A System of Logic* (London 1843), Book 6, Ch. 5.
25. These ideas crop up at various points in Lacan's work; but see, for an important source, 'The Subversion of the Subject and the Dialectic of Desire in the Freudian Unconscious', in *Ecrits: A Selection* (London, 1977). For an excellent exposition of Lacan's thinking on these matters, see Peter Dews, *Logics of Disintegration* (London, 1987), Ch. 2. The Young Irelander John Mitchel remarks in his *Jail Journal* of the Cape Colony that 'whatever is done here can only be said to be inchoate, provisional, and not a perfect act, until news of it go to England, and an answer return' (*Jail Journal*, reprinted Dublin 1982, p. 210).
26. The point has often been made with regard to feminism: if a woman speaks intelligibly she has been co-opted; if she remains on the margin her discourse is dismissed as senseless. John Mitchel makes much the same point from a nation-

alist perspective: 'If I profess myself a disbeliever in that gospel [of success], the Enlightened Age will only smile, and say, "The defeated always are." Britain being in possession of the floor, any hostile comment upon her way of telling our story is an unmannerly interruption; nay, is nothing short of an *Irish howl*' (*Jail Journal*, p. xxxvii).

8.   JOE CLEARY, 'MISPLACED IDEAS? COLONIALISM, LOCATION AND DISLOCATION IN IRISH STUDIES'

(From Clare Carroll [ed.], *The Last Ditch: Ireland and the Postcolonial World* [forthcoming, Cork, 2002].)

Summary

In this essay Cleary reflects critically on the turn to postcolonial modes of analysis in Ireland. Drawing on the writings of Brazilian cultural critic Roberto Schwarz and his account of place and ideology, Cleary contends that such readings have the potential to dislocate Irish Studies. With this in mind, he embarks on a detailed account of the meanings and relevance of colonialism in the Irish context. The essay analyses the implications of different concepts of development for Ireland. Itself working within a Marxist framework, the argument moves towards envisioning Ireland as a site of contradictory and competing economic and political interests.

Notes

1. For a more detailed analysis of modernization theory, see Jorge Larrain, *Theories of Development, Capitalism, Colonialism and Dependency* (Oxford, 1989), especially pp. 85–110. For an incisive and cogent account of the origins of modernization theory and its limits as a mode of comparative social analysis, see Dean C. Tipps, 'Modernization Theory and the Comparative Study of Societies: A Critical Perspective', *Comparative Studies in Society and History*, 15 (1973), 199–226.
2. For an incisive critique of modernization discourse in the Irish context, a discourse he terms 'the cultural dominant of the nineties' and 'the preferred code of advocacy and dissent', see Francis Mulhern's *The Present Lasts A Long Time: Essays in Cultural Politics* (Cork, 1998), pp. 1–28, 20. For another take, see Luke Gibbons, 'Coming Out of Hibernation? The Myth of Modernization in Irish Culture', in his *Transformations in Irish Culture* (Cork, 1996), pp. 82–93.
3. Mulhern, *The Present Lasts a Long Time*, p. 20. Mulhern's critique is drawn on Peter Osborne's *The Politics of Time: Modernity and Avant-Garde* (London, 1995).
4. For a leftist overview of Southern Irish society informed by a modernization perspective, see Ellen Hazelkorn and Henry Patterson, 'The New Politics of the Irish Republic', *New Left Review*, 207 (Sept.–Oct., 1994), 49–71.
5. This aspect of the postcolonial studies project is developed most forcefully by David Lloyd in the essays 'Regarding Ireland in a Postcolonial Frame' and

'Outside History: Irish New Histories and the "Subalternity Effect"', both of
which are collected in *Ireland After History* (Cork, 1999).

6. For examples of such critique, see Liam Kennedy, 'Post-Colonial Society or
    Post-Colonial Pretensions?' in his *Colonialism, Religion and Nationalism in Ire-
    land* (Belfast, 1996), pp. 167–81, and Edna Longley, *The Living Stream: Litera-
    ture and Revisionism in Ireland* (Newcastle upon Tyne, 1994), pp. 22–44. For a
    critique from the left, see Francis Mulhern, 'Postcolonial Melancholy,' in *The
    Present Lasts a Long Time*, pp. 158–63.

7. Roberto Schwarz, 'Misplaced Ideas', in *Misplaced Ideas: Essays on Brazilian
    Culture*, ed. and introd. John Gledson (London, 1992), pp. 19–32, 25. My
    reading of Schwarz's essay has been informed by several commentaries. See
    especially Adriana Johnson's 'Reading Roberto Schwarz: Outside Out-of-Place
    Ideas', *Journal of Latin American Cultural Studies*, 8, 1 (1999), 21–33 and Neil
    Larson, 'Brazilian Critical Theory and the Question of Cultural Studies', in his
    Reading North by South: On Latin American Literature, Culture and Politics
    (Minneapolis, 1995), pp. 205–16. See also the comments by Mulhern in *The
    Present Lasts A Long Time*, pp. 159–60.

8. For Schwarz: 'Ideas are in place when they represent abstractions of the process
    they refer to, and it is a fatal consequence of our cultural dependency that we are
    always representing our reality with conceptual systems created somewhere else,
    whose basis lies in other social processes.' Schwarz, 'Beware of Alien Ideologies',
    in *Misplaced Ideas*, pp. 33–40, 39.

9. The case against considering Ireland a colony is cogently developed in Thomas
    Bartlett, ' "What Ish My Nation?" Themes in Irish History: 1550–1850', in Tom
    Bartlett et al. (eds), *Irish Studies: A General Introduction* (Dublin, 1988), pp. 44–
    59 and in Tom Dunne, 'New Histories: Beyond Revisionism', *The Irish Review*,
    12 (Spring/Summer 1992), 1–12.

10. Lloyd, *Ireland After History*, p. 7.

11. See Arghiri Emmanuel, 'White-Settler Colonialism and the Myth of Investment
    Imperialism', *New Left Review*, 73 (May–June, 1972), 35–57. Emmanuel does
    not, however, mention some significant exceptions such as the slave rebellion in
    Haiti or the Great Indian Mutiny.

12. Gibbons, *Transformations in Irish Culture*, p. 17.

13. See Robert J. Hind, ' "We Have No Colonies" – Similarities within the British
    Imperial Experience', *Comparative Studies in Society and History*, 26 (1984), 3–35.

14. D. K. Fieldhouse, *The Colonial Empires: A Comparative Survey from the Eight-
    eenth Century* (London, 1965), pp. 7–13; George Fredrickson, *The Arrogance of
    Race: Historical Perspectives on Slavery, Racism and Social Inequality* (Middle-
    town, CT, 1985), pp. 216–35. My own taxonomy borrows heavily on Fredrick-
    son's reworking of Fieldhouse's work. For another attempt at a typology, see
    Jürgen Osterhammel, *Colonialism: A Theoretical Overview*, trans. Shelley
    L. Frisch (Princeton, NJ, 1997), pp. 10–12.

15. On the plantation colonies, see Philip D. Curtin, *The Rise and Fall of the
    Plantation Complex: Essays in Atlantic History* (Cambridge, 1990) and David
    Watts, *The West Indies: Patterns of Development, Culture and Environmental
    Change since 1492* (Cambridge, 1987).

16. For overviews of colonial South America, see James Lockhart and Stuart
    B. Schwarz, *Early Latin America: A History of Colonial Latin America and Brazil*
    (Cambridge, 1983) and Mark A. Burkholder and Lyman L. Johnson, *Colonial
    Latin America* (Oxford, 1994).

17. On these issues, see R. Cole Harris, 'The Simplification of Europe Overseas', *Annals of the Association of American Geographers*, 67, 4 (Dec. 1977), 469–83, and R. Cole Harris and Leonard Guelke, 'Land and Society in early Canada and South Africa', *Journal of Historical Geography*, 3, 2 (1977), 135–53.
18. See George M. Fredrickson, *White Supremacy: A Comparative Study in American and South African History* (Oxford, 1988). On Palestine, see Gershon Shafir, *Land, Labor and the Origins of the Israeli-Palestinian Conflict 1882–1914* (Cambridge, 1989).
19. On these continuities, see Edwin Williamson, *The Penguin History of Latin America* (London, 1992), pp. 55–75.
20. Immanuel Wallerstein's *The Modern World System, II, Mercantilism and the Consolidation of the European World-Economy, 1600–1750* (New York, 1980), is the classic study of this development. For an alternative account, which seeks to remedy the theoretical weaknesses in Wallerstein's work and to correct its North European bias, see Giovanni Arrighi, *The Long Twentieth Century: Money, Power, and the Origins of Our Times* (London, 1994).
21. Kevin Whelan, 'Ireland in the World-System 1600–1800,' in Hans-Jürgen Nitz (ed.), *The Early-Modern World-System in Geographical Perspective* (Stuttgart, 1993), pp. 204–18, 205.
22. Ibid., p. 204.
23. Robert Brenner, 'The Origins of Capitalist Development: A Critique of Neo-Smithian Marxism', *New Left Review*, 104 (July/August, 1977), 63–118. Quotes from Brenner cited in Eamonn Slater and Terrence McDonough, 'Bulwark of Landlordism and Capitalism: The Dynamics of Feudalism in Nineteenth Century Ireland', *Research in Political Economy*, 14 (1994), 63–118, 64–5.
24. Slater and McDonough, 'Bulwark of Landlordism and Capitalism', 111.
25. Larson, *Reading North by South*, pp. 214–15.
26. Mulhern, *The Present Lasts a Long Time*, p. 24.
27. Several works in comparative sociology locate Northern Ireland within a wider colonial settler context. These include Ian Lustick's *Unsettled States, Disputed Lands: Britian and Ireland, France and Algeria, Israel and the West Bank-Gaza* (Ithaca, NY, 1993); Ronald Weitzer, *Transforming Settler States: Communal Conflict and Internal Security in Northern Ireland and Zimbabwe* (London, 1990); Michael MacDonald, *Children of Wrath: Political Violence in Northern Ireland* (Oxford, 1986); Hermann Giliomee and Jannie Gagiano (eds), *The Elusive Search For Peace: South Africa, Israel, Northern Ireland* (Cape Town, 1990); and Pamela Clayton, *Enemies and Passing Friends: Settler Ideologies in Twentieth Century Ulster* (London, 1996). Some leading political scientists and sociologists of the Northern conflict have also attributed some importance to settler colonialism as a shaping influence on the contemporary period, though the degree of salience they attach to it varies. See Liam O'Dowd, 'New Introduction' to Albert Memmi, *The Colonizer and the Colonized*, trans. Howard Greenfeld (London, 1990); John McGarry and Brendan O'Leary, *Explaining Northern Ireland: Broken Images* (Oxford, 1995); Joseph Ruane and Jennifer Todd, *The Dynamics of Power in Northern Ireland: Power Conflict and Emancipation* (Cambridge, 1996). For a related view, which situates Northern Ireland in terms of other 'ethnic frontiers' in Europe and elsewhere, see Frank Wright, *Northern Ireland: A Comparative Analysis* (Dublin, 1987).

9. SIOBHÁN KILFEATHER, 'SEX AND SENSATION IN THE NINETEENTH-CENTURY NOVEL'

(From Margaret Kelleher and James H. Murphy [eds], *Gender Perspectives in Nineteenth-Century Ireland* [Dublin, 1997], pp. 83–92.)

Summary

Where many postcolonial critics see issues such as sex, love and marriage as an escape from the political, Kilfeather reads sexuality and colonialism in dynamic relation with one another. Her focus on bodies and sexuality in nineteenth-century Irish fiction causes her to dismantle oppositions between private and public arenas. In the process, Kilfeather moves away from a view of nineteenth-century fiction as evincing the viewpoint of the colonizer and inevitably stereotyping those represented. Her focus on genres normally thought of as 'fantasy' (sensation fiction, melodrama) enables her to reject Terry Eagleton's account of the failure of Irish realism and to produce a more complex picture of the 'reality' that was being represented.

Notes

1. Jane (Lady) Wilde, *Ancient Legends, Mystic Charms, and Superstitions of Ireland. With Sketches of the Past* (1888; republished Galway, 1971), p. 208.
2. Emily Lawless, *Grania: The Story of an Island* (London, 1892), p. 249.
3. Terry Eagleton, *Heathcliff and the Great Hunger: Studies in Irish Culture* (London, 1995), p. 227.
4. Ibid., p. 209; William Carleton, *The Black Prophet: A Tale of Irish Famine* (Belfast, 1847), p. 118. Eagleton slightly mis-remembers here: the speaker is young Dick but the elaborate performance of speechlessness is the relevant point.
5. See Thomas Flanagan, *The Irish Novelists, 1800–1850* (New York, 1959); John Cronin, *The Anglo-Irish Novel, Volume One: The Nineteenth Century* (Belfast, 1980); Seamus Deane, *A Short History of Irish Literature* (London, 1986); Barry Sloan, *The Pioneers of Anglo-Irish Fiction: 1800–1850* (Gerrard's Cross, 1986); Seamus Deane (ed.), *The Field Day Anthology of Irish Writing* (3 vols; Derry, 1991).
6. 'The sensationalists made crime and violence domestic, modern, and suburban; but their secrets were not simply solutions to mysteries and crimes; they were the secrets of women's dislike of their roles as daughters, wives, and mothers. These women made a powerful appeal to the female audience by subverting the traditions of feminine fiction to suit their own imaginative impulses, by expressing a wide range of suppressed female emotion, and by tapping and satisfying fantasies of protest and escape'; see Elaine Showalter, *A Literature of Their Own: British Women Novelists from Brontë to Lessing* (1977; revised edn, London, 1984), pp. 158–9.
7. Jenny Bourne Taylor, *In the Secret Theatre of Home: Wilkie Collins, Sensation Narrative and Nineteenth-century Psychology* (London, 1988), p. 1.
8. See W. J. McCormack, *Sheridan Le Fanu and Victorian Ireland* (Oxford, 1980) and McCormack's introduction to 'Language, Class and Genre' in *The Field Day Anthology of Irish Writing*, i, pp. 1070–82.
9. Eagleton, *Heathcliff and the Great Hunger*, p. 187.
10. Ibid., p. 212.
11. Flanagan, *The Irish Novelists*, p. 334.

12. Cronin, *The Anglo-Irish Novel*, p. 92.
13. Margaret Oliphant, article in *Blackwood's Edinburgh Magazine* 1862, quoted by Taylor, *In the Secret Theatre of Home*, p. 3.
14. Siobhán Kilfeather, 'Origins of the Irish Female Gothic' in *Bullán*, i, 2 (Autumn 1994), 35–45.
15. Taylor, *In the Secret Theatre of Home*, p. 17.
16. For a discussion of the western landscape, and particularly Killarney, in Victorian melodrama, see Luke Gibbons, 'Landscape and character in Irish romantic melodrama', in Kevin Rockett, Luke Gibbons and John Hill, *Cinema and Ireland* (London, 1987), pp. 210–21.
17. Gerald Griffin, *The Collegians: A Tale of Garryowen* (1829; London, [1842]), p. 242.
18. Luke Gibbons, 'Topographies of Terror: Killarney and the Politics of the Sublime', in *SAQ*, 95, 1 (Winter 1996), 23–44, 38; Tzvetan Todorov, *The Fantastic: A Structural Approach to a Literary Genre* (Ithaca, NY, 1975), p. 33.
19. Griffin, *The Collegians*, p. 243.
20. For accounts of this phenomenon in different periods see Anna Clark, *Women's Silence, Men's Violence: Sexual Assault in England 1770–1845* (London, 1987); Keith Soothill and Sylvia Walby, *Sex Crime in the News* (London, 1991); Judith Walkowitz, *City of Dreadful Delight* (London, 1992); James Kelly, '"A Most Inhuman and Barbarous Piece of Villainy": An Exploration of the Crime of Rape in Eighteenth-Century Ireland', in *Eighteenth-Century Ireland / Iris an dá chultúr*, 10 (1995), 78–107.
21. Griffin, *The Collegians*, p. 126.
22. Sarah Grand, *The Heavenly Twins* (London, 1893; reprinted Ann Arbor, 1992), pp. 157; 'The face rose up to hers. She looked into the subtle eyes, and the thrill of the lips, just touching hers, awakened a sense of sin, and her eyes when they opened were frightened and weary', George Moore, *Evelyn Innes* (London, 1898) p. 33.
23. Sheridan Le Fanu, *Uncle Silas: A Tale of Bartram-Haugh* (1864; reprinted with an introduction by Elizabeth Bowen, London, 1947). Introduction reprinted in *Collected Impressions* (London, 1950) and in *The Mulberry Tree*, ed. Hermione Lee (London, 1986) pp. 100–13; 101–2.
24. Le Fanu, *Uncle Silas*, ch. 29.
25. Christian Johnstone, *True Tales of the Irish Peasantry, As Related by Themselves, Selected from the Report of the Poor Law Commissioners* (Edinburgh, 2nd edn, 1836), preface; Frances Power Cobbe, *Essays on the Pursuits of Women Reprinted from Fraser's and Macmillan's Magazines* (London, 1862); Annie Besant, *Coercion in Ireland and Its Results* (London, 1882); Josephine E. Butler, *Our Christianity Tested by the Irish Question* (London, 1887).
26. Cobbe, *Essays on the Pursuits of Women*, p. 192. I must emphasize that I am interested here primarily in modes of representation. For a discussion of women's historical experience, see Maria Luddy and Clíona Murphy (eds), *Women Surviving: Studies in Irish Women's History in the Nineteenth and Twentieth Centuries* (Dublin, 1989), particularly chapters by Luddy on prostitution and by Dympna McLoughlin on workhouses.
27. Frances Browne, *The Hidden Sin* (3 vols; London, 1866), iii, pp. 101–2.
28. D. A. Miller, *The Novel and the Police* (California, 1988), p. x.
29. Griffin, *The Collegians*, p. 282.
30. Horace Plunkett, *Ireland in the New Century* (London, 1904; revised edn, London, 1905), p. 116.

10.   CHRISTOPHER MORASH, 'TANTALIZED BY PROGRESS'

(From *Writing the Irish Famine* [Oxford, 1995], pp. 52–66.)

Summary

Morash argues that a distinctive political situation – nineteenth-century Ireland – produces a self-aware linguistic practice which can be read in tandem with the counter-Enlightenment textuality of Foucault and Nietzsche. He relates the narrative texture of John Mitchel's *Jail Journal*, written when Young Irelander Mitchel was a convict in Tasmania, to the Irish Famine, arguing that Mitchel's refusal of an end-point to Irish history may be seen in counterpoint to nineteenth-century political economy and the doctrine of progress.

Notes

1. D. F. MacCarthy, 'Advance', *Nation*, IV, 189 (23 May 1846), 505. MacCarthy glosses 'Ajalon' thus: 'Move not, O Sun, towards Gibeon, nor thou, O Moon, toward the Valley of Ajalon'. Joshua 10: 12.
2. W. Drennan, Jr, '1848', in *Glendalloch and Other Poems* (Dublin, 1859), p. 151. Drennan's father had framed the manifesto of the United Irishman a half-century earlier.
3. J. S. Donnelly, Jr, describes Mitchel's reading of the Famine as 'by far the dominant popular interpretation among Irish Catholics at home and abroad'. J. S. Donnelly, Jr, 'The Great Famine', *History Ireland*, I, 3 (Autumn 1993), 33.
4. T. B. Macaulay, 'Sir James Mackintosh', in *Critical and Historical Essays Contributed to the Edinburgh Review* (London, 1903), ii. 72–3.
5. A. Briggs, *Iron Bridge to Crystal Palace* (London, 1979), p. 167.
6. W. M. Thackeray, 'Mr. Malony's Account of the Crystal Palace', in *Ballads and Contributions to 'Punch' 1842–1850* (Oxford, 1908), p. 160.
7. 'Dives and Lazarus', *Nation*, VIII, 37 (10 May 1851), 585.
8. William Shakespeare, *Richard II*, 11. i. 40–66.
9. 'The Day After the Storm', *Dublin University Magazine*, XXXVIII, 223 (July 1851), 108.
10. *The Exhibition of Art-Industry in Dublin* (London, 1853), p. vii.
11. 'The Opening of the Exhibition', *Nation*, XI, 37 (14 May 1853), 584.
12. 'The History of Ten Years', *Nation*, VIII, 46 (12 July 1851), 728.
13. 'The Age We Live In', *Irishman*, I, 29 (21 July 1849), 49.
14. 'The Pauperisation of Ireland', *Irishman*, I, 1 (6 Jan. 1849), 9.
15. J. Bentham, *Fragment on Government* ([1776]; Oxford, 1948), p. 28.
16. 'Democracy', *Irishman*, I, 36 (8 Sept. 1849), 569.
17. J. Bentham, 'Summary of Basic Principles', in *Bentham's Political Thought*, ed. B. Parekh (London, 1972), p. 295. Bentham's ideas were very much at the forefront of public debate in the decade before the Famine as a consequence of James Mill's controversy with Macaulay. See Jack Lively and John Rees (eds), *Utilitarian Logic and Politics* (Oxford, 1978).
18. A. Smith, *An Inquiry Into the Nature and Causes of the Wealth of Nations* ([1776]; Oxford, 1976), i. p. 532.
19. J. R. Hill, 'The Intelligentsia and Irish Nationalism in the 1840s', *Studia Hibernica*, 20 (1980), 104. See also O. MacDonagh, *The Emancipist: Daniel O'Connell, 1830–47* (London, 1989), 19.

20. The phrase was Thomas Wilson's of *The Economist*; cited in C. Ó Gráda, *The Great Irish Famine* (Dublin, 1989), p. 52.
21. 'The Railway Scheme', *Nation*, V, 227 (13 Feb. 1847), 297.
22. M. Foucault, 'What is Enlightenment', in *The Foucault Reader* (Harmondsworth, 1984), 42–3.
23. T. Davis, 'The History of Ireland', in *Thomas Davis: Literary and Historical Essays*, ed. C. G. Duffy ([1846]; Dublin, 1883), p. 28.
24. J. Mitchel, *Jail Journal* ([1854]; Shannon, 1982), p. lix.
25. D. Lloyd, *Nationalism and Minor Literature* (Berkeley, CA, 1987), pp. 51, 70.
26. J. Mitchel, *Jail Journal* (New York, 1854); J. Mitchel, *Jail Journal* (New York, 1868).
27. 'Let no man write my epitaph... Let my character and my motives repose in obscurity and peace, till other times and other men can do them justice... Then may my epitaph be written.' R. Emmet, 'Speech from the Dock', in S. Deane (ed.), *The Field Day Anthology of Irish Writing* (Derry, 1991), i. p. 939.
28. H. White, *Metahistory* (Baltimore, MD, 1973), p. 281.
29. H. Butterfield, *The Whig Interpretation of History* ([1931]; London, 1951), pp. 88–9.
30. By contrast, 'in comedy time plays a redeeming role'. N. Frye, *Anatomy of Criticism* (Princeton, NJ, 1957), p. 213.
31. J. Mitchel, *The Last Conquest of Ireland (Perhaps)* ([1861]; London, n.d.), p. 220.
32. I. Davies, *Writers in Prison* (Oxford, 1990), p. 235.
33. Mitchel, *Jail Journal*, p. 121.
34. Mitchel, *Last Conquest*, p. 117.
35. Lloyd, *Nationalism and Minor Literature*, p. 58.
36. For a useful account of Lalor's by no means simple relationship to the nationalist movement, see D. Buckley, *James Fintan Lalor* (Cork, 1990).
37. J. F. Lalor, 'A New Nation', *Nation*, V, 237 (24 Apr. 1847), 457. It is worth noting that later in the same essay, Lalor develops his ideas along modified Benthamite lines, arguing that once 'an active and affluent' agricultural community exists, 'any further interference with the course and process of natural laws would be useless and mischievous'.
38. Mitchel, *Last Conquest*, pp. 115–16.
39. Lalor, 'A New Nation', p. 457.
40. Mitchel, *Last Conquest*, p. 92.
41. M. Brown, *The Politics of Irish Literature* (Seattle, 1972), p. 105.
42. M. Foucault, *Madness and Civilization* ([1961]; London, 1967), p. 63.
43. Mitchel, *Last Conquest*, pp. 179, 218.
44. Mitchel, *Jail Journal*, p. xli.

11. CLAIR WILLS, 'THE POLITICS OF POETIC FORM'

(From *Improprieties: Politics and Sexuality in Northern Irish Poetry*
[Oxford, 1993], pp. 13–27.)

Summary

Wills analyses the work of three of the post-Heaney generation of Northern Irish poets: Tom Paulin, Medbh McGuckian and Paul Muldoon. She identifies and argues against a perceived need to make a critical choice between reading the poems in terms of either postmodern textuality on the one hand, or their Irish content and political relevance on the other. Wills draws together these approaches and insists that formal complexity carries a political charge. Her essay confronts the move from lyric into obscurity and difficulty and argues that reticence and privacy should be read as narrative strategies in their own right, rather than as a retreat from the public world. The poets Wills writes about have produced new work since this essay was written; some of this is discussed in her most recent book, *Paul Muldoon* (1999).

Notes

1. Paul Muldoon, *Meeting the British* (London, 1987), p. 50.
2. Seamus Heaney, *The Government of the Tongue* (London, 1988), p. xxii.
3. Seamus Heaney, *The Government of the Tongue*, p. 14.
4. Muldoon's link with Heaney at this stage was a very important one. He attended meetings of the poetry Group which had been set up in the early 1960s in Belfast by Philip Hobsbaum, then also a lecturer at Queen's, on the lines of the London poetry Group which he had started in the late 1950s with Edward Lucie-Smith, although by the time Muldoon went to Queen's in 1969 Hobsbaum had left. See the *Honest Ulsterman*, 52, for a retrospective by Belfast poets on the Group. The *Honest Ulsterman* itself, which was started by James Simmons in 1968, was an important forum for new writing and literary discussion, as was the Belfast Arts Festival, which helped to consolidate artistic confidence in the region.
5. Blake Morrison, 'Tropical Storms', rev. of Medbh McGuckian, *Venus and the Rain*, in *London Review of Books* (6–19 Sept. 1984), 22.
6. Medbh McGuckian, *Venus and the Rain* (Oxford, 1984); p. 33. For a detailed analysis of this poem see Clair Wills, 'The Perfect Mother: Authority in the Poetry of Medbh McGuckian', *Text and Context*, 3 (1988), 91–111.
7. Martin Mooney notes the incongruity between logical grammatical structures and a seemingly arbitrary selection of images in 'Body Logic: Some Notes on the Poetry of Medbh McGuckian', *Gown Literary Supplement* (1988), 16–18. See for example the poems 'Harem Trousers' and 'Death of a Ceiling', in *On Ballycastle Beach*.
8. Paul Muldoon, interview with John Haffenden, in John Haffenden (ed.), *Viewpoints: Poets in Conversation with John Haffenden* (London, 1981), p. 133.
9. *Mules* (London, 1977), p. 52. On Muldoon's use of tense see Edna Longley, *Poetry in the Wars* (Newcastle upon Tyne, 1986), pp. 222–4.
10. Muldoon notes in his interview with John Haffenden his interest in stories that can be juxtaposed against each other, like mirrors, thereby creating new narrative possibilities (Haffenden (ed.), *Viewpoints*, p. 136).
11. John Goodby, 'Elephantiasis and Essentialism', *Irish Review*, 10 (1991), 133.
12. Tom Paulin, 'Mount Stewart', *Fivemiletown* (London, 1987), p. 38.
13. Blake Morrison and Andrew Motion (eds), *The Penguin Book of Contemporary British Poetry* (Harmondsworth, 1982). It should be stressed that this anthology deals solely with mainstream poetry, published by major British publishing houses, and consequently ignores the vigorous tradition of experimental and avant-garde poetry in English. However, part of my aim here is to question the sharp division between experimental work such as LANGUAGE writing and the seemingly more traditional forms these poets use. For a recent anthology which does represent the experimental tradition see Gillian Allnutt, Fred D'Aguiar, Ken Edwards, and Eric Mottram (eds), *The New British Poetry* (London, 1988).

14. See Fredric Jameson, 'Postmodernism, or The Cultural Logic of Late Capitalism', *New Left Review*, 146 (July–Aug. 1984), 53–92. Another, equally influential, variant of Morrison and Motion's claim is John Kerrigan's argument for the existence of the new narrative, 'Reflexive, aleatory and cornucopian, the New Narrative deploys its fragmented and ramifying fictions to image the unpredictability of life, and its continuous shadowing of What Might Be'. Kerrigan formulated this description in a review of Muldoon's *Quoof* so it is not perhaps surprising that it should so snugly fit poems such as 'The More a Man Has'; however, he draws a further link between postmodern style and the political. In arguing for 'the essential interdependence, of a metaphoric emphasis in poetry and narrative Post-modernism', he makes the case for the style's natural alliance with feminism in that both reject the received structure of myths and narratives. See *London Review of Books* (16–29 Feb. 1984), 22–3.

15. Alan Robinson, *Instabilities in Contemporary British Poetry* (Basingstoke, 1988), p. 7.

16. Dillon Johnston, *Irish Poetry After Joyce* (Bloomington, IN; Mountrath, 1985), p. 250. In fact Johnston rightly intimates that such 'unity of culture' never existed, but was simply claimed as both result and evidence of Ireland's traditional communal identity.

17. As Liam O'Dowd has noted, perhaps the major stumbling-block for all these positions is that they lack a material or economic dimension of analysis, 'Neglecting the Material Dimension: Irish Intellectuals and the Problem of Identity', *Irish Review*, 3 (1988), 8–17.

18. Seamus Deane, 'Remembering the Irish Future', *Crane Bag*, 8,1 (1984), 81–92. Deane's essay is itself an attempt to conceptualize a means of transcending this division, although his work, and that of other politically engaged cultural critics, has been read both as too tender (i.e. nationalist) and as too tough minded (i.e. rationalist), by critics such as Edna Longley and Witoszek and Sheeran respectively. See Edna Longley, 'Poetry and Politics in Northern Ireland', *Crane Bag*, 9,1 (1985), 26–37, and Nina Witoszek and Pat Sheeran, 'From Explanations to Intervention', in the same volume, 83–6.

19. As the most well known of its current practitioners, Roy Foster, points out, to call it a 'school' is in fact a misnomer, since 'To the Scholars, it is quite simply a desire to eliminate as much as possible of the retrospectively "Whig" view of history which sees every event and process in the light of what followed it rather than what went before'. Yet Foster's consequent insistence that revisionists are not, as a body, hostile to Irish nationalism is somewhat belied by his claim that what they are hostile to is the 'old pieties' which are the mark of the popular understanding of Irish history: 'as regards political history, the old pieties have it their own way and historians tread carefully for fear of the "anti-nationalist" smear' (Roy Foster, 'We Are All Revisionists Now', *Irish Review*, 1 [1986], 2).

20. See the introduction to Roy Foster's *Modern Ireland, 1600–1972* (Harmondsworth, 1988).

21. Richard Kearney, 'Myth and Motherland', *Ireland's Field Day*, ed. Field Day Theatre Company (London, 1985), p. 79. Kearney and others have been accused both of valuing Irish tradition only in so far as it contributes to their postmodernist project, and of seeking a purely and genuinely Irish tradition only.

22. Luke Gibbons, 'Montage, Modernism and the City', *Irish Review*, 10 (1991), 5–6.

23. On theories of nationalism which question atavistic and irrational interpretations see Ernest Gellner, *Nations and Nationalism* (Oxford, 1983); Benedict Anderson, *Imagined Communities* (London, 1983); for an analysis of Irish nationalism in

this light see Tom Garvin, 'The Return of History: Collective Myths and Modern Nationalisms', *Irish Review*, 9 (1990), 16–30.

## 12.	RICHARD KIRKLAND, ' "IN THE MIDST OF ALL THIS DROSS": ESTABLISHING THE GROUNDS OF DISSENT'

(From *Literature and Culture in Northern Ireland Since 1965: Moments of Danger* [London, 1996], pp. 19–33.)

Summary

The Ulster Folk and Transport Museum provides the occasion for Kirkland's discussion of rootedness and the grounding of identity. He analyses the various attempts at authenticity inherent in the museum's layout and design. The museum is organized around Ulster (the ancient nine-county province) rather than Northern Ireland (the six-county statelet created at the end of the Irish War of Independence in 1922), a contradiction Kirkland explores in relation to the meanings of tradition, still a much cited concept in debates on Northern Ireland. Kirkland carries this interest in place and identity over into a discussion of regionalism, offered by many as an alternative to the rigid oppositions generated by nationalist and unionist debates. The deployment of land and ground as the means of establishing communal identity is explicitly politicized in a close analysis of Rhonda Paisley's *Ian Paisley: My Father*.

Notes

1.	'[Folk] museums do not look for the unique building having no historical or cultural significance other than as the manifestation of its builder's eccentric ideas. The criterion of typicality is all important, for the individual building chosen must represent something more than itself.' Trefor M. Owen, 'The Role of a Folk Museum' in A. Gailey (ed.), *The Use of Tradition: Essays Presented to G. B. Thompson* (Cultra: Ulster Folk and Transport Museum, 1988), pp. 76–7.
2.	This is significant if one credits the assertion of George Thompson, the first director of the museum, that funds intended for the development of a National Museum were 'diverted to defensive measures against militant anti-partitionists' in 1921, in M. Longley (ed.), *Causeway: The Arts in Ulster* (Belfast, 1971), p. 153.
3.	S. Wichert, *Northern Ireland Since 1945* (Harlow, 1991), p. 66.
4.	Gailey (ed.), *The Use of Tradition: Essays Presented to G. B. Thompson*, p. vii.
5.	In Longley (ed.), *Causeway: The Arts in Ulster*, p. 154.
6.	Ibid.
7.	Phillipe Hoyau, 'L'année du patrimoine ou la société de conservation', *Les Révoltes Logiques*, 12 (Summer 1980), 70–7, cited in P. Wright, *On Living in an Old Country: The National Past in Contemporary Britain* (London, 1991), p. 25.
8.	In Longley (ed.), *Causeway: The Arts in Ulster*, pp. 153–65.
9.	Ibid., pp. 163–4.
10.	Gailey (ed.), *The Use of Tradition: Essays Presented to G. B. Thompson*, p. 64.
11.	Care has to be exercised with such a model as, despite the strategies inherent to the Museum, I wish to maintain that there is still a distinction between the 'real' and the 'fictive' within socio-cultural discourse; a distinction that Baudrillard in

his reading of Disneyland ultimately seeks to deny. See Chris Norris, *What's Wrong with Postmodernism: Critical Theory and the Ends of Philosophy* (London, 1990), p. 174.

12. J. Baudrillard, *Selected Writings*, ed. M. Poster (Cambridge, 1988), p. 22.
13. Baudrillard, *Selected Writings*, p. 22. The relationship of the subject to this play of difference is illustrated by the distance which the visitor must cover to 'find' each artefact in its physical setting. The individual labour required to 'discover' the inherent bonds between the subject and the object-symbol conceals the actual process by which the closed and self-referential system of relationships between the signs is consumed.
14. Wright, *On Living in an Old Country: The National Past in Contemporary Britain*, p. 25.
15. Baudrillard, *Selected Writings*, p. 171.
16. Ibid.
17. A. Gramsci, *Selections From the Prison Notebooks*, trans. and ed. Q. Hoare and G. Nowell Smith (London, 1971), p. 276.
18. 'Tea Lane (Urban terrace). From Rowland Street, off Sandy Row, Belfast. Six terrace houses built in the 1820s representing the oldest surviving terrace housing in Belfast. From the 1820s until the 1880s the street was known as Tea Lane.' From the Visitor's Broadsheet, Ulster Folk and Transport Museum (Cultra: Ulster Folk and Transport Museum, 1994).
19. Wright, *On Living in an Old Country: The National Past in Contemporary Britain*, pp. 229–30.
20. Ibid., p. 253.
21. D. Lloyd, *Anomalous States: Irish Writing and the Post-colonial Moment* (Dublin, 1993), p. 16.
22. See R. F. Foster, *Modern Ireland: 1600–1972* (London, 1989), p. 526: 'Partition was now a fact, though its British architects had expected it to be temporary, and built in several unrealistic inducements to future unity.'
23. J. Hewitt, *Collected Poems*, ed. F. Ormsby (Belfast, 1991), p. 187.
24. For example, Patrick Marrinan, *Paisley: Man of Wrath* (London, 1973) or Ed Molony and Andy Pollak, *Paisley* (Dublin, 1986).
25. R. Paisley, *Ian Paisley My Father* (Basingstoke, 1988), p. 31.
26. 'Whatever you may think of my father's political aims or religious beliefs, I trust that you will not permit those views to rob you of the view of him in the softer tones of a husband, father and friend.' R. Paisley, *Ian Paisley My Father*, p. 147.
27. Ibid., pp. 42–3.
28. It seems necessary to qualify the use of 'England' in this context rather than 'Britain'. Loyalism, in the face of renewed calls for Scottish self-determination and the strong historical links between Scotland and Ulster, would seem to accept, and despair of, the essentially Anglocentric composition of the British constitution, and therefore to locate the prospect of betrayal as coming from the (largely despised) Westminster intent on denying the destiny of the imagined Union.
29. R. Paisley, 'A Struggle About Identity, Loyalty, Government and, above all, Territory', *Irish Times* (28 October 1993), 14.
30. 'I always remember when he (Ian Paisley Junior) was younger he was having an in-depth discussion about the troubles with Mum, Sharon, and me. With the clear and confident logic of a politically-aware eight-year-old he affirmed, "What this country needs is a dictator, and I'm the man to do it!" His political awareness is no less astute but his logic, I'm glad to say, has matured somewhat.' Paisley, *Ian Paisley My Father*, p. 3.

31. D. Lloyd, *Anomalous States: Irish Writing and the Post-colonial Moment*, p. 16.
32. J. Hewitt, *Ancestral Voices: The Selected Prose of John Hewitt*, ed. T. Clyde (Belfast, 1987), p. 146.
33. Ibid., pp. 116–17.
34. Ibid., p. 122.
35. Such as, for instance, The Tennessee Valley Authority. J. Hewitt, *Ancestral Voices*, p. 123.
36. It is worth noting that Hewitt, again like The Ulster Folk and Transport Museum, establishes his proposals from a (presumably) nine-county Ulster rather than from the administratively convenient Northern Ireland. This is possibly because, despite the specious modernity which clings to the essay, it was and is easier to give individual loyalty to a concept of Ulsterness. See J. Whyte, *Interpreting Northern Ireland* (Oxford, 1991), pp. 69–70.
37. 'Ulster, considered as a region and not as the symbol of any particular creed, can, I believe, command the loyalty of every one of its inhabitants.' J. Hewitt, *Ancestral Voices*, p. 125.
38. Ibid., p. 123. Lewis Mumford was central to Hewitt's thinking on this issue; for a useful example of his belief in settlement as organic creation see L. Mumford, *The City in History* (London, 1961).
39. In relation to this point it is worth noting that Hewitt, despite his refusal to accept the reality of partition, recognized Dublin as 'our literary capital' and was encouraged in his urge to write by letters and comments from AE. J. Hewitt, *Ancestral Voices*, p. 150.
40. See Hewitt's 'The Colony' in Hewitt, *Collected Poems*, p. 78, which can be read either as a masterly lesson in the use of contradiction and reduction within the poetic artefact or as quite confused. In the absence of arguments to support the former I would suggest the latter.
41. In G. Dawe and J. W. Foster (eds), *The Poet's Place: Ulster Literature and Society. Essays in Honour of John Hewitt 1907–87* (Belfast, 1991), p. 176. It is worth noting that McFadden had no better ideas.
42. Dawe and Foster (eds), *The Poet's Place: Ulster Literature and Society*, pp. 174–5, 303.
43. J. Montague, *Poisoned Lands* (London, 1961). My reference copy for this work was inscribed with the handwritten dedication 'John Montague for John Hewitt; some Ulster poetry'.
44. J. Montague, *Poisoned Lands* (London, 1961), p. 56. The poem reappeared in the 1977 edition of this volume divided into six-line stanzas and shorn of the title 'Regionalism', J. Montague, *Poisoned Lands*, rev. edn (Dublin, 1977).
45. Hewitt, *Collected Poems*, p. 78. See note 40.
46. Ibid., p. 225.
47. P. Muldoon, *Meeting the British* (London, 1987), p. 9.
48. S. Heaney, *North* (London, 1975), p. 10.
49. In R. P. Draper (ed.), *The Literature of Region and Nation* (London, 1989), pp. 10–23.
50. Draper (ed.), *The Literature of Region and Nation*, p. 12.
51. Ibid.
52. Dawe and Foster (eds), *The Poet's Place: Ulster Literature and Society*, p. 179.
53. See Tom Clyde, 'A Stirring in the Dry Bones: John Hewitt's Regionalism' in Dawe and Foster (eds), *The Poet's Place: Ulster Literature and Society*, pp. 249–58. Clyde is perhaps the chief promulgator of this pervasive mythology.

13. COLIN GRAHAM, 'SUBALTERNITY AND GENDER: PROBLEMS OF POSTCOLONIAL IRISHNESS'

(From *Journal of Gender Studies*, 5 [1996], 363–70, 372–3.)

Summary

Gender and nationality co-exist as categories of identity and yet the question of how to read the one in relation to the other is fraught with difficulties. Diagnosing a tendency within some forms of postcolonial thinking to align gender with nationality under the general rubric of the 'subaltern' or the oppressed, Graham argues for a more nuanced understanding of the theoretical concept of subalternity. Returning to Gramsci's writings on hegemony, Graham contends that the subaltern should be understood as affiliated to dominant power structures, rather than as simply opposed to them. This allows him to argue for gender and nationality as separate identities, and to further point to how questions of gender can be used to interrogate nationalist politics.

Notes

1. Ailbhe Smyth, 'The Floozie in the Jacuzzi', *Irish Review*, 6 (1989), 7–24 (p. 7).
2. Quoted in M. Kelly, 'Women in the North' in T. Caherty (ed.), *Is Ireland a Third World Country?* (Belfast, 1992), p. 53.
3. Antonio Gramsci, *Selections from the Prison Notebooks* (London, 1971), p. 55.
4. Ibid., p. 52.
5. Ibid.
6. Ibid.
7. Ibid.
8. R. Guha (ed.), *Subaltern Studies*, 7 vols to date (Delhi, 1982).
9. R. Guha, 'On some aspects of the historiography of colonial India', in Guha, *Subaltern Studies*, Vol. I, p. 7.
10. Gayatri Chakravorty Spivak, 'Subaltern studies: deconstructing historiography' in Guha, *Subaltern Studies*, Vol. IV.
11. Ibid., p. 338.
12. See G. C. Spivak, *In Other Worlds: Essays in Cultural Politics* (London, 1988); G. C. Spivak, 'Can the subaltern speak?' in P. Williams and L. Chrisman (eds), *Colonial Discourse and Post-Colonial Theory: a Reader* (Hemel Hempstead, 1993), and G. C. Spivak, *Outside in the Teaching Machine* (London, 1993). See also L. E. Donaldson, *Decolonizing Feminisms: Race, Gender and Empire Building* (London, 1992), and R. S. Rajan, *Real and Imagined Women: Gender, Culture and Postcolonialism* (London, 1993).
13. Guha, 'On some aspects of the historiography of colonial India', p. 1.
14. G. Meaney, *Sex and Nation: Women in Irish Culture and Politics* (Dublin, 1991), p. 17. Similar assumptions about the relationship of nationalism and gender in Ireland can be found in E. Longley, *From Cathleen to Anorexia: the Breakdown of Irelands* (Dublin, 1990), M. Ward, *The Missing Sex: Putting Women into Irish History* (Dublin, 1991), Smyth, 'The Floozie in the Jacuzzi', and C. Wills, *Improprieties: Politics and Sexuality in Northern Irish Poetry* (Oxford, 1993), though all of these writers tend to disagree beyond this basic notion of incompatibility.

15. D. Kandiyoti, 'Identity and its discontents: women and the nation', in Williams and Chrisman, *Colonial Discourse and Post-colonial Theory*, p. 376.
16. Ibid., p. 380.
17. R. Radhakrishnan, 'Nationalism, gender and the narrative of identity', in A. Parker, M. Russo, D. Summer and P. Yaeger (eds), *Nationalisms and Sexualities* (London, 1992), p. 78.
18. Quoted in T. Brown, *Ireland: A Social and Cultural History, 1922–1985* (London, 1985), p. 146.
19. D. Lloyd, 'Nationalisms Against the State: Towards a critique of the anti-nationalist prejudice', in T. P. Foley, L. Pilkington, S. Ryder and E. Tilley (eds), *Gender and Colonialism* (Galway, 1995), p. 257.
20. Lloyd, 'Nationalisms Against the State'.
21. D. Lloyd, *Anomalous States: Irish Writing and the Post-colonial Moment* (Dublin, 1993), p. 127.
22. C. Coulter, *The Hidden Tradition: Feminism, Women and Nationalism in Ireland* (Cork, 1993).
23. Ibid., p. 2.
24. Coulter sees this division as part of the de-nationalization of Irish debate, 'emancipating Ireland from the shackles of its obsessions with the past and [allowing] it to take its place among the nations of the new Europe'. Ibid.
25. Ibid., p. 3.
26. Ibid.
27. Ibid., p. 54.
28. G. C. Spivak, 'Can the subaltern speak?', p. 69.
29. Ibid., p. 87.
30. Lloyd, *Anomalous States*.
31. Lloyd, 'Nationalisms Against the State', p. 276.
32. Coulter, *The Hidden Tradition*.
33. Spivak, 'Can the subaltern speak?', p. 79.
34. Spivak, 'Subaltern studies: deconstructing historiography', p. 358.
35. Ibid., p. 340.
36. Spivak, 'Can the subaltern speak?', p. 87.
37. Ibid., p. 90.
38. Smyth, 'The Floozie in the Jacuzzi', p. 16.
39. Ibid., pp. 20–1.
40. Spivak, 'Can the subaltern speak?', p. 79.

14.   DAVID LLOYD, 'THE SPIRIT OF THE NATION'

(From *Nationalism and Minor Literature: James Clarence Mangan and the Emergence of Irish Cultural Nationalism* [Berkeley, Los Angeles and London, 1987], pp. 54–72.)

Summary

Lloyd analyses the construction of nationalism in nineteenth-century Europe and traces the political and cultural roots of the Young Ireland movement. He shows how the Irish nation of nineteenth-century Irish nationalism is imagined in the first instance as already under threat, on the point of being lost. This gives rise to an aesthetics of fragmentation, with debility and loss being positively valued. The Irish language is exemplary in this respect, imagined as irretrievably lost and in the same moment fetishized as the guarantor of national identity. Lloyd illuminates the thinking of Young Ireland by comparison with movements within German romanticism. A central thread of his argument is that Irish nationalism was significantly shaped by its relations with the British state. This concept is developed in Lloyd's later work, which seeks to distinguish between state-forming and other nationalisms.

Notes

1. See, further, E. Kamenka (ed.), *Nationalism: The Nature and Evolution of an Idea* (London, 1975), pp. 9–10, and Elie Kedourie, *Nationalism* (London, 1960), p. 9.
2. See John Breuilly, *Nationalism and the State* (New York, 1982), pp. 349–50. It is this aspect of Hegel's theory of the state that Marx attacks most forcefully in his 'Critique of Hegel's Doctrine of the State', in Karl Marx, *Early Writings*, introduction by Lucio Colletti, trans. Rodney Livingstone and Gregor Benton (New York, 1974), pp. 90–1: rather than expressing the particular manifestation of a transcendental idea, the bourgeois state emerges, for Marx, at the point when 'private spheres have achieved an independent existence', necessitating their reconciliation in a political constitution. Paul Thomas, *Marx and the Anarchists* (London, 1980), pp. 31–40, gives an excellent account of both Hegel's and Marx's arguments.
3. This transition is most obvious in Coleridge's reformulation of Burke's constitutional theory in *Church and State*. See David Lloyd, 'James Clarence Mangan and "A Broken Constitution" ', *Cornucopia*, 3 (1981–82), 71–115, 74–83, on this transition and its influence on unionism in Ireland.
4. See, for example, the anonymous article 'Notabilities of the Times', *The Nation*, 13 April 1843, p. 426.
5. I derive the term 'deterritorialization' from Gilles Deleuze and Félix Guattari's usage of it in *Anti-Oedipus: Capitalism and Schizophrenia* (New York, 1977), where the effect of cultural and psychic dislocation is seen as the product of capitalism's unleashing of economic flows which were formerly 'territorialized'. The term's metaphoric reach usefully connects cultural and social with economic phenomena. For a general discussion of Deleuze and Guattari's concepts of de- and reterritorialization, see Vincent Descombes, *Le Même et l'Autre: Quarante-cinq Ans de philosophie française, 1933–1978* (Paris, 1979), pp. 205–6.
6. Thomas Meagher, quoted in Denis Gwynn, *Young Ireland and 1848* (Cork, 1949), p. 77. Cf., for this general argument concerning the difference between nationalist and constitutionalist states, Breuilly, *Nationalism and the State*, p. 62.
7. Kamenka, *Nationalism*, p. 14.
8. Joseph Mazzini, *The Duties of Man and Other Essays*, introduction by Thomas Jones, trans. Ella Noyes, L. Martineau, and Thomas Okey (London, 1907), p. 55.
9. Ibid., p. 52.
10. J. G. Fichte, *Addresses to the German Nation*, trans. R. F. Jones and G. H. Turnbull (London, 1922); hereafter cited as Fichte. Kedourie discusses Fichte's contribution to nationalist thought throughout *Nationalism*.
11. Fichte, pp. 223–4.
12. Fichte, p. 55.
13. Fichte, p. 63. Arnold, in this tradition, makes a similar remark in *On the Study of Celtic Literature*, in R. H. Super (ed.), *The Complete Prose Works of Matthew Arnold*, vol. 3, pp. 292–3, in relation to the Gallo-Celtic origin of the French.
14. Fichte, p. 127.

15. Fichte, p. 57. See S. T. Coleridge, *The Friend*, ed. Barbara Rooke, Bollingen Series (Princeton, NJ, 1969), I: 476.
16. Fichte, pp. 60–1.
17. This analogy is made implicitly in Fichte, pp. 58–9.
18. Fichte, p. 110.
19. Wilhelm von Humboldt, *Über den Nationalcharacter des Spraches*, quoted in R. L. Brown, *Wilhelm von Humboldt's Conception of Linguistic Relativity*, p. 80.
20. According to Akenson, 'Irish had ceased to be the national language long before mid-century'. His assertion is deduced from census figures of 1851. See *The Irish Education Experiment* (London, 1970), pp. 378–80.
21. Thomas Davis, 'Our National Language', *The Nation*, 1 April 1843, p. 394.
22. Ibid., p. 394. D. George Boyce, *Nationalism in Ireland* (London, 1982), pp. 155 and 187n., points out the influence of German Romanticism on Davis, as does Brown, *Politics of Irish Literature* (Seattle, 1972), p. 56, who argues his relationship to other European nationalists such as Mazzini. See more generally, Giovanni Costigan, 'Romantic Nationalism: Ireland and Europe', *Irish University Review* 3, 2 (Autumn 1973), 141–52.
23. Thomas Davis, 'Academical Education', *The Nation*, 17 May 1845, p. 520.
24. Charles Gavan Duffy, *Young Ireland* (London, 1880), pp. 153, 155.
25. Such criticisms were voiced by Young Irelanders themselves at the time: see Gwynn, *Young Ireland*, pp. 151, 191, 258, and *JJ*, pp. 143–5. For more recent criticisms, see Owen Dudley Edwards, 'Ireland' in O. Dudley Edwards, G. Evans, J. Rhys and H. Macdiarmaid, *Celtic Nationalism* (London, 1968), pp. 107–18, p. 144, and E. Strauss, *Irish Nationalism and British Democracy* (London, 1957), p. 105.
26. Strauss, *Irish Nationalism and British Democracy*, p. 89.
27. 'Union against the Union', *The Nation*, 11 March 1848, p. 168.
28. Mazzini, *Duties of Man*, pp. 131–2. Emphasis in the original.
29. See Edwards, 'Ireland', p. 83.
30. S. T. Coleridge, 'The Statesman's Manual', in *Lay Sermons*, ed. R. J. White, Bollingen Series (Princeton, NJ, 1972), p. 30.
31. Edwards, 'Ireland', p. 85. Cf. Brown, *Politics of Irish Literature*, p. 55, for comments on the necessarily 'amorphous idealism' developed by Irish nationalism to overcome actual division. Such a remark should not, however, blind one to the powerful *formal* consistency of Young Ireland ideology.
32. 'The Individuality of a Native Literature', *The Nation*, 21 August 1847, p. 731.
33. Ibid.
34. Quoted in Charles Gavan Duffy, *Four Years of Irish History* (London, 1883), p. 72.
35. On this German tradition, see André Lefevere, *Translating Literature: The German Tradition* (Amsterdam, 1977), passim, and W. W. Chambers, 'Language and Nationality in German Pre-Romantic and Romantic Thought', *MLR*, 41 (October 1946), 382–92.
36. Thomas Davis, 'Irish Songs', *The Nation*, 4 January 1845, p. 202.
37. 'Ballad Poetry of Ireland', *The Nation*, 2 August 1845, p. 698.
38. Denis Florence McCarthy (ed.), *The Book of Irish Ballads* (Dublin, 1846), pp. 12, 21–2.
39. Ibid., pp. 22–3.
40. 'Recent English Poets, No. 1: Alfred Tennyson and E. B. Browning', *The Nation*, 15 February 1845, p. 314.
41. Ibid.

42. Padraic Fallon, 'The Poetry of Thomas Davis', in *Thomas Davis and Young Ireland*, ed. M. J. MacManus (Dublin, 1945), p. 25. On the scorn with which the street ballad was regarded, see Duffy, *Young Ireland*, p. 756. Patrick C. Power, *The Story of Anglo-Irish Poetry, 1800–1922* (Cork, 1972), discusses the development of the street ballad out of Anglo-Gaelic crossings, pp. 116–25, and the refined character of the *Nation* ballads, pp. 33–5.

43. According to Duffy, *Young Ireland*, p. 285, a new edition was required every year between 1843 and 1880.

Glossary

Note: Words or phrases given in italics are also defined in their alphabetical place in the glossary.

Authenticity Much-appealed-to category in Irish debates, now being revalued according to the theories of Jacob Golomb and Theodor Adorno. Both show how authenticity eludes any single moment in which it can be captured or defined. *Postcolonial* critics such as David Lloyd argue that because the colonizer finds inauthenticity in colonial societies (or, to put it differently, misrecognizes the other culture as less than fully human), the nationalist response is often to fetishize attributes seen as 'genuine' or 'natural'. Adorno's study, *The Jargon of Authenticity* ([1964] London, 1986), enables a sceptical approach to authenticity, exposed as embedded in hierarchical power relations. Colin Graham however, drawing on Golomb, argues for authenticity as an enabling category, its uncertainty and flexibility possessing the power to disturb the teleologies of *postcolonialism*. See Jacob Golomb, *In Search of Authenticity: From Kierkegaard to Camus* (London, 1995); Colin Graham, ' "...maybe that's just Blarney": Irish Culture and the Persistence of Authenticity', in Colin Graham and Richard Kirkland (eds), *Ireland and Cultural Theory: The Mechanics of Authenticity* (Basingstoke, 1999), pp. 7–28.

Colonialism Colonialism refers to a global phenomenon whereby countries in the West have invaded and systematically exploited other polities. Ireland is sometimes described as the first European colony, under some form of British influence from the twelfth century. Some historians, however, dispute the applicability of the label 'colony' to Ireland, arguing instead for a more diffuse and stratified version of Anglo-Irish relations. Once united with Britain by the 1801 Act of Union, Ireland was represented in Westminster in a manner which distinguishes it from other kinds of settler colonialisms. The persistence of the link with Britain into the twentieth century has, however, led to a characterization of the North of Ireland as a colonial or at least neo-colonial state.

Enlightenment In historical terms the Enlightenment describes the turn away from religious faith and towards science which took place in the eighteenth century; in part a response to the wars of religion which had raged across seventeenth-century Europe. The concept is more broadly associated with such qualities as progress, truth and cosmopolitanism. Poststructuralist critics have tried to relativize the universalist claims of the Enlightenment and to shake its faith in linear teleologies. From a different perspective, *postcolonialism* has been concerned to relativize also, pointing to the geographical and racial limits of Enlightenment definitions of humanity. Luke Gibbons' work calls for Irish critics to develop a notion of 'alternative' Enlightenments. Luke Gibbons, 'Alternative Enlightenments: the United Irishmen, Cultural Diversity and the Republic of Letters', in Mary Cullen (ed.), *1798, 200 Years of Resonance: Essays and Contributions on the History and Relevance of the United Irishmen and the 1798 Revolution* (Dublin, 1998), pp. 119–27.

Foucault, Michel   French historian of ideas and philosopher who has charted the histories of sexuality, discipline and punishment in his writings. His work shows how bodies and sexuality belong to the world of power relations. See, for example, *The History of Sexuality*, Vol. 1, trans. Robert Hurley (Harmondsworth, 1979).

Gramsci, Antonio   Italian Marxist critic whose conceptualization of power relations in terms of hegemony has influenced many *postcolonial* critics. Gramsci's writings on Italian history develop the notion of a *subaltern* position, originally applied to classes not assimilated to the State. See *Selections from the Prison Notebooks of Antonio Gramsci*, ed. and trans. by Quintin Hoare and Geoffrey Nowell Smith (London, 1971). First introduced into Irish debates by David Cairns and Shaun Richards, in their study *Writing Ireland: Colonialism, Nationalism and Culture* (Manchester, 1988).

Hybridity   The version of *postcolonial* criticism most influenced by poststructuralism has tried to move away from thinking about power within a self/other dynamic, and to deconstruct the binary opposition between colonizer and colonized by focusing on hybridity, and the closely related concept of ambivalence. The critic most associated with this thinking is Homi Bhabha, who outlines a concept of hybridity as a state of in-between-ness. See his *The Location of Culture* (London, 1994). Others, most notably Robert Young, have criticized the metaphor for its organicist associations, arguing that metaphors of mixing cannot spring free of imperial notions of impurity. Robert Young, *White Mythologies: Writing History and the West* (London, 1990).

Nationalism   Nationalism in its modern form was developed in the nineteenth century, and is associated with the formation of new states and power structures in the aftermath of the bourgeois challenges to dynastic powers across Europe in the 1840s. Voicing a powerful appeal to origins, however, nationalism also claims for itself a much older history and even a timelessness, what Homi Bhabha identifies as the vanishing point within the temporality of nationalist thought. See his edited collection of essays, *Nation and Narration* (London, 1990), which translates Benedict Anderson's theory of nationalism as the triumph of print culture into poststructuralist terms. Revisionary accounts of nationalism stress its invention of tradition, and yet a theory of nationalism as culturally constructed no longer seems an adequate response to its still-powerful rallying cry. Writing about Ireland, David Lloyd has argued for a distinction between state-forming and other kinds of nationalisms. See his 'Nationalisms Against the State', *Ireland After History* (Cork, 1999), pp. 19–36.

Postcolonialism   Postcolonialism describes both a temporal relation to the colonial (that which comes after it) and also a critical approach that traces the impact and influence of colonialist assumptions. Northern Ireland's role within the Union means that some nationalists and republicans are unhappy with the designation postcolonial (in this first sense) for Ireland as a whole. From a different perspective, the economist Liam Kennedy has suggested that any comparison between Ireland and Third World countries is invalid. See his book, *Colonialism, Religion and Nationalism in Ireland* (Belfast, 1996). The role of culture has come to occupy a central place in discussions of Ireland and the postcolonial, with critics like Kennedy and Stephen Howe accusing creative writers and cultural critics alike of irresponsibility, seeking the emotional satisfaction to be found in converting the complex movements of historical change into loose metaphors of oppression and resistance.

Postnationalism   The postnationalist agenda seeks to relativize the significance of the nation state while replacing emotional ties to the nation with other allegiances. What it offers is at once a move beyond the frontiers of the nation state (usually in the direction of the European Union) and a retrenchment to local allegiances, in the shape of the region. One of the most attractive aspects of postnationalism has been its promise of a new perspective on the North/South border.

Subaltern   Antonio *Gramsci* developed his concept of the subaltern position to account for class formations other than those legitimized by the State or the dominant classes. Different groupings may be meant by this designation, and subaltern classes are conceived of as disparate, only united with each other in the eyes of the State. *Postcolonial* critics, most notably the Indian historians writing for the journal *Subaltern Studies*, have appropriated the term to describe oppressed groups under colonialism. See Colin Graham's essay (13) in this Reader, which insists that Gramsci conceived of subaltern groups as affiliated to the dominant class, not as radically estranged.

Tradition   Tradition refers to customs, habits and cultural forms of a group or society, understood to be always in the past for the present incarnation of that society. As a description of certain enduring modes of life or behaviour, this appeal to qualities which have always been there and are thus out of time is a constitutive element of 'tradition'. See Seamus Deane's essay (2) in this Reader.

Suggestions for Further Reading

ACCESSIBLE

Boland, Eavan, *Object Lessons: The Life of The Woman and The Poet In Our Time* (London, 1996). A poet reflecting on the literary and political tradition she has inherited, one which addresses women as the passive objects of discourse.

Bourke, Angela, *The Burning of Bridget Cleary: A True Story* (London, 1999). Valuable work of social history which reads an incident of a man burning his wife to death in late nineteenth-century Tipperary through the lens of feminism, folklore and colonialism.

Bradley, Anthony and Maryann Gialanella Valiulis (eds), *Gender and Sexuality in Modern Ireland* (Amherst, MA, 1997). Essays which read masculinity and femininity within the context of colonialism, ranging from the Revival to the present.

Brewster, Scott, Virginia Crossman, Fiona Becket and David Alderson (eds), *Ireland in Proximity: History, Gender, Space* (London, 1999). Clear and well-framed essays, introducing readers to recent theoretical issues as they have been taken up in Irish literature and historiography.

Briggs, Sarah, Paul Hyland and Neil Sammells, *Reviewing Ireland: Essays and Interviews from Irish Studies Review* (Bath, 1988). Somewhat eclectic collection which captures many of the trends in Irish Studies since the 1980s. Chronologically arranged.

Brown, Terence, *Ireland: A Social and Cultural History, 1922–1979* (London, 1981). Laid the foundations for cultural materialist readings of Irish texts.

——, *Ireland's Literature: Selected Essays* (Dublin, 1988). Essays covering aspects of nineteenth- and twentieth-century writing, offering insights into the relationship between history and literature as it has taken shape in Irish culture.

Cairns, David and Shaun Richards, *Writing Ireland: Colonialism, Nationalism and Culture* (Manchester, 1988). The first sustained attempt to address Irish literature (from the early modern period onwards) in terms of its colonial contexts, drawing on Gramsci's theories of culture and criticism.

Connolly, Claire (ed.), *Postcolonial Ireland? European Journal for English Studies*, 3 (1999). Collection of essays which interrogate the usefulness of postcolonial approaches to Irish culture with reference to nineteenth-century culture, Joyce, Yeats and contemporary film and theatre.

Coulter, Carol, *Ireland: Between First and Third Worlds*, LIP pamphlet (Dublin, 1990). Polemical call to connect Ireland's historical experience with that of other colonized countries.

——, *The Hidden Tradition: Feminism, Women, and Nationalism in Ireland* (Cork, 1993). Part of ongoing debate seeking to establish a new relationship between feminism and nationalism.

Deane, Seamus (ed. and introd.) *Nationalism, Colonialism and Literature* (Minneapolis, 1990). Deane introduces essays by Terry Eagleton, Edward Said and Fredric Jameson; all invited by Field Day to contribute to the emerging discussion of postcolonial Ireland.

——, *Strange Country: Modernity and Nationhood in Irish Writing Since 1790* (Oxford, 1997). Lectures which find in nineteenth-century Irish writing solutions (both treacherous and enabling) to current dilemmas, notably the relationship between culture and politics.

Dorgan, Theo and Máirín Ní Dhonnchadha (eds), *Revising the Rising* (Derry, 1991). Collection which includes essays by Deane, Kiberd and Longley; all reflecting on problems of making current sense of past events, especially in the light of the 1916 rising and its commemoration.

Dunne, Tom, 'New Histories: "Beyond Revisionism"', *The Irish Review*, 12 (1992), 1–12. Wishes to see history writing move beyond the nationalist versus revisionist debate and admit a more expansive understanding of the past.

Eagleton, Terry, 'History and Myth in Yeats' "Easter 1916"', *The Eagleton Reader*, ed. Stephen Regan (Oxford, 1998), pp. 350–8. Discovers a dialectic between history and myth in Yeats' poem.

Gibbons, Luke, *Transformations in Irish Culture* (Cork, 1996). Stylish and engaged essays which question the applicability of modernization discourse to Ireland and in the process extend the field of culture to include television soaps, film, advertising and postcards.

Kearney, Richard, *Transitions: Narratives in Modern Irish Culture* (Dublin, 1988). Lucid introduction to the metanarratives which continue to structure the debate.

——, *Postnationalist Ireland: Politics, Culture, Philosophy* (London, 1997). Sets out an agenda for a hybridized Irish future structured according to overlapping identifications: regional, national, federal.

Kelleher, Margaret, *The Feminization of Famine: Expressions of the Inexpressible* (Cork, 1997). Reads selected accounts of famine (literary, journalistic, historical) in terms of the intertwined problematics of representation and gender.

Kiberd, Declan, *Synge and The Irish Language*, second edition (Basingstoke, 1994). The introduction relates Fanon's three stages of decolonization to Synge's *Playboy of the Western World*.

——, *Inventing Ireland: the Literature of the Modern Nation* (London, 1995). Argues persuasively that Irish literature from the Revival onwards has been in the forefront of decolonization.

Longley, Edna, *Poetry in the Wars* (Newcastle upon Tyne, 1986). Polemical call for poetry to be removed from the field of politics.

——, *The Living Stream: Literature and Revisionism in Ireland* (Newcastle, 1994). Adversarial and engaged essays in the history and politics of Irish literary criticism.

McCarthy, Conor, *Modernisation, Crisis and Culture in Ireland, 1969–1992* (Dublin, 2000). Charts a history of cultural attempts to come to terms with both the language and the experience of modernization.

McCormack, W. J., *The Battle of the Books: Two Decades of Irish Cultural Debate* (Dublin, 1986). Provisional judgements on emerging trends in Irish Studies in the 1980s, with chapters on Conor Cruise O'Brien, Terence Brown, Field Day, Edna Longley and *The Crane Bag*.

Meaney, Geraldine, *Sex and Nation: Women in Irish Culture and Politics*, LIP
Pamphlet (Dublin, 1991).
——, 'Myth, History, and the Politics of Subjectivity: Eavan Boland and Irish
Women's Writing', *Women: a Cultural Review*, 4 (1993), 136–53. Uses theory to
read against the grain of Boland's own account of her formation as a poet.
——, 'Landscapes of Desire: Women and Ireland on Film', *Women: A Cultural
Review*, 9 (1998), 237–51. Reads representations of women and landscape in Irish
film in terms of recent trends in feminist criticism.
O'Toole, Fintan, *A Mass for Jesse James: A Journey Through 1980s Ireland* (Dublin,
1990). Witty and informative essays that consider the issue of modernization.
——, *Black Hole, Green Card: The Disappearance of Ireland* (Dublin, 1994). Argues
through wide-ranging and linked essays that Ireland's sense of itself is now diasporic.
Pettit, Lance, *Screening Ireland: Film and Television Representation* (Manchester,
2000). Comprehensive introduction to debates around Irish cinema and television.
Richards, Shaun, 'Field Day's Fifth Province: Avenue or Impasse', in Eamonn
Hughes (ed.), *Culture and Politics in Northern Ireland, 1960–1990* (Milton Keynes
and Philadephia, 1991), pp. 139–50. Evaluates the success of Field Day's appeal to
the 'fifth province'.
Smyth, Gerry, *Decolonisation and Criticism: The Construction of Irish Literature*
(London, 1988). Plots a history for Irish criticism from the foundation of the state.
Walshe, Éibhear (ed.), *Sex, Nation and Dissent in Irish Writing* (Cork, 1997). Essays
which begin to map out connections between dissident sexuality and the discourses
of nationalism.
Whelan, Kevin, 'Come All You Staunch Revisionists: Towards a Post-Revisionist
Agenda for Irish History', *Irish Reporter*, 2 (1991), 23–6. Lively analysis of Irish
historiography and its complicity in programmes of state formation.

MORE DIFFICULT, BUT WORTH IT

Attridge, Derek and Marjorie Howes (eds), *Semicolonial Joyce* (Cambridge, 2000).
Essays on Joyce which seek to connect readings of the main texts with recent issues
in postcolonial criticism.
Cullingford, Elizabeth Butler, ' "Thinking of Her ... as ... Ireland": Yeats, Pearse
and Heaney', *Textual Practice*, 4 (1990), 1–22. Astute reading of Irish texts
which objectify or ventriloquize women. Cullingford suggests that, in spite of
themselves, such texts may open up a critical approach to mythologies of purity
and authenticity.
Eagleton, Terry, *Crazy John and the Bishop and Other Essays on Irish Culture* (Cork,
1998). Essays which recuperate neglected figures and traditions in Irish writing and
reflect on current critical practices in Irish Studies.
Foster, John Wilson, 'The Critical Condition of Ulster', *Colonial Consequences:
Essays in Irish Literature and Culture* (Dublin, 1991), pp. 215–47. Calls for a
more flexible critical sphere and queries Field Day's achievements in shifting the
grounds of debate.
Graham, Colin, *Deconstructing Ireland* (Edinburgh, 2001). A series of linked essays
that consider how Ireland is an imagined entity, constantly projected into a
deferred future.

Graham, Colin and Richard Kirkland (eds), *Ireland and Cultural Theory: The Mechanics of Authenticity* (Basingstoke, 1999). A collection of essays all of which use theory in order to problematize existing critical patterns within Irish Studies.

Herr, Cheryl, 'A State o' Chassis: Mobile Capital, Ireland, and the Question of Postmodernity', in John S. Rickard (ed.), *Irishness and (Post) Modernism* (London and Toronto, 1994), pp. 195–229. Critically relates postmodernism to Irishness via an analysis of Ford cars.

——, *Critical Regionalism and Cultural Studies: From Ireland To The American Midwest* (Gainesville, FL, 1996). Considers issues such as emigration and rural life in the context of contemporary cultural representation.

Howes, Marjorie, *Yeats' Nations: Gender, Class and Irishness* (Cambridge, 1996). Locates contradictions in Yeats' writing at the points where gender, sexuality and class intersect.

Hughes, Eamonn, 'Leavis and Ireland: an Adequate Criticism?', *Text and Context* (Autumn 1988), 112–32. Considers Leavisite literary scholarship in relation to Ireland.

Kearney, Richard, 'An Irish Intellectual Tradition: Philosophical and Cultural Contexts', Introduction to Richard Kearney (ed.), *The Irish Mind: Exploring Intellectual Traditions* (Dublin, 1985), pp. 7–14. Clear and stimulating introduction to the history of ideas in Ireland which frames the turn to theory within a broader context.

Kirby, Peadar, Luke Gibbons and Michael Cronin (eds), *Reinventing Ireland: Culture, Society and the Global Economy* (London and Sterling, VA, 2002). Collected essays that seek to establish a more complex theoretical framework within which the Ireland of the 'Celtic Tiger' can be analysed.

Leerssen, Joep, *Mere Irish and Fíor-Ghael: Studies in the Idea of Irish Nationality, its Development and Literary Expression Prior to the Nineteenth Century* (1986) (Cork, 1996). Structuralist-inspired study of images of Ireland found in both Irish and English language texts.

——, *Remembrance and Imagination: Patterns in the Historical and Literary Representation of Ireland in the Nineteenth Century* (Cork, 1996). Large-scale cultural history which offers a theory of nineteenth-century Irish culture as 'auto-exotic'.

Lloyd, David, *Anomalous States: Irish Writing and the Post-Colonial Moment* (Dublin, 1993). Essays expressing a scrupulous suspicion of the aesthethics of cultural nationalism.

——, *Ireland After History* (Cork, 1999). Selected essays which map out a new departure in Lloyd's work, in the direction of forms of cultural expression which seem to defy the dictates of 'modernity'. The essays cover a variety of topics including terrorism and technological surveillance, emigration, cinema and kitsch art.

McCormack, W. J., *From Burke to Beckett: Ascendancy, Tradition and Betrayal in Literary History* (Cork, 1994). Complex reflections on the processes of literary and cultural history.

Mulhern, Francis, *The Present Lasts a Long Time: Essays in Cultural Politics* (Cork, 1998). Collected essays which consider modernization and the turn towards Europe alongside such issues as translation and education.

O'Dowd, Liam, *On Intellectuals and Intellectual Life in Ireland: International, Comparative and Historical Contexts* (Belfast, 1996). Essays which consider the institutionalization of various kinds of knowledges about Ireland, from the eighteenth century to the present.

Oxford Literary Review, Special Issue on Neocolonialism (1991). Includes essays by Wills, Gibbons and Lloyd, all establishing the grounds on which postcolonial criticism of Ireland might proceed. With a focus on the issue of 'race'.

Richards, Shaun, 'Placed Identities for Placeless Times: Brian Friel and Postcolonial Criticism', *Irish University Review*, 27 (1997), 55–68. Finds a convergence between recent trends in postcolonial theory and the dramas of Brian Friel.

Ryan, Ray (ed.), *Writing in the Irish Republic: Literature, Culture, Politics 1949–1999* (Basingstoke, 2000). Unusual in treating the Irish Republic (officially in place since 1949) as a new and distinct political and social entity, rather than as a timeless truth awaiting full territorial expression. Some essays stand out for their blend of formal and ideological analysis: Chris Morash's reading of theatre in terms of the Republic of Ireland Act, Joe Cleary's interpretation of 'Modernization and Aesthetic Ideology in Contemporary Irish Culture' and Michael Cronin and Barbara O'Connor's incisive analysis of tourism, 'From Gombeen to Gubeen: Tourism, Identity and Class in Ireland, 1949–99'.

Viswanathan, Gauri, *Outside the Fold: Conversion, Modernity and Belief* (Princeton, NJ, 1998). A detailed study of religious conversion in the nineteenth and twentieth centuries which argues for conversion as a form of cultural criticism and includes reference to some significant Irish texts and figures.

Waters, John Paul (ed.), *Ireland and Irish Cultural Studies*, Special Issue, *The South Atlantic Quarterly*, 95, 1 (1996). A rare discussion of what Irish cultural studies might look like. Includes essays on prostitution, museum practice and tourism.

Watson, George J., *Irish Identity and The Literary Revival: Synge, Yeats, Joyce, and O'Casey* (London and New York; Washington, DC, 1979; 1994). A materialist reading of the late nineteenth- and early twentieth-century culture which analyses the rhetorics of the Revival.

Notes on Contributors

Angela Bourke is a Senior Lecturer in Irish at NUI Dublin. She has published extensively on feminism, oral tradition and literature, and her book *The Burning of Bridget Cleary* was published in 1999. A collection of her short stories, *By Salt Water*, appeared in 1996.

Joe Cleary is a lecturer in English Literature at NUI Maynooth. He has published essays on contemporary Irish film, drama and fiction, and the development of postcolonial studies in Ireland, and a book, *Literature, Partition and the Nation-State: Culture and Conflict in Ireland, Israel and Palestine* (Cambridge, 2002).

Patricia Coughlan is Associate Professor of English Literature at NUI Cork and has published extensively in the fields of sixteenth- and seventeenth-century writing, nineteenth-century Anglo-Irish literature, and modern Irish culture and gender. She edited *Spenser and Ireland* (1989), and, with Alex Davis, *Modernism and Ireland* (1995).

Seamus Deane is Keough Professor of Irish Studies at the University of Notre Dame. A founder member of the Field Day company, he has published pamphlets with the company, edited and introduced the Field Day lectures of Terry Eagleton, Fredric Jameson and Edward Said (1990), and acted as general editor for the three-volume *Field Day Anthology of Irish Writing* (1991). He is currently general editor of the Field Day *Critical Conditions* series (1996–?). His books include *Celtic Revivals* (1985), *A Short History of Irish Literature* (1986), *The French Revolution and Enlightenment in England* (1988), and, most recently, *Strange Country: Modernity and Nationhood in Irish Writing since 1790* (1995). A novel, *Reading in the Dark*, appeared in 1996.

Terry Eagleton is Professor of Cultural Theory and John Rylands Fellow at Manchester University and author of a great many books on literary theory, Marxism and culture. He has published extensively in the area of Irish studies, and in 1988 contributed a pamphlet entitled *Nationalism, Irony and Commitment* to the Field Day series. More recently he was written *Heathcliff and the Great Hunger* (1995), *Crazy John and the Bishop* (1998) and *Scholars and Rebels in Nineteenth-Century Ireland* (1999). He is also the author of fiction and plays, including *Saints and Scholars* (1987) and *Saint Oscar* (1989).

Luke Gibbons is Professor of English and Film, Theatre and Television at the University of Notre Dame. He has published widely on Irish culture, especially cinema, and has written many essays on Irish romanticism. He is co-author, with Kevin Rockett and John Hill, of *Cinema and Ireland* (1988), and author of

Transformations in Irish Culture (1996). His book *Edmund Burke and Ireland: Aesthetics, Politics and the Colonial Sublime* is forthcoming in 2003.

Colin Graham lectures in the School of English, Queen's University, Belfast. He has published a number of essays on postcolonial theory and Ireland and a book, *Ideologies of Epic: Nation, Empire and Victorian Epic Poetry* (1998). With Richard Kirkland, he co-edited *Ireland and Cultural Theory: The Mechanics of Authenticity* (1999).

Siobhán Kilfeather is a lecturer in English literature at Sussex University. She has published a number of essays on eighteenth- and nineteenth-century Irish literature, especially women's writing and the Gothic.

Richard Kirkland lectures in the School of English, Manchester University. His books include, *Literature and Culture in Northern Ireland since 1965: Moments of Danger* (1996) and *Identity Parades: Northern Irish Culture and Dissident Subjects* (Liverpool, 2002). With Colin Graham, he co-edited *Ireland and Cultural Theory: The Mechanics of Authenticity* (1999).

David Lloyd is Hartley Burr Alexander Chair in the Humanities at Scripps College, Claremont, California. His books include *Nationalism and Minor Literature* (1987), *Anomalous States: Irish Writing and the Post-Colonial Moment* (1993), and *Ireland after History* (1999). He has edited two collections of essays: *The Nature and Context of Minority Discourse* (1990) with Abdul R. JanMohamed, and, with Lisa Lowe, *The Politics of Culture in the Shadow of Capital* (1997).

Chris Morash is a Senior Lecturer in English Literature at NUI Maynooth. He has published many essays on nineteenth-century Irish culture, and his book, *Writing the Irish Famine*, appeared in 1995. He edited *The Hungry Voice* (1989) and co-edited (with Richard Hayes) a collection of essays on the Famine, *Fearful Realities*. He has also written *A History of Irish Theatre, 1600–2001* (Cambridge, 2002).

Shaun Richards is Professor of Irish Studies in Staffordshire University. He co-authored *Writing Ireland* with David Cairns in 1988. Since then he has published widely on Irish literature and culture, especially theatre, and is currently completing *The Dramas of Modern Ireland: An Infinite Rehearsal*, to be published by Palgrave Macmillan.

Clair Wills is a Reader in Modern Poetry at Queen Mary and Westfield College, London. She has published essays on Joyce and on twentieth-century Irish poetry. Her book, *Improprieties*, appeared in 1993, followed by *Reading Paul Muldoon* in 1998.

Index